Engineering a Hospital Turnaround

Proven Strategies for Reinvigorating Financial and Operating Performance

Edited by Richard A. Baehr
for Ernst & Young

AHA

AHA books are published by American Hospital Publishing, Inc., an American Hospital Association company

Library of Congress Cataloging-in-Publication Data

Engineering a hospital turnaround : proven strategies for reinvigorating financial and operating performance / edited by Richard A. Baehr for Ernst & Young.
p. cm.
Includes bibliographical references.
ISBN 1-55648-102-0 (pbk.)
1. Hospitals—United States—Business management. 2. Corporate turnarounds—United States—Management. I. Baehr, Richard A. II. Ernst & Young.
[DNLM: 1. Hospital Administration—methods—United States. WK 157 E57 1993]
RA971.3.E54 1993
362.1'1'0681—dc20
DNLM/DLC
for Library of Congress 93-9622
CIP

Catalog no. 001120

Printed in the USA

AHA is a service mark of the American Hospital Association used under license by American Hospital Publishing, Inc.

Text set in English Times
2.5M—05/93—0342

Richard Hill, Acquisitions and Development Editor
Anne Hermann, Production Editor
Peggy DuMais, Production Coordinator
Luke Smith, Cover Designer
Marcia Bottoms, Books Division Assistant Director
Brian Schenk, Books Division Director

This book is dedicated to the memory of my parents, Kurt and Betty Baehr. Whatever I have achieved I owe in large part to their love, their attention, and the effort they made to ensure that I valued the things that were important to my family and my people.

Contents

List of Figures

About the Editor

Richard A. Baehr is president of Richard A. Baehr & Associates, Highland Park, Illinois. Mr. Baehr has been a health care consultant for more than 18 years, primarily at Amherst Associates, Inc., where he served as chairman of the board and chief operating officer, and at Ernst & Young, where he was a partner specializing in financial and strategic planning for health care organizations. He was a founding investor and board member of Mobile Technology, Inc., the nation's largest provider of mobile magnetic resonance imaging services.

Mr. Baehr served from 1985 to 1988 as a member of the board of trustees of Mt. Sinai Hospital Medical Center in Chicago, Illinois. He has presented more than 100 seminars on various financial and strategic topics and has written several articles on these topics as well. He holds a master of science degree in management from the Sloan School of Management at the Massachusetts Institute of Technology, Cambridge, and a bachelor of arts degree in political science from Kenyon College, Gambier, Ohio.

Contributors

Patricia C. Breault is manager of health care business advisory services at Ernst & Young. She was formerly associate director for finance and systems at the University of Chicago Physicians Group, Chicago, Illinois. She holds a master of business administration degree from the University of Chicago.

Bonnie Brickell is a senior manager in the Chicago office of Ernst & Young. She was formerly vice-president of affiliate operations for Memorial Medical Center in Savannah, Georgia. She holds a master's degree in public administration.

Thomas Collier, M.D., is a senior advisor for health care consulting with the Cleveland office of Ernst & Young. A board-certified orthopedic surgeon and holder of a master of business administration degree, Dr. Collier is a recognized authority in process improvement for hospital surgical services.

Robert M. Fishman, J.D., is a partner with the business insolvency practice group of Ross & Hardies, Chicago, Illinois. His practice is concentrated in the areas of debtor–creditor relations, insolvency, and bankruptcy. He is also vice-president for education of the American Bankruptcy Institute (ABI) and is a member of ABI's board of directors and executive committee.

Roger Green is vice-president of marketing at HealthEast, St. Paul, Minnesota.

Mark E. Grube is associate vice-president for strategy/program development at Mercy Health Services in Farmington, Michigan. He was previously a senior manager of health care consulting in the Chicago office of Ernst & Young. He holds a master of business administration degree from the University of Chicago.

Loree Lewan Hanas is a project manager in the financial operations division of Northwestern Memorial Hospital, Chicago, Illinois. She was formerly a consulting manager in the health care practice of Ernst & Young, where she specialized in receivables management and cash acceleration for hospitals and physician group practices. She is a certified public accountant.

Tim Hanson is president and chief executive officer of HealthEast, St. Paul, Minnesota.

Lauren Jones, Ph.D., R.N., is a principal at the Organizational Learning Group, Covington, Kentucky. She is also a lead faculty member for the Joint Commission on Accreditation of Healthcare Organizations, for which she designs and delivers executive retreats and seminars on continuous quality improvement. She was formerly a senior manager of the organizational behavior practice at Ernst & Young.

Olivia A. Kirk is a senior manager in the health care consulting practice of Ernst & Young, Chicago, Illinois. She specializes in strategic financial planning, financial feasibility studies, and program business planning. She is a certified public accountant.

Catherine Mazanec is a partner of the Northeast Ohio Health Care Consulting Group of Ernst & Young, Cleveland, Ohio. She holds a master of business administration degree from the Wharton School, Philadelphia, Pennsylvania.

Charles Musfeldt, M.D., is senior manager of health care consulting in the Chicago office of Ernst & Young. He holds a master of business administration degree and practices family medicine on a part-time basis.

Steven C. Renn, J.D., is a first vice-president of AMBAC Indemnity Corporation, a leading municipal bond insurer, where he is involved in the underwriting and risk management of health care issuers. He is also a cofounder and managing director of Health Care Investment Analysts, Inc., Baltimore, Maryland. He was previously a faculty member of the Johns Hopkins Medical Institutions in the Department of Health Policy and Management, as well as a research associate in the Center for Hospital Finance and Management.

James B. Riley, Jr., is a partner and vice-chairman of the health care law department of Ross & Hardies, Chicago, Illinois. He serves on the Health

Law Advisory Board of the DePaul University School of Law, also located in Chicago.

Sandra Shelley, R.N., D.N.Sc., is an independent consultant in the Chicago area. She was previously senior manager of the health care operations and performance improvement practice in the Chicago office of Ernst & Young.

Darrell J. Tamosuinas is coordinating partner of special services in the Minneapolis, Minnesota, office of Ernst & Young. In this capacity he specializes in health care restructuring and reorganization, litigation support, valuation, and corporate finance. He holds a master of business administration degree from California State Polytechnic University, Pomona.

Mark Van Sumeren is senior manager of Ernst & Young's health care performance improvement practice, where he is responsible for directing performance improvement engagements in hospitals and physician groups. He was formerly manager of management engineering for Harper-Grace Hospitals in Detroit, Michigan. He holds a master of business administration degree from the University of Michigan, Ann Arbor.

Kimberly A. Warnke, J.D., is an associate with the law firm of Ross & Hardies, Chicago, Illinois. Her practice focuses on bankruptcy and debtor–creditor relations. She holds a law degree from Washington University, St. Louis, Missouri.

Preface

Whether Bill Clinton's election as the 42nd president of the United States has provided a mandate for change will be debated by political scientists, some of whom might challenge the strength of that mandate when he received only 43 percent of the popular vote in a three-man race. Regardless of the conventional wisdom on this subject, the early signs are that his administration will be one that starts from the premise that government can be a powerful and positive agent of change and can help solve significant national problems. The president and his team have also already demonstrated that they are not afraid to shake things up if they believe they can convince the public and the Congress (probably in that order) that radical transformation is required.

In no area has the bar for success been raised higher than health care. The appointment of an interagency task force to create a health reform package for submission to the Congress, headed by Hillary Rodham Clinton and including some of the most powerful cabinet and executive office appointees, makes quite clear that this will be an early and perhaps crucial test of the administration's ability to fashion new solutions to extremely complex problems. The health care debate will also provide significant evidence as to whether this administration will fare better than the previous ones in creating a consensus for change, when change means indirect benefit for many, but direct pain for some.

If the administration is successful in slowing down the health care cost spiral, corporations and governmental payers will see more moderate rates of increase in their health insurance premiums. But small businesses, which in many cases now do not provide health insurance coverage, may not be as much of an engine for job growth in the future if they are required to provide this coverage as a result of new mandates. Similarly, the health care industry itself, which has been a strong creator of new jobs during the very weak economic period of the past four years, could see contraction in its work force if new health care financing programs (for example, heavier reliance on managed care and the use of capitation arrangements) provide sharp incentives for providers to practice more serious cost reduction efforts.

The administration's promise to cut costs will also be tested by the equally strong commitment to expand access to the almost 40 million uninsured, by the promise to expand programs for child immunizations and prenatal care, and by the need (probably as much political as clinical) to expand research efforts to fight AIDS. There are also fierce fights ahead as to the appropriate way to cut health care costs—whether government-set national health spending limits, rationing, and price setting are required or whether private-market, more competitive solutions offer greater promise. Political constituencies attached to each approach, or to hybrids of the two, can be expected to make their case with great purpose, given the dollars at stake, and the likelihood that the change that is coming may be more global than the tinkering that has occurred for the most part over the past two decades.

Hospitals will come under great pressure from serious reform agendas, whether they are top-down government mandates or more free-market managed-competition approaches. It is possible to foresee a health care marketplace in which integrated delivery networks of hospitals, physicians, ambulatory care centers, nursing homes, home health agencies, hospices, and retirement centers share economic risk by accepting a capitation contract for the total health care needs of a specific population. In this kind of world, hospitals will no longer worry about filling beds or generating patient revenues. They will be interested in being able to package a network of providers that shares a common treatment philosophy and is organized so that care can be delivered efficiently, in the most appropriate setting, to produce high-quality outcomes at the least possible price.

The risk of failure and the likelihood of the closure of significant hospital capacity is very high in the coming years. This book, written before the outlines of the proposed health care reform agenda are clear, provides guidance for strengthening an institution during the nervous transitional period ahead. Hospitals that understand the general direction of the reform effort—and its imperatives to become a lower-cost, higher-quality, more integrated provider of care—can position themselves so that their chances of survival in the reformed health care system are enhanced. As several articles suggest, however, there are many hospitals that cannot realistically expect to be winners in the next decade, and planning for an orderly withdrawal from the market may be the best strategic move for some institutions.

It is our hope that this book will assist the managers of hospitals who will need to engineer a turnaround to improve financial and operational performance, as well as those already struggling with such an effort. Organizational change has become the price of participation in the nation's health care system, and the speed of the change that must be encompassed and acted on will accelerate in the next few years. On behalf of all my coauthors, I wish our readers success in managing the change effort and hope that our book will make the job a little easier.

Richard A. Baehr

Acknowledgments

This book is the result of the efforts of many people. Nineteen people authored or coauthored chapters, and I thank them for their interest in participating in this venture, which competed for the little time left over from their very crowded schedules. I would like to thank American Hospital Publishing, Inc., in particular Rick Hill and Anne Hermann, for providing me the opportunity to develop this book and for their skillful involvement in seeing it through. I would like to thank my family for permitting me to undertake another project that took time away from them.

Finally, I would like to thank Ron Mills, formerly of Ernst & Young. Ron is a talented professional editor who has made my job much easier throughout the course of the preparation of this book. He has also greatly enhanced the quality of the final product by his suggestions and his critical review of the individual articles.

Chapter 1

Introduction

Richard A. Baehr

Any dramatic change in the financing and delivery of health care in the United States must consider the future role of acute care hospitals, still the centerpiece of this nation's health care system. Acute care hospitals quickly assumed this central role during the Johnson administration with the advent of the Medicare and Medicaid programs, which significantly increased access to hospitals and physicians for the elderly and the poor. Today, acute care hospitals receive by far the largest share (38.4 percent in 1989[1]) of total U.S. health care expenditures.

The focus of the health care industry shifted in the 1980s after the implementation of the diagnosis-related group (DRG) system for Medicare inpatient care and the rapid growth of managed care payment systems. Both these changes served to limit hospital inpatient utilization and to spur the growth of outpatient and ambulatory services. Many hospitals, particularly those in poor urban areas and small hospitals in rural areas, closed their doors. Record numbers of hospitals closed in the 1980s – 698 in all, with a one-year record of 106 shutting down in 1988.[2] Similarly, total hospital financial performance dropped precipitously from the mid- to late 1980s, with operating income margins slipping to less than 2 percent of net patient revenue in 1989. Many health care analysts have predicted a very gloomy future for hospitals, based merely on a continuation of the trends in evidence in the last half of the previous decade. Various surveys have suggested that as many as half of all hospital administrators believe their hospitals are at risk of failure in the next five years, though less than 15 percent of all nonfederal hospitals closed in the 10 years between 1980 and 1989.[3,4]

The Call for Substantive Health Care Reform

Although hospital financial performance has edged up slightly since 1989 and fewer hospitals closed in the years after 1988 than in previous years, there is still great trepidation among hospital administrators over the future role and viability of their institutions. For one thing, substantive health care reform became a serious issue in the 1992 presidential campaign, and most of the reform proposals addressed hospital cost containment as one component of the plan. With the exception of the 1983 DRG program, which was appended to the Social Security reforms passed the same year, virtually all legislation affecting the industry in the past 20 years has worked around the edges of the system rather than challenging its fundamental character. In no small part, this reflects the paralysis of the nation's major political institutions, particularly the fact that in only four years since 1969 has a sitting president had a congressional majority to work with.

However, no matter who won the 1992 presidential election, the pace of health care change at the federal level would likely have accelerated. Even the incumbent, George Bush, felt it necessary to stake out a "reform" program considerably more aggressive than any offered by recent presidents.

In recent years, most of the substantive change in health care policy has come at the state level. Hawaii, Vermont, and, to a lesser extent, Minnesota have adopted universal access programs; others have begun to ration certain very expensive tertiary procedures for their Medicaid programs (for example, transplantation services in Oregon); and still others have contracted with managed care providers for their Medicaid patient populations. In essence, the states and the federal government are grappling with certain fundamental issues, none of which will be easy to resolve:

- How does the government ensure access to health care for all Americans without spurring the already substantial health care inflation rate?
- How can the government and other major third-party payers encourage providers to establish a lower cost structure per unit of service (thereby limiting required third-party payments), and still maintain the financial health of these providers and their access to capital for replacement and new technology? In essence, what do hospitals need to earn, and what is the most efficient way for third-party payers to contract for their services? Should third parties pay per individual unit of service or on a capitation basis, discharging to the providers the risk of paying for the cost of care?
- Can third-party payment programs achieve their cost control goals only by significantly limiting consumer choice to particular physicians and hospitals?
- Should the financing of health care be a mixed public–private system, as it is now, or move to an all-public or all-private financing system?
- How can the enormous outlays already made for health care in this country (far higher than other countries per capita or as a percentage

of GNP) be used more effectively to improve outcomes and quality? What incentives can be created to promote preventive medicine rather than treatment, and to direct resources to providers (hospitals, physicians, nursing homes, hospices, home health care agencies) that can demonstrate high-quality care with favorable outcomes at reasonable prices?
- How will the technology explosion—particularly the growth of products from the biotechnology industry—affect the future need for hospital beds, operating room suites, and other elements of the current health care system?

This book does not attempt to answer all these questions, many of which are more policy-oriented than pragmatic. Rather, it assumes that change is not the enemy of successful hospital administrators but a potential ally. Those who can adapt, who can understand the incentives created by a new system, will not only survive but potentially thrive in the new environment.

The Need for Hospital Performance Turnaround

As indicated in the previous section, many hospital administrators and their boards are nervously concerned about the future of their institutions, in part because the plans for future federal and state health care reform are so unclear. The health care industry has already experienced powerful shocks in the past 10 years, and many hospitals have not adequately adjusted their operating patterns or strategic visions to confront the changes that have occurred. Although ratios of average hospital financial performance in 1990 are only slightly lower than similar numbers for 1980, such comparisons mask the much wider distribution of performance today, which generates an average that is not a norm for many hospitals.[5] In other words, the industry has developed distinct performance tiers: some superb performers, some average performers, and some laggards.

Traditionally, hospital turnarounds have been associated with institutions on the verge of failure. This book addresses a much broader market: hospitals that are failing, hospitals whose performance is declining, and hospitals whose performance is stable but mediocre. In an environment where the only constant is rapid change, mediocre performers can decline quickly and declining performers quickly confront failure.

Thus, many of the chapters in this book address ways to reinvigorate a hospital's performance and are not aimed specifically at institutions that might be characterized as distressed. The message is that all hospitals need not feel the boom of the worsening payment climate and utilization shifts away from their core business. Institutions that can improve quality, reduce cost structures, maximize revenues and cash flow, and package and promote services to address the community's service needs will likely outperform less well-managed providers that share their market area. Hospitals certainly must improve performance if the goal is not only to survive but also to succeed.

Although certain performance improvement strategies and approaches should be helpful to virtually all hospitals, it is nonetheless true that many hospitals start at a significant demographic disadvantage and have to work harder to either remain in business or succeed. For example, the administrator of a hospital on the West Side of Chicago has greater difficulty generating an operating profit than the administrator of a hospital located in Chicago's North Shore suburbs, due mainly to the very different payer mix associated with their respective patient populations. Similarly, a hospital in a heavily penetrated managed care market, such as Minneapolis, has less pricing flexibility than hospitals in metropolitan areas in many other states where managed care represents 10 percent or less of insured patients. A hospital in a rate control state (particularly in the northeastern section of the country) has greater difficulty achieving an adequate financial return-on-invested assets and equity than an institution in a less restrictive financial environment.

All these circumstances and comparisons are meant to forewarn the reader against translating the contents of this book into simple recipes for improved operating performance. The environment in which a hospital is situated—characterized by population growth, age distribution, income levels, managed care activity, payer mix, Medicaid payment levels, and competition from other hospital and nonhospital providers—is very influential in determining performance. It is also true, however, that within those areas where demography poses a disadvantage, the more efficient providers will continue to outperform the inefficient ones. In fact, good management is more critical in a difficult environment than in a favorable location.

Several of the chapters in this book also recognize the more traditional distressed hospital situation. In these cases, hospitals need to determine if they have a viable future under the best of circumstances, and with the best management direction and strategic positioning. In many cases, the odds against realizing a successful future as a traditional acute care hospital will be very long.

The Change in Hospital Use Rates

It can be argued that the United States will require substantially fewer hospitals to meet its health care needs in the next decade. Between 1980 and 1990, hospital occupancy dropped from 75.9 to 64.5 percent, despite a reduction in overall bed capacity of approximately 50,000 beds.[6] Assuming that 75 percent was an acceptable occupancy level on an average basis for all the capacity in the country, this suggests that there were 129,000 excess beds in 1990. In other words, 430 300-bed hospitals or 645 200-bed hospitals could shut down if the goal were to eliminate excess capacity and drive the fixed costs associated with this capacity out of the system. Looking forward, it is difficult to be optimistic about volume growing to fill the available capacity. More likely, metropolitan areas that have had low managed care penetration rates will see a growth in these plans, at the expense of inpatient utilization and intensive outpatient diagnostic and treatment services. Similarly, it is likely that all major third-party payers, and newly formed business coalitions in many cities, will work to push down inpatient use rates in markets where these rates are well above the national average (including many cities in the Northeast and the Midwest). The experience of the low-use-rate markets (many West Coast cities) will become the national model for the goals established by purchasers of care. As a result, the national average use rate will continue to decline, until most high-use-rate markets are more in line with the national pattern. It is also likely that payers, armed with information on resource consumption and outcomes at individual institutions, will increasingly direct resources within a market to those institutions with better performance records for both inpatient and outpatient services. This, too, will have the effect of suppressing overall demand. Finally, the sheer volume of certain expensive procedures, such as open-heart surgery, can be expected to be challenged. Various studies have argued that as many as one-third of all open-heart procedures performed in hospitals were not necessary, at a cost of $25,000 or more per procedure. Closer scrutiny of the necessity for these and other expensive, largely inpatient-intensive procedures can be expected.

In recent years, physician fees have grown at a faster rate than hospital inpatient expenditures. Some of this growth can be explained by the rapid growth of the physician population and, in particular, the concentration of new physicians in specialty and subspecialty areas. As with hospital supply, additional physician supply pulls demand along with it. Much of the explosive growth in outpatient diagnostic and treatment services has been fueled by the proliferation of these physician specialists. The DRG system for Medicare inpatients has allowed the program to control inpatient costs per admission, and has provided incentives for reduced lengths of stay. One proposal to address the volume and expenditure growth in the physician component that has received increased attention in the past few years would create DRG payment rates that include the physician component. Such a change would almost certainly lead to reduced resource consumption, shorter lengths of stay, and more empty inpatient beds.

The recent introduction of the resource-based relative value scale (RBRVS) payment methodology for Medicare physician fees was designed in part to address the imbalance of physician earnings between primary care doctors and specialists. The change may also provide greater incentives for new doctors to consider primary care as a practice. The expected continued growth in managed care penetration rates will also give primary care physicians more leverage by making them the gatekeepers controlling utilization and resource consumption. For many years hospitals have had to pay the cost of providing the resources required to support the practice patterns of physicians who were on staff but who were only minimally controlled by the hospital, and whose financial interests in many cases were in conflict with the hospital's. Although hospitals had incentives to minimize resource consumption, particularly for fixed-rate payers, physicians continued to bill on either a fee-for-service basis or a discounted fee-for-service basis, with minimal volume constraints. Hospitals that have been able to establish more direct linkages with their physicians—optimally, as salaried employees or as a dedicated multispecialty group practice—will have a much greater ability to achieve their future strategies in consonance with their physicians.

Another inhibitor to inpatient and outpatient demand in the next 10 years could come from significant changes in the way care may be delivered. If the federal government were to challenge the hospital expenditures associated with patients (primarily Medicare patients) who are unlikely to survive beyond a few months, it would have a dramatic impact on the volume of home health care and hospice services, but at the expense of hospital and physician utilization. In addition, technology changes are working against inpatient utilization. Sophisticated procedures, such as cardiac catheterization and lithotripsy, are now performed routinely on outpatients. Advanced diagnostic capabilities (such as magnetic resonance imaging [MRI] and positron emission tomography [PET] scanners) combined with chemotherapy and radiation therapy delivered on an outpatient basis are replacing the need for invasive exploratory or cancer surgery. Most significant would be health care reform initiatives designed to equalize the access to ambulatory and preventive medicine and to provide prenatal care for many low-income citizens. Hospitals now offer the first medical intervention for many of these people, generally through outpatient clinics or the emergency department, with resulting inpatient use rates and costs well above the average for similar age segments of the population.[7]

Another factor that argues for greater excess capacity in the next 10 years is that the substitution of specialty care units for traditional inpatient acute units has probably run its course. The growth of inpatient capacity and utilization for behavioral medicine (psychiatric beds, and alcohol and chemical dependency units) as well as for other specialty facilities or units (rehabilitation, long-term care) served to cushion hospitals against very steep rates of decline in their traditional acute care business. From 1980 to 1989, general acute inpatient days declined by 67 million days (27 percent), whereas total inpatient days declined by only 48 million days (18 percent).[8] It is likely, in fact, that specialty hospital utilization will decline in the coming years. The negative publicity surrounding the psychiatric hospital business (tainted by payoffs to individuals who referred patients for admission to inpatient units) has only reinforced the general inclination on the part of third-party payers to more aggressively challenge the growth in psychiatric and chemical dependency program expenditures. In the past two years, inpatient utilization for these facilities has shrunk substantially, largely due to marked reductions in lengths of stay.

The Impact of Hospital Closures

If it is accepted that many hospitals should close, will the distribution of these closures be fairly widespread or, instead, limited to the types of hospitals that have been the predominant victims in the past decade? In Chicago, 16 hospitals closed in five years, many after a very restrictive state Medicaid initiative was launched. Most of the closures were in inner-city neighborhoods that suffered payment reductions due to their heavy reliance on the Medicaid system. A few were in higher-income neighborhoods but with many competitive institutions located nearby, and failed largely because they were disproportionately affected by the drop-off in inpatient volume. A second large category of closed hospitals in the 1980s was rural institutions, particularly very small hospitals (under 100 beds). Over half the community hospital closures each year between 1986 and 1990 were rural hospitals. Several financing initiatives passed by Congress in the past few years were designed to steer more Medicare money to these hospitals. It is possible that many of the smallest hospitals (under 50 beds) may only be able to survive as outpatient and day-surgery facilities, with overnight stays used primarily for holding patients to be transferred.

The rationalization of the nation's health care system, which may occur in the next decade, will need to include finding a way to identify institutions that fill a critical patient care role in specific geographic areas and to keep them in business. In the inner cities, some hospitals surely must remain open or access problems will mount. Similarly, rural hospitals in areas far from other providers fulfill an indispensable role in ambulatory medicine and can be linked to larger institutions in cities for inpatient care or more sophisticated outpatient treatment when it is needed.

But many hospitals sharing markets with more successful providers will close in the next 10 years, without significant social cost to their communities. This is true for several reasons, but primarily because there is unlikely to be enough business to support keeping open all the capacity that is presently available. In larger metropolitan areas with a few million total population, this could mean 10 to 12 hospitals remaining where there are 15 today. In smaller communities, it might mean three hospitals today, but only two in five years. Hence, the great majority of patients and physicians will still enjoy several convenient choices, even after a particular hospital closes. It can also be argued that the high-quality hospitals will not likely be the ones that fail in saturated markets. Hospitals with low census typically have poor financial performance, and low census is frequently associated with a lower quality of care. Patients formerly associated with these hospitals will, in general, be redirected to higher-quality, more financially stable institutions.

There is also a strong financial incentive for third-party payers to drive out excess capacity from markets having several providers. A third-party payer that is billed for a patient stay at a low-occupancy hospital will be paying a very high percentage of that bill to support an overhead structure rather than direct patient care. If patients at these low-volume hospitals are transferred to larger facilities, the incremental revenue from these patients need only be greater than the marginal cost of treating them at the larger recipient facility for the business to be profitable. Thus, if many fewer hospitals were treating the same or a slightly declining volume of inpatient business as is now treated at many more facilities, the required cost per inpatient unit (admission or day) should decline. In certain states (Illinois is one), the payment programs of Medicaid and managed care companies have seemed designed to reduce capacity by offering blocks of patient business to the lowest bidders. In general, low-census hospitals are unable to bid successfully for blocks of business and, as a result, lose what they already have.

Strategies for the Future

All this suggests that one of the most successful strategies for many hospitals in competitive markets will be to take steps that will position them more effectively. If health care reform produces a national payment system that controls total expenditures for all providers, the aggressive pursuit of this strategy will become even more advantageous. Some health care organizations in selected markets are already buying up other institutions only to close them, figuring that the return on investment from the incremental business secured will pay for the initial capital expenditure in a relatively short period of time. A quick return is particularly likely in a case where the acquired hospital is quickly closed, because the cost associated with the additional volume will only be the variable cost of serving additional patients at the existing institution.

It can also be expected that the pace of hospital mergers will accelerate in the coming decade, especially if the Justice Department and the Federal Trade Commission decide to pursue a less aggressive policy toward hospital merger activity. Many potential mergers, particularly those considered by institutions in smaller communities (five or fewer hospitals), have been put on hold as a result of the chilling effect of government challenges to mergers of hospitals in Rockford, Illinois; Roanoke, Virginia; and Ukiah, California. In the late 1980s, the only substantive antitrust cases pursued by various governmental bodies were health care cases, whereas the megamergers of airlines, food companies, and the like went unchallenged. Many hospital mergers were initially organized to distribute services more rationally among two or more hospitals in a community and to avoid costly technological or service duplication. Over time, however, many of these mergers led to the closure of inpatient acute care capacity, with one of the facilities renovated for alternative use (for example, long-term care or specialty care) or, in some cases, closed or put up for sale. It is likely that the time period between merger and capacity consolidation will shrink as the financial burden of maintaining duplicate inpatient capacity increases.

Again, much of this book is aimed at helping hospital administrators and their boards position their institutions to be winners in the end game that will be played out among the weaker hospitals in many communities. For these hospitals, survival is not assured—but neither is failure. Strategies and actions to reinvigorate an institution will need to address both short-term financial and operating issues as well as longer-term concerns. In some cases, survival will depend on affiliation, merger, or strategic partnership with another acute care provider, or perhaps a more formal and direct relationship between the hospital and its medical staff. Hospitals that can position themselves to be strategic partners with their medical staffs and with major third-party purchasers will, in general, have better prospects than those that have distant or adversarial relationships with these other major players.

One of the keys to successfully navigating the next series of health care shakeups will be for hospitals to better understand what they can do well and in what areas they can efficiently serve their communities. More than 800 hospitals now perform open-heart surgery, more than 500 do organ transplants, and more than 1,300 have cardiac catheterization programs.[9] Rather than continued proliferation of these tertiary services to more and more community hospitals, the 1990s are likely to see a reduction in the number of facilities with these services, as third-party payers direct business to selected institutions, primarily those with already high volumes and better-than-average cost and outcome profiles. Increasingly, hospitals will begin to fill three distinct roles: primarily outpatient providers, community hospitals with very modest tertiary capability, and very intensive medical centers designed to handle most of the tertiary-level care. Even within these categories, hospitals will need to select areas for focus—the specialized services or centers of excellence that will be the drawing card for the institution with major purchasers of care. For these services, the hospital will need to be a high-quality, low-cost provider in order to secure the additional volume that makes it easier to provide high quality at a low cost. It is already apparent that in many communities managed care companies are negotiating contracts with specific hospitals for particular services, rather than general facilitywide contracts. This will increasingly become the case in markets where there are many providers and where third-party-payer leverage is greatest. Hospitals in competitive markets will need to excel at something to stay in business in the difficult environment that appears to be ahead.

Conclusion

Although the true theme of much of this book has a positive tone—how to engineer a hospital turnaround to ensure that it is one of the survivors—this introductory chapter has focused on why there will likely be fewer hospitals in the years ahead. The reason for this is twofold: First, even if all hospitals do everything well, some hospitals will fail. This is primarily attributable to the large amount of overcapacity in the industry, which will likely grow over the next decade. With rapid growth in health care expenditures becoming a matter of national urgency, third-party payers will not continue to pay for this overcapacity and will assist in its elimination. Because hospitals that attempt a turnaround need to exert much energy and investment, one message cannot be overemphasized: It is simply not worth it for some institutions to try.

The second point relates to two somewhat contradictory trends that are likely to develop over the next decade: both greater collaboration and greater competition among providers. If the message about elimination of capacity is correct, the competition theme will dominate until much of the excess capacity is eliminated. Once this very difficult process has run its course, the remaining institutions are likely to find it in their interest to be more collaborative, a model that is currently playing out in the airline industry, where deregulation has led to the birth of almost 100 new carriers. Today, fewer than 15 years later, seven carriers account for almost 90 percent of all domestic traffic, and only two of the new airlines are in business, one of them operating under Chapter 11 protection. The major carriers that are well positioned for the future behave like oligopolists, imitating each other's pricing strategies and for the most part avoiding other strong competitors' markets. Once the weaker carriers are driven out of business, it can be expected that prices will rise and the industry will behave more like a public utility, with predictable profit margins and more even year-to-year performance. This model for the hospital industry would suggest that, after a nasty competitive period, the resulting shakeout will leave a somewhat smaller group of providers that are leaner, of higher quality, and clearer about their function. This phase will bring down the "production cost" of providing care and, with greater rationalization of individual hospitals' roles and service offerings, help reduce the very costly duplication of services and technology that is now so evident.

These macro themes need to be understood at the micro level of the individual hospital turnaround. Hospitals will be tested in the years ahead to deliver high-quality services for a fixed price, particularly in the specific areas identified by hospital management as those in which the hospital has a better chance of performing successfully. Accomplishing this will require great effort to improve performance, accelerate cash flow, maximize income from third-party payers, operate more productively and with higher quality, and improve the hospital's relations and coordination with medical staff and third-party payers. Not all hospitals will be up to the task, but it is hoped that this book will provide some insight into how to assemble the building blocks that must be in place for a turnaround to succeed.

References

1. Waldo, D. (for the Health Care Financing Administration). National health care expenditures. *Health Care Financing Review,* Fall 1991.
2. American Hospital Association. *Chicago Hospital Closures 1980–1990.* Chicago: AHA, 1991.
3. AHA.
4. Touche Ross & Co. *U.S. Hospitals: The Future of Health Care.* New York City: Touche Ross & Co., 1988.
5. Healthcare Financial Management Association. *Financial Report of the Hospital Industry.* Chicago: HFMA, 1991.
6. American Hospital Association. *National Hospital Panel Survey.* Chicago: AHA, 1991.
7. United States Congress. *1990 Green Book.* Washington, DC: U.S. Congress, 1990.
8. National Center for Health Statistics. *Health United States 1990.* DHHS Publication No. 91-1232. Washington, DC: NCHS, 1991.
9. American Hospital Association. *1990 Hospital Statistics.* Chicago: AHA, 1991.

Chapter 2

Identifying the Financially Distressed Hospital

Steven C. Renn and Olivia A. Kirk

In the years ahead, hospitals that have been able to maintain strong operating performance and amass substantial cash reserves will surely prevail over hospitals that have suffered cumulative annual losses and exhausted all of their available cash and lines of credit. Among today's failing hospitals, those that hope to survive must act swiftly and with purpose. How early a hospital is diagnosed as financially distressed can be crucial to employing the least disruptive and most workable solution. The sooner the symptoms are identified, the less imposing the adoption and implementation of a feasible plan of action.

The analysis of specific performance indicators and other information can pinpoint the reasons for financial distress. Beginning with the evaluation of key financial ratios, operational performance trends, market position, environmental characteristics, medical staff composition, and management attributes, management *can* diagnose problems before they become irreversible. But a wide diversity among hospitals can be expected due to differences in their size, location, ownership structures, and other commitments and functional strategies. Associated with these differences are differences in payer mix, managed care penetration, the regulatory environment, physician practice patterns, and organizational culture. Considering these profound differences, a successful approach to identifying distress begins by evaluating a hospital's performance against a carefully constructed peer group.

This chapter is divided into two parts. Part 1 identifies some of the major concerned parties, or stakeholders, in a hospital's success or failure, their major causes for concern, and the internal indicators that may trigger alarm among external parties. Part 2 identifies the warning signals of financial distress, including the performance areas to investigate and how to construct appropriate comparison groups for benchmarking. The warning signals in specific performance areas focus on market and environmental factors, internal operational measures, and financial statement indicators of distress.

Part 1: Identifying the Hospital's Internal and External Stakeholders

A hospital has numerous constituencies to keep apprised of its current financial affairs, financial position, and future viability. These concerned parties, or stakeholders, include both internal entities (such as the board of directors, management, medical staff, and employees) and external entities (such as trade creditors, bondholders, bond insurers, rating agencies, financing authorities, and bond trustees). With increasing hospital closures, bankruptcy filings, and bond rating downgrades, hospitals' stakeholders are becoming more involved in analyzing financial performance on an ongoing basis in order to avert financial deterioration and potential closure.

Internal Concerned Parties

The hospital's internal entities include the board of trustees, management, medical staff, and employees. The following sections describe these positions and how the hospital's financial distress can affect them.

Board of Trustees

The hospital trustees have a legal obligation to ensure that the hospital's mission is being carried out, that its strategic plan is operational, and that quality of care standards are being met. The trustees are also responsible for safeguarding the hospital's assets and managing the affairs of the hospital through a competent and experienced management team.

Indicators of financial distress at the board level include the board's general unawareness of the hospital's financial, operating, and strategic situation. This lack of attention to the affairs of the hospital and inadequate guardianship and support of management can lead to legal liability exposure. On the other hand, the board can become too involved in the day-to-day management of the hospital and neglect its governance function. This excessive involvement may stem from the need to overcompensate for weak management, but ultimately will prevent management from performing effectively. The manner in which the board effectuates decisions can also be revealing. A board that does not adequately discuss major issues and yet approves plans unanimously or shelves them indefinitely may lack decisive leadership.

Other indicators of hospital distress at the board level include the lack of board self-evaluations, which provide a process to improve the board's overall effectiveness, and the lack of management evaluation, which provides a regular process to appraise the chief executive officer's performance. These evaluation requirements can provide a mechanism to improve the governance of the hospital and can provide invaluable feedback to management.

Financial distress may be further complicated by the board's reaction to the general business planning process in the hospital. From time to time, independent assessments of proposals must be demanded so that assumptions and conclusions can be tested objectively. Not involving outside parties to verify results can lead to governance by administration rather than by the board and may cause unwise investing of the hospital's cash reserves. In other cases, hospital management may be misusing outside consultants merely to support its own views and circumvent an objective analysis. There must be a mechanism in place to counterbalance management's proposals and ensure that plans discussed at the board level are implemented and monitored.

In order to make sound business decisions, the board must be provided with useful financial and statistical information. The lack of regular reports to monitor key performance indicators is a source of concern because it may indicate inadequate management reporting at all levels or corroborate management's desire to conceal important information from the board. In any event, the lack of adequate information at the board level may cause problems to go undetected for too long.

Management

Management has the overall responsibility to carry out the mission of the hospital, manage its financial affairs effectively and efficiently, ensure that quality of care standards are being met, and implement sound business strategies. Financial distress is a major concern for hospital managers because the deterioration of cash reserves will imperil their ability to make necessary operational and facility improvements. This delay in making necessary improvements and the overall lack of focus on future viability may provoke some key management personnel to look elsewhere for employment.

On the other hand, management may be the root of the problem. Management's failure to obtain Joint Commission on Accreditation of Healthcare Organizations (JCAHO) accreditation, for example, may cause the health care and medical community to question the overall quality of care provided at the hospital. An equally or more devastating noncompliance issue is the threatened decertification by the Medicare and Medicaid programs. Failing to comply with these government standards not only causes quality of care concerns and damages a hospital's reputation, it also jeopardizes reimbursement, potentially creating a cash flow problem. This is particularly important when a hospital depends on Medicare and Medicaid for a large percentage of its revenues.

Able managers have a firm grasp of major environmental conditions such as reimbursement changes, charity care, deteriorating physician relations, the shift from inpatient to outpatient settings, and managed care; and they effectively control or make decisions to counterbalance the impact of these external forces. When management lacks a plan of action to address these conditions, financial performance suffers.

Persisting organizational issues may elicit a surprise "going-concern" audit. Such qualified audit opinions may be rare, but consistent major year-end audit adjustments are cause for worry and do warrant investigation. Issues raised in the auditor's management letter also require immediate attention. These basic organizational issues may be indicative of a poorly managed accounting and business office. When a hospital is experiencing financial distress, the entire organization is affected; but the real pressure point is the strength of the accounting and business office and its ability to provide timely financial results in addition to managing cash on a daily basis through improved accounts receivable collections, coordinating short-term financing, and carefully stretching payment cycles.

In order to assess weaknesses in organizational structure, the hospital's information system may also need to be evaluated. The lack of adequate management reporting may leave problems undetected. General areas of concern regarding management reporting include inconsistent reports, lack of timely reporting, and inaccurate and insufficient reporting. One of the major issues typically raised by top management is its inability to procure decision support information on a routine and timely basis. The lack of adequate management reporting may be caused by poor data input or inadequate programming capabilities.

Financial reporting also includes a comprehensive budget process with appropriate variance reports and department head accountability. A hospital that does not involve department heads in its budget process may lack adequate controls on operating expenses and shows a disregard for overall financial planning. This absence of financial planning will become more problematic as utilization declines, and a flexible budgeting process must be instituted immediately to reduce operating costs in proportion to volume declines.

Medical Staff

A hospital's medical staff is primarily concerned with the overall quality of care provided to the patients admitted to the hospital. Another area of concern is the lack of adequate capital to sustain a safe and modern patient care environment, provide state-of-the-art equipment, and maintain a good reputation in the community.

Although the medical staff is a concerned internal party, early indicators of financial distress may be traced to medical staff activities. If utilization declines persist, the hospital should review medical staff activities and performance. Some common areas of concern include a history of poor medical staff planning, as evidenced by a high average age of active physicians, and a low concentration of individual practices at the hospital, which may indicate ineffective marketing efforts and poor communication among the existing medical staff membership. Another medical staff symptom that can contribute to financial distress is medical malpractice experience, which exposes the hospital to legal and financial liability, as well as quality of care problems. Lastly, hospitals in financial distress may look for a quick fix by entering into unprofitable ventures and excessive payment contracts with outside physicians, thereby undermining existing medical staff relations.

Employees

Hospital employees are concerned about the financial stability of the hospital because of the potential loss of salary and benefits. Early indicators of poor employee relations that can contribute to financial distress include high employee turnover, particularly in critical professional positions that may be difficult to replace because of shortages in the industry. These unfilled positions will force the hospital to depend heavily on more costly agency staff. Another symptom is excessive overtime, which contributes to poor morale and possibly leads to heavy unionization and negative publicity.

External Concerned Parties

External stakeholders or concerned parties include a variety of outside creditors, bondholders and bond insurers, bond trustees, rating agencies, and financing authorities. Creditors and investors share a common concern of financial exposure when a hospital is in financial distress. Other external parties, such as financing authorities, are concerned about their fiduciary responsibilities and relationships with outside investors.

Financial distress will hamper the hospital's relationship with vendors when credit is discontinued or when the hospital cannot renew its line of credit with the local bank to meet payroll. Severe cash flow shortages will become most apparent when payroll taxes cease to be funded, creating a legal exposure for those making the decision to avoid paying taxes. When all outside sources of cash have been exhausted, the hospital may resort to using its debt service reserve fund, which will trigger an automatic technical default and serve as public notice to a "cast of thousands" of concerned parties.

Trade Creditors

Trade creditors are probably the first to suspect that a hospital may be experiencing a cash shortage. Typically, a hospital operates with a 35- to

50-day accounts payable cycle. The first signs of distress may occur when this payment cycle lags beyond 60 days and telephone calls to the hospital go unreturned. The relationship begins to deteriorate when commitments to make payment are not kept. This severing of relations is troublesome to both the vendor and hospital management. The vendor will not want to lose a large account, whereas management will be most concerned about the delivery of needed goods to maintain operations.

Bondholders and Bond Insurers

Tax-exempt bonds are a low-cost method of obtaining capital for hospital replacement or modernization or for refinancing existing debt. The lower cost of borrowing is due to the federal tax-exemption benefit to the bondholder, which allows the bonds to be sold at a lower interest rate than a taxable bond offering. After the bonds have been sold, the bondholders or registered owners receive payments of principal and interest until scheduled maturity. The hospital's ability to make these payments is contingent on its future revenue stream. Bonds sold by health care entities carry a certain amount of risk due to various factors in the industry, such as federal and state changes in reimbursement policies; state regulatory changes that affect licensure; increasing managed care and employer contracting, which constrain price flexibility; professional staff shortages, which increase employee wages; the hospital's position within its market area; advances in technology that lower the use of hospital care; and the capability of the management team.

Bondholders want to avoid the financial exposure created by a default on bond payments and the potential that the hospital may have to file for bankruptcy and/or to close. They are therefore concerned about the hospital's financial stability. When a bond payment is not made, the bondholders are typically notified immediately by the bond trustee that the hospital is in default. As added protection, bondholders may be notified before the hospital even misses a payment; falling below a certain financial target specified in the loan covenants can put the hospital in technical default. Such loan covenants include a required minimum performance on certain financial ratios, such as the hospital's current ratio, debt service coverage ratio, long-term debt to capitalization ratio, and/or operating margin.

Bond Trustees

The bond trustee, who is appointed at the time of the sale of bonds, has a fiduciary responsibility to collect scheduled principal and interest payments from the hospital, transfer payment to the bondholders, and maintain escrowed bond funds as required in the bond indenture. When the hospital withholds payment, the bond trustee is typically responsible for declaring the outstanding portion of the debt due immediately and may have to pursue any available remedy to collect the payments. The bond trustee has overall responsibility to ensure that required bond funds, payments, and covenants are being met by the borrower.

Financing Authority

In a tax-exempt bond issue, a municipal issuer is required because a tax-exempt hospital cannot sell bonds unless it is done through a state agency or state health care financing authority. Under the U.S. Constitution, only states can issue debt exempt from federal taxes. Even though the debt is issued through the authority, the authority is not liable for the repayment of the debt. The financing authority does, however, take an active role in structuring the transaction. A public financing authority has a fiduciary duty to ensure that the health care financing is in the public interest, alleviates a financial hardship, or may be expected to lessen the cost of patient care to third-party payers and consumers.

Financing authorities are typically notified when a hospital is in default. Even though they do not have any financial exposure or legal obligation, they are concerned about the financial stability of the hospitals they have approved for tax-exempt financing.

Rating Agencies

Rating agencies have a responsibility to the bond purchasers because they have provided the hospital with a bond rating based on its creditworthiness. Investors, in part, base their decision to purchase the bonds on this rating. Rating agencies assign a rating based on their judgment of the creditworthiness of the hospital and the capability of management to carry out its plan. The rating is determined based on the agency's investigation, available studies, other information and assumptions, and general trends within the industry. There is no assurance that the rating will not be lowered or withdrawn at any time; however, in light of their role in the investor community, rating agencies are most concerned about the hospital's ability to maintain acceptable financial performance.

This section has identified the hospital's key stakeholders—those concerned parties who are most involved in the organization's present and future performance. The remainder of this chapter explains how to discern the signs and indicators of possible financial distress and presents an approach that can be used to facilitate the identification process.

Part 2: Identifying the Warning Signals of Financial Distress

Identifying a hospital in financial distress, or one likely to become distressed, is not an easy undertaking. Although the term *financial distress* is frequently heard in the industry, there is unfortunately no generally accepted definition of the term or any precise consensus as to what it means. Nor is there any recognized or reliable litmus test that can be applied to reveal a failing financial condition in a hospital.

In some instances, there are unmistakably apparent signs that a hospital is in financial distress. At the extreme end of the spectrum, a hospital that closes or ceases to offer patient services or otherwise fails to survive can safely be identified as distressed. Similarly, hospitals that suspend interest payments or default on their bonded indebtedness or are unable to pay their short-term creditors are probably suffering from severe financial pressures. By the same token, hospitals that are forced to take extraordinary actions, such as curtailing or eliminating services, closing a substantial proportion of beds, laying off large numbers of employees, or searching for a merger partner, may be experiencing distress.[1]

For the vast majority of hospitals, though, discovering the signals of financial distress requires a thorough investigation of many factors. The following presents a general approach that can be used to identify a variety of early warning signals and other indicators associated with current financial distress or with the strong probability of subsequent deterioration in financial performance. This approach involves making comparisons between a target hospital and appropriate national, regional, and local peer groups of hospitals that are similar to the target facility or share its market area in order to identify those areas in which the hospital's performance is notably deficient compared with its peers and to assess whether these deficiencies are signalling distress. The final section of this chapter discusses the importance and interpretation of warning signals in specific performance areas, including a hospital's market position, reimbursement and regulatory environment, management, utilization, pricing, efficiency of internal operations and clinical practice, profitability, liquidity, capital structure, and solvency.

Using a Comparative Approach to Identify the Signals of Distress

The comparative approach to identifying financially distressed hospitals relies in large part on the quantitative analysis of financial, operating, and other empirical information. Because a hospital's performance can be measured in a variety of ways, some guidance is first needed in determining which performance areas should be analyzed.

Determining Performance Areas to Investigate

A thorough understanding of the business fundamentals of operating a hospital, an awareness of the national and local trends that are shaping a hospital's environment, and some lessons learned from the history of other hospitals that have experienced financial distress are the starting points for determining which areas of an individual hospital's performance should be investigated. Additional guidance is provided by prior empirical research that has quantified the factors that predict or predispose a facility to financial distress.

For example, several published studies have sought to identify the factors that are associated with a downgrade in a hospital's bond rating.[2] Standard & Poor's has analyzed some of the common quantitative and qualitative factors that may have been responsible for six recent defaults by hospitals and has also published a review of the guidelines it uses to assign a credit rating to hospital debt.[3] A number of studies have examined the factors responsible for the recent closures of acute care hospitals in the United States.[4]

A quantitative approach should involve the review of a broad array of measures of facility performance, illuminating such diverse areas as utilization, market share, patient and payer mix, capital structure, liquidity, pricing strategies, productivity and efficiency, and profitability. In some areas, such as the hospital's market share for a particular service line, quantitative data are often not readily available and difficult to obtain. For other areas, such as the relationship between the hospital's medical staff and management, performance may be impossible to quantify. Nonetheless, for these and many other important areas, whatever information that is available to address the concern should be examined, even if the analysis requires qualitative or subjective judgments.

Assessing Leading Indicators versus Lagging Indicators

Traditionally, unfavorable values for certain financial ratios calculated from a hospital's income statement and balance sheet are deemed to be clear signals of hospital distress. However, performance measures derived from a hospital's financial statements—because they chart its history—may not provide the earliest warning of impending distress. For example, by the time undesirable levels of profitability, liquidity, or financial leverage are recorded on an audit, or even on interim financial or utilization reports, certain "leading" signals of distress may have been apparent for some time. Moreover, because deterioration in these leading areas is frequently the *cause* for the poor performance ultimately reflected in financial statement measures, they are more susceptible to remedial efforts, as well as earlier intervention.

Thus, an investigation of other areas, especially those related to a hospital's market position, utilization, management, and internal operations, may prove more fruitful, because poor performance in these areas tends to predate—often well in advance—the deterioration seen later in the hospital's financial statements. Because they illuminate the underlying causes of unfavorable financial performance, identifying these leading indicators is of greater use in shaping a turnaround plan.

Another important perspective on causality is gained by distinguishing between factors beyond the control of management and those factors within its ability to change or correct. For example, in the short run, management has little ability to radically change a hospital's mission, affect the demographic trends in the hospital's service area, or rectify an unfavorable reduction in payment level under a major reimbursement program such as Medicare. However, over the long run, management certainly should be able to at least anticipate and plan for most exogenous factors.

Constructing Appropriate Comparison Groups

The early identification of a distressed facility begins with an examination of the performance of that hospital compared with the performance of similarly situated facilities. The first step in such an undertaking is to construct one or more appropriately defined peer groups.

As noted previously, an extremely wide variation in financial performance is to be expected among individual hospitals. Substantial differences exist among hospitals in terms of their size, location, regulatory environment, market position, ownership, mission, organizational form, patient and payer mix, provision of medical education, and similar structural and functional attributes. Many of these differences are the result of external or exogenous factors or forces, which a hospital has little ability to affect or control, whereas others may be within management's province to change. Regardless of their source, such fundamental external factors have a tremendous impact on the financial and operating performance of a particular facility.

Most large public hospitals, for example, can be expected to demonstrate weak earnings or even losses from patient care operations, in part because of the large amount of indigent care they typically provide and because they historically have been able to rely on substantial subsidies from their local or municipal governments. It would be inappropriate, then, to hold a large government hospital to a national average standard for operating profitability in attempting to determine whether it is distressed. Similarly, major teaching hospitals, in part because of their size, complex service offerings, and added teaching costs, incur average operating costs per case that are well in excess of smaller, suburban, nonteaching hospitals; but it would be a mistake to conclude that they are inefficient from that information alone.

Thus, before developing benchmarks or desired values for the financial and operating performance of a particular facility, in order to determine whether it appears distressed and to identify in which areas, it is crucial that the hospital be evaluated against a comparison group of similarly situated (or "peer") hospitals. Once one or more peer groups of similar hospitals have been assembled, the performance of the subject hospital should be roughly comparable to its peers, and significant unfavorable variances may be indicative of financial distress. Moreover, identifying and highlighting the initial areas in which a hospital appears, on the surface, to be underperforming similar hospitals serves to focus attention on these performance differences and may obviate the need to investigate areas whose relevance may be negligible. Sharpening the focus on these areas also increases the chances for uncovering the root causes of distress and formulating successful corrective actions.

A number of criteria based on a hospital's structure, location, and mission traditionally have been used to develop appropriate and sound comparison groups of hospitals that, all other things being equal, are subject to basically the same external constraints and thus can be expected to demonstrate similar performance. Listed below are some of the attributes most frequently used to construct hospital peer groups, along with a brief explanation of the rationale for using the criteria to select similar hospitals:

- *Bed size.* Hospitals are typically grouped into size categories, based on the number of beds in service they operate. Larger hospitals typically provide a more extensive, sophisticated, and resource-intensive array of services and, as a result, treat a more acutely ill mix of patients. Larger hospitals are also more often located in urban areas and more frequently operate teaching and research programs. As a result, larger hospitals tend to have higher per-patient operating costs, higher charges, and higher net revenues than smaller hospitals.
- *Location.* Typically, urban and rural hospitals are not grouped together. Primarily because of their higher labor costs, but also due to their larger size and higher case-mix complexity, urban hospitals have higher total and per-patient costs and revenues than rural hospitals. Other standard geographic categories include hospitals located in the same city, metropolitan statistical area, or state. Another important location group is that of other facilities in the hospital's local or market area.
- *Ownership.* Usually, distinctions are made between the ownership types of not-for-profit, investor-owned, and government hospitals. Investor-owned hospitals tend to show more aggressive pricing and marketing, better access to capital, newer facilities, and more centralized management than not-for-profit and government hospitals. Government hospitals are frequently able to rely on direct appropriations and subsidies to offset operating deficits and are often located in inner cities or outlying rural areas with greater proportions of uninsured patients, which serves to increase the amount of uncompensated care they provide.
- *System affiliation status.* System-affiliated hospitals often demonstrate the practice of managing cash and other current assets at their parent

organization, which may make certain liquidity measures, such as the number of days of cash on hand and current ratio, appear lower than those of freestanding hospitals.

- *Teaching status.* Usually, distinctions are made between major teaching, minor teaching, and nonteaching hospitals. Major and minor teaching hospitals tend to be larger, urban hospitals, and they incur additional costs as a result of the graduate medical education and research programs they sponsor. They also provide disproportional amounts of uncompensated care to indigent patients. As a result of their broader and more resource-intensive service offerings, they treat a more complex mix of patients and tend to have higher per-patient expenses and revenues.

Other frequently used hospital comparison groups include:

- Standard & Poor's or Moody's bond rating category
- Payer mix range (for example, proportion of Medicare plus Medicaid patient days above a certain threshold)
- Case-mix complexity range (for example, Medicare case-mix index above a certain threshold)
- Payment classification groups (for example, rural referral centers, disproportionate-share hospitals, or sole community providers)

Examining Sources of Data

A variety of sources of information may need to be examined in order to assess a hospital's current and projected future operating and financial performance. Some of the sources of information that may need to be analyzed include audited and interim financial statements, financial forecasts, capital and operating budgets, strategic plans, feasibility studies, certificates of need, reports by consultants or auditors, information on patient origin and service use, trust indentures and similar legal documents governing long-term indebtedness, and related supplemental materials. Other sources of data include services provided by health care information companies (such as Health Care Investment Analysts, Inc.), as well as data bases maintained by industry trade associations (such as the American Hospital Association and the Healthcare Financial Management Association).

Establishing Benchmarks and Making Comparisons

Comparisons should include the most currently available data, which at a minimum should include the facility's most recently ended fiscal year. Interim (year-to-date) financial and operating statistics should also be sought. Analyses should include at least three, and preferably five, years of historical data.

The benchmarks or standards of the "typical" hospital's performance in the comparison group are usually expressed as median, average, or weighted-average values. Median values are often preferred over average values for describing central tendency, or the typical hospital, because they are not as greatly affected by extreme or "outlier" values as are averages.

Percentage variances between a hospital's performance measure and the median or average for its peer group are often calculated in order to quantify the magnitude of the difference. Frequently, determining only that a hospital's performance is "below average" provides insufficient information, and quartile and percentile rankings may need to be calculated. Quartile values divide a group of observations into four subgroups that are equal in number; the bottom quartile value (often called the 25th percentile) is the value for which 75 percent of the hospitals in the group have higher values and only 25 percent have lower values. Determining that a hospital ranks in the bottom quartile of a peer group (or in the bottom decile, that is, the lowest 10 percent) provides a greater confidence level that the facility's poor performance is not due to random variation.

Heeding Certain Caveats

Finally, several caveats should be kept in mind when undertaking a comparative analysis of a hospital's operating and financial performance measures. First, the examination of only a small number of measures by themselves may not always lead to reliable conclusions. A broad array of measures should be examined and the various ratios interpreted in conjunction with one another and in the context of the mission, operations, and circumstances of the individual hospital. Even results suggesting conformance in most or all areas should not reflexively lead to the conclusion that the facility is completely healthy. Second, comparative ratio analyses may not completely determine the fundamental, underlying causes of distress. They rarely provide detailed explanations, suggest mitigating factors, or describe extraordinary events that may have occurred. Instead, such analyses often serve to identify the most fruitful areas for additional inquiry. Finally, comparative analyses cannot replace careful review of financial statements or the notes to financial statements. Neither can they obviate the need for investigating the hospital's external environment, market area, management, and internal operations.

Examining the Impact of Market and Environmental Factors on Hospital Performance

One of the first discrete areas to investigate for warning signals of distress is composed largely of external market and environmental factors. The following sections discuss the importance of examining the impact of such factors as market share, third-party reimbursement systems, compliance with external regulatory bodies, changing demographics and economic conditions within the hospital's service area, and trends in hospital utilization.

Market Position

Competition among hospitals intensified during the 1980s and early 1990s, spurred on by accelerating advances in technology, a growing surplus of hospital beds, an increasing number of physicians and other providers, and the proliferation of "prudent purchasing" arrangements and price-sensitive insurers, all set against a backdrop of persistent declines in the number of patients using inpatient services. Hospitals attract patients on the basis of the breadth of their service offerings, levels of patient convenience and amenities, sophistication of technology and medical programs, prices charged to private insurers, and the perceived quality of care they provide, among many other attributes. Increasingly, hospitals are promoting their strengths, reputation, and uniqueness through formal marketing and advertising in an effort to make themselves attractive to patients, physicians, business and employer groups, private insurers, and other purchasers of hospital services.

As hospitals attempt to attract more and more patients, the risk to facilities that fare poorly in this effort is assuming much greater importance. The loss of market share for a hospital in a stable or declining market translates directly into a loss of admissions. Significant or persistent declines in admissions to a hospital, as discussed further below, almost inevitably have an adverse effect on financial performance. At the same time that net revenues drop, expenses drop less, thus reducing the hospital's earnings and cash flow. The deterioration of a hospital's position in its market is one of the earliest warning signals of financial distress, often predating subsequent utilization declines of greater magnitude and even more distant symptoms of financial distress.

At the same time, the erosion of market share is also one of the hardest trends to reverse. A hospital whose market position is declining often finds itself trapped in a vicious circle. The loss of patients reduces the facility's earnings and cash flow, making it difficult to accumulate or borrow the funds that are continually needed to upgrade its physical plant, acquire equipment, and develop new services and thus recruit and retain the physicians needed to maintain its market position. As a usual consequence, a hospital viewed as being outmoded, lacking key facilities or services, or being behind alternative facilities in its service area will see its market position slide further, exacerbating its loss of patients. At an extreme point, there may develop a perception among patients, physicians, and the community at large that the hospital is failing, which may be one of the more difficult images to correct.

As intimated above, the erosion of market share can be the result of myriad factors: an aging, outmoded, or unattractive physical plant; an inability to acquire the latest equipment; failure to adopt current medical practice styles; failure to develop responsive service offerings; an inadequate number of primary care physicians or specialists in certain fields; the dissatisfaction of admitting physicians; stronger positions of other hospitals in the market area; new services offered by alternative providers, such as within ambulatory or subacute settings; a change in the demographics of the service area; or the growth of managed care arrangements.

A cursory investigation of market-based distress signals should begin with an assessment of the structure of the hospital's market, its position within and share of that market, and the perceptions of the hospital's position in that market by patients and physicians. The investigation can be expanded to include an analysis of the financial performance of other market-area hospitals, the changes in market shares that have occurred over the past several years, and any anticipated future strategies of other area hospitals, including proposed new services, renovations, alliances, or joint ventures.

Service overlaps with other market-area hospitals and possibly exploitable service offerings should be identified. The investigation should also attempt to identify the presence of "centers of excellence" or other specialized, high-technology programs at other area hospitals that may be drawing patients away from the subject hospital. In those market areas for which more detailed patient-level discharge data are available, the review should include specific information on the loss of market share by geographic area (such as a ZIP code or census tract) for individual diagnosis-related groups (DRGs), clinical service categories, or product lines.

Another area of inquiry is the extent of nonhospital facilities in the service area. The steady proliferation of ambulatory, outpatient, community-based, home-based, and specialty providers; the advancing sophistication of medical technologies; as well as the burgeoning supply of physicians increasingly have provided alternatives to inpatient settings that may be eroding a hospital's market share.

Finally, an investigation of the success of any efforts at related or unrelated horizontal diversification and vertical integration should be undertaken. Even though such ventures may be responsible for increasing admissions to more profitable services and for maintaining physician allegiance, or otherwise promoting the hospital's image as a full-service provider, they may represent a significant financial drain on a facility.

Reimbursement Environment and Payer Mix

Especially in the reimbursement environment of the 1990s, hospitals may be gradually or abruptly put at risk of distress as a result of changes in the prevailing payment systems employed by their patients' third-party payers. After more than two decades of searching for solutions, the United States has not solved the problem of disproportionately higher rates of hospital cost inflation compared with the general economy. During the last half of the 1980s, however, a series of growing concerns—the unavoidable need to rein in ballooning federal budget deficits; the political infeasibility of increasing taxes; fear that the increasing share of gross national product (GNP) devoted to health care was displacing more "desirable" areas of national production or investment, such as education, research and development, or infrastructure; and the handicap that health care costs represent to U.S. business in an accelerating movement toward a global economy—indicate that efforts at cost containment by business and government can only intensify in the future.

Over the past half-decade, the major third-party payers—the federal Medicare program, state Medicaid programs, Blue Cross plans, commercial insurers, and self-insured employers—have tightened their payment methodologies and significantly slowed the rate of increase in their outlays for hospital care. Thus, financial viability may be integrally related to the source of third-party reimbursement for patient services and the nature of the reimbursement methodology used by the third-party payer.

Medicare Prospective Payment System

Since 1984, the federal Medicare program has relied on a prospective, DRG-based, fixed-price reimbursement methodology referred to as the Medicare prospective payment system (PPS).[5] Generally speaking, PPS represents a technically sophisticated reimbursement methodology that recognizes in its payment rates differences in DRG-level case-mix complexity, local prevailing wage rates, teaching costs, capital-related costs, outlier-case costs, and other factors that vary among hospitals. However, since the mid-1980s, federal expenditures under the Medicare program (like several other large categories of federal spending) have continued to be an unavoidable target for federal budget-deficit reduction pressures. Between 1985 and 1991, the cumulative increase in Medicare payments per Medicare beneficiary was 35 percent, whereas the cost per Medicare patient jumped nearly 70 percent.[6] As a result, and not surprisingly, the average profit margin generated under Medicare dropped precipitously, from 14 percent in 1985 to an estimated −10 percent in 1992.[7]

Because further savings from the Medicare program will continue to be sought from Congress and, more important, because Medicare represents, on average, 40 percent of the revenue to the typical hospital, a hospital's current reliance on PPS and likely changes to aspects of the PPS reimbursement methodology should be examined. The assessment should include quantifying the profitability of the facility under PPS; determining whether reimbursement has been maximized under existing payment regulations; assessing the importance and future reliability of reimbursement for capital-related costs and direct and indirect teaching costs, outlier payments, and disproportionate-share payments; and evaluating the future impact on overall earnings of a hospital's PPS profits or losses. The share of Medicare discharges, Medicare inpatient days, or Medicare net revenues at a hospital as a percentage of total discharges, days, or net revenues are several reliable indicators of the hospital's dependence on PPS and its vulnerability to payment shortfalls or cutbacks in reimbursement.

State Medicaid Program

For hospitals that depend significantly on revenue from the provision of care to Medicaid patients, an assessment of the hospital's state Medicaid program may also be required. Many states have recently begun to experience severe fiscal and budgetary pressures. Because state spending on Medicaid is often the second largest and fastest-growing item in their budgets, the states' common response has been to implement stringent cost-containment mechanisms for their Medicaid expenditures, to the extent that insufficient rates of reimbursement under Medicaid may be the most prevalent among the major payers. At the same time, Medicaid patients may require more care because of attendant socioeconomic problems. A recent study has suggested that, in 1989, hospitals were paid less than their costs for Medicaid in all but three states.[8]

A hospital's share of Medicaid discharges, inpatient days, or revenues as a percentage of total discharges, inpatient days, or revenues is a measure of its vulnerability to payment shortfalls under its state's Medicaid program. Because of the fairly dramatic changes to Medicaid programs and increasing litigation in the area, it may be advisable to analyze the impact of a significant proposed change to a Medicaid reimbursement methodology on a particular hospital. Also, although the sufficiency of payment rates may not suggest an adverse impact, several state Medicaid programs have significantly lengthened their payment cycles, and others frequently exhaust their budgeted funds before the end of the state's fiscal year.

Furthermore, for many hospitals, treating a relatively large proportion of Medicaid patients is associated with a disproportional burden of indigent patients. If this is the case, an investigation of financial cost of the provision of uncompensated care should be undertaken. Since both the Medicare and Medicaid programs tend to reimburse hospitals according to less generous methodologies than do Blue Cross plans, commercial insurers, and other private-sector payers, analogous ratios measuring the proportions of "government payer" discharges, days, or revenues should be examined.

Managed Care Penetration

Unlike the federal government's approach of unilaterally and prospectively setting prices, third-party payers in the private sector control their expenditures for hospital care by focusing on curtailing the use of hospitals by the patients they insure. Since the mid-1980s, hospital utilization by private patients has been reduced significantly through a combination of greater cost-sharing requirements imposed on insureds; stronger incentives to use alternative, less expensive, noninpatient settings for treatment; vigorous application of utilization review techniques; the use of prudent purchasing or selective contracting arrangements (such as preferred provider organizations, or PPOs); and the adoption of capitated financing schemes (such as health maintenance organizations, or HMOs) that offer providers strong incentives to avoid unnecessary hospitalizations.

The penetration of managed care varies dramatically by region of the country and local market area. More than half of all U.S. HMO members, for example, live in 30 large metropolitan areas, where the average market penetration is 22 percent. In the larger metropolitan areas of California, Minnesota, Oregon, Washington, and Wisconsin, HMOs have captured between 30 and 50 percent of the market.[9] Although even in smaller metropolitan market areas HMOs can command between 10 and 15 percent of the patient population, the presence of a strong managed care environment tends to be a local phenomenon.

More important, the steady trend of commercial insurers, Blue Cross plans, and self-insured employers to increase the incentives for their insureds to join HMOs, PPOs, and other kinds of managed care insurance arrangements is expected to continue throughout the 1990s. As of January 1, 1992, traditional and open-ended HMOs enrolled nearly 38 million Americans, or more than 14 percent of the U.S. population.[10] Although growth in enrollment has slowed in recent years (HMO enrollment increased about 5.0 percent in 1991, compared with an annualized growth rate of 14 percent per year between 1980 and 1990), the HMO industry demonstrated significant financial gains in 1990 and 1991, increasing net income to more than $1.0 billion in each of the two years.[11] Moreover, the recent consolidation of HMO plans and the significant amount of unused capacity in the hospital industry has strengthened the bargaining power of managed care organizations. Consequently, the impact of a heavy managed care reimbursement environment, or the particular contracts that a hospital has negotiated, is more likely today to be among the factors that might predispose a facility to distress.

Generally speaking, managed care arrangements, if they are to be financially successful, must be able to extract a discount from a hospital's retail prices, limit their members' utilization of hospital services, and/or discourage their enrollees from using high-cost hospitals. At a minimum, a qualitative investigation of the perceived attractiveness of the hospital to HMOs and PPOs should be undertaken, including whether negotiated rates are sufficient, whether increased utilization will offset any substantial discounts, and the reasons for a hospital's exclusion from any plans. If data are available, further investigation should be made of the magnitude of additional administrative burdens, such as utilization review; whether the magnitude of any discounts granted are economically justified; whether the hospital has calculated the average or marginal costs of providing care to the managed care population, and whether those costs are covered by the negotiated rates; and whether the additional volume will materialize and, if so, whether it would occur regardless of the discounts granted.

In some cases, the price competition introduced into a market by the entry of managed care arrangements may lead to a widespread tempering of prices, even when payers may be more interested in appropriate service offerings, quality, or other competitive attributes. Finally, it may be advisable to investigate the financial condition and net worth of a managed care organization, as the recent insolvencies of several HMOs and at least one Blue Cross plan have made clear.

Pricing Strategies

Besides the efficiency with which it delivers care, a hospital's ability to generate earnings is also a function of its pricing strategies. For some hospitals, distress may result in part from not charging enough for some or all of the services provided to patients. On the other hand, as discussed immediately above, as private-sector insurers become more sensitive to differences in prices among providers, hospitals may be excluded from selective contracting arrangements as a result of overly aggressive pricing strategies. Even if not warranted by the existence of managed care arrangements, selective contracting, or other evidence of pricing differences among hospitals or price sensitivity on the part of private insurers in the hospital's service area, an investigation of distress should include an evaluation of the hospital's pricing policies, especially for its non-Medicare patients, compared with those of other hospitals in its service area.

One measure of the average overall price per case is gross patient revenue per adjusted discharge. Because of the strong positive relationship between case-mix complexity and average price per discharge, it is usually advisable to adjust raw charges for differences among hospitals in the complexity of care provided before comparing hospitals on the basis of price.

Other circumstantial evidence of noncompetitive prices may be gleaned by examining the charge-to-cost markup ratios for certain high-volume ancillary services (such as pharmaceuticals and medical supplies). Hospitals have traditionally chosen these less visible services (compared with the prices for routine services) for higher markups.

Regulatory Environment

Difficulty in complying with the regulations of state, federal, and private bodies governing the hospital industry—such as losing JCAHO accreditation—or in adjusting to a radical or hostile change in the regulatory environment—such as the adoption of a state-administered rate-setting program—can also contribute to financial distress.

Accreditation Status from JCAHO
Since a frequent early manifestation of distress may be deterioration in the facilities, processes, and standards employed for providing patient care, the report from the latest JCAHO survey of the hospital should be examined. Conditional or limited accreditation or significant instances of minimal compliance or noncompliance, especially in direct patient care areas, should be cause for concern and further investigation.

State Rate-Setting Systems
Although the popularity of state-level commissions that regulate the amount of revenue that hospitals can receive has waned in recent years, a number of states, mainly in the Northeast, continue to operate fairly stringent rate-setting programs. The enabling or related legislation establishing the commissions in most of the states explicitly or implicitly requires that rates set by the commission will be sufficient to maintain the financial viability of the regulated hospitals.

In a few states, however, the stringency of payment rates or the rate-setting agencies' aggressiveness in penalizing inefficient providers has been a contributing factor to financial distress. In at least one state, a hospital's default has been blamed in part on its inability to adapt to a new rate-setting methodology.[12]

Other Regulatory Programs
Other regulatory initiatives possibly having an adverse impact on hospital performance include the presence and stringency of a state certificate-of-need program, the existence of state-level indigent care "pools" or financing programs, the introduction of PPO licensing or enabling legislation, and the hospital's compliance with the requirements of the Medicare and Medicaid fraud and abuse laws, IRS regulations governing tax-exempt status, state and federal antitrust laws, and state licensing requirements.

Service-Area Demographics and Economics

Other warning signals of distress can come from changes in the demographic characteristics of and economic conditions in a hospital's local service area. In the mid-1980s, for example, many areas in the "oil patch" states of Arkansas, Louisiana, Oklahoma, and Texas suffered downturns in their local economies, resulting in business failures, high unemployment, slumping real estate prices, and a significant migration of the population out of these areas. Partly as a result, a number of local hospitals experienced severe financial distress. Between 1985 and 1991, Texas led the nation in the number of hospital closures, with a cumulative total of almost 90, or more than 20 percent of all hospitals that closed in the United States during that period.[13]

Although on a less drastic scale, the economic base and population mix and growth rate of most hospitals' service areas are constantly changing.

Consequently, it often may make sense to review or update projections of hospital demand and service utilization in future years in the hospital's market area in light of new information on population growth, changes in age cohorts, local unemployment rates, per-capita income levels, physician supply and distribution, the nature of the major employers in the service area, new industries entering or leaving the area, and similar demographic trends.

Similarly, current and projected market supply and demand should be evaluated against national, regional, and local benchmarks for per-capita admission and inpatient day rates, other service demand rates, per-capita bed supply rates, and trends in those rates.

Hospital Size and Utilization

In the current era of declining use of hospitals, trends in the utilization of inpatient services by patients may be among the most reliable warning signals of financial distress. At a minimum, an investigation should analyze the most recent five-year trend in the number of acute care admissions to or discharges from the hospital, including detail on admissions by major hospital service category. If data are available, an examination of trends in the use of specific programs and ancillary services may reveal areas where demand has softened. Although the core business of most hospitals is still the provision of acute care inpatient services, it is increasingly important to investigate the utilization of outpatient services. A relatively small share of outpatient revenue as a percentage of total patient revenue may imply that the hospital has not sufficiently developed outpatient lines of business.

The size of a hospital is an important factor in assessing susceptibility to distress. Several recent studies investigating the factors associated with hospital closure and the reasons for downgrades in credit ratings have concluded that smaller hospitals are more prone to distress.[14,15] Smaller hospitals typically offer a less extensive array of services than larger ones, and may not provide many of the newer, more medically sophisticated, and more technologically advanced services and programs more often found in larger hospitals, such as neonatal and other specialized intensive care units; cardiac and other rehabilitative services; and magnetic resonance imaging (MRI), ultrasound, and similar diagnostic services. As a result of their narrower range of services, smaller hospitals may be unable to treat more complex illnesses or perform sophisticated procedures. Smaller hospitals are less likely to operate teaching programs, and the absence of the interns and residents available to assist physicians and the associated prestige of a teaching or research program may also disadvantage them. Moreover, the quality of care provided by smaller hospitals may be perceived as being lower by patients, physicians, or payers. Consequently, smaller hospitals sharing a market area with larger hospitals may be at a disadvantage.

The occupancy rate of a hospital, and the trends in its occupancy rate, are key predictors of financial distress. An occupancy rate expresses the average number of occupied beds as a proportion of the number of available beds (preferably, beds set up and staffed for use, as opposed to licensed beds) and thus measures the extent to which the hospital's inpatient capacity is being utilized.

A declining trend in a hospital's occupancy rate, besides indicating that the hospital is becoming less attractive to patients, implies that the hospital's fixed costs must be apportioned over a smaller number of patients, which is frequently responsible for increases in the average cost per discharge. As a result, occupancy rate declines make it more difficult for the hospital to avoid losses, especially under fixed-price reimbursement systems. Low or declining occupancy rates, especially when caused by low or decreasing volumes of admissions, nearly always have an adverse impact on productivity, efficiency, and profitability, and thus tend to predate deteriorating financial performance in the areas of liquidity, debt service coverage, and solvency.

A hospital's occupancy rate is directly related to five underlying factors: the population of the hospital's market area, the admission rate in that market, the hospital's market share of admissions, the average length of stay for those admissions, and the number of beds set up and staffed for admissions. The first three of these factors are discussed above; of the last two, which are more within management's control, the receptiveness of management to closing or reducing the expenses associated with unused beds is an important inquiry. In a potentially distressed facility with a low occupancy rate, it is important to determine whether there are plans to scale down the size of the hospital, convert underutilized capacity to more productive uses, change the service offering of the hospital, or affiliate with other hospitals and physician groups.

Assessing the Impact of Internal and Operating Factors on Hospital Performance

Declining market share, declining inpatient utilization, and payment systems that reward increased efficiency have meant that, for many hospitals, the factors responsible for the greatest risk of distress are a result of internal and operational problems. Analyzing the appropriateness of clinical practice, the efficiency of internal operations, the productivity of employees, and the quality of management often holds the greatest promise for identifying specific warning signals of distress.

Clinical Efficiency

As mentioned above, the unmistakable trend of the major third-party insurers is to promote reimbursement systems that encourage clinical efficiency in a hospital—generally, those practices that avoid delivering an excessively high intensity of services per case or excessively long lengths of stay. The major government payers—Medicare and most Medicaid programs—accomplish this through fixed-price, per-case reimbursement systems that reward shorter stays and lower resource consumption and penalize the opposite behavior. Private insurers achieve this through multiple approaches to utilization review and selective contracting. Besides impairing a hospital's ability to survive under fixed-price or managed care reimbursement arrangements, inappropriate or inefficient clinical practice styles may threaten the quality of care delivered.

A patient's average length of stay at a hospital is primarily a function of the complexity of the hospital's case mix, the customary periods of hospitalization for particular diagnoses in the area, the availability of long-term and home health care for those needing support after discharge, and the clinical efficiency with which a hospital treats its patients. All other things being equal, longer average lengths of stay are associated with higher measures of case-mix intensity, higher resource consumption, and higher average costs per discharge.

Hospital-level average lengths of stay should be investigated by payer category, or at least based on separate calculations for Medicare and non-Medicare patients, and may need to be explicitly adjusted for the relative complexity of care provided by the hospital. The average length of stay for Medicare patients is particularly important to examine, because it correlates well with the hospital's ability to generate profits under PPS.

Lengths of stay that are significantly longer than a peer group's values and not justified by a more complex case mix may be interpreted as evidence of clinical inefficiencies in operation. Relatively long or increasing lengths of stay may indicate poor utilization management; problems with scheduling patient services; the need for improved monitoring, communication, and feedback mechanisms for admitting physicians or house staff; or the lack of available alternatives for subacute or nursing home services. If warranted, the analysis of patient-level discharge data may be necessary to investigate potential problems with specific service areas, DRGs, or individual physicians. Another measure of clinical efficiency is the proportion of inpatient days that are special-care days (days spent in coronary care, burn care, and other intensive care units); higher values, if not justified by a more complex case mix, are undesirable.

Productivity and Operational Efficiency

As noted above, measures of productivity and efficiency often illuminate the underlying causes of unfavorable financial performance. Generally speaking, indicators of productivity and efficiency compare a measure of hospital output (such as revenues, discharges, inpatient days, or volumes of individual ancillary services) with a measure of the inputs required to produce that output. For example, an overall hospital staffing ratio, such as the number of employees per occupied bed, measures the average number of personnel used to provide an inpatient day of hospital care; a measure of asset efficiency, such as the total asset turnover ratio, compares the amount of net patient revenue with the asset base required to generate that revenue.

Total operating expense per discharge, which is a measure of the average inpatient production cost of a hospital, is one of the first overall measures of hospital efficiency that should be examined in order to obtain a preliminary sense of whether low productivity may be contributing to distress. Values for case-mix and wage-adjusted average expense per case that are high or increasing significantly faster than hospital market-basket cost inflation may predispose a facility to distress.

Hospital-level staffing ratios (either measured on the basis of full-time-equivalent personnel per adjusted average daily census or per 100 adjusted discharges) are among the next indicators that should be reviewed. Because of the positive relationship between case-mix complexity and hospital staffing, it may be advisable to adjust an average cost per case value or a staffing ratio in order to take into account the relative complexity of care provided in the hospital. Tertiary care hospitals and other facilities that treat more acutely ill patients may also require a higher skill mix of personnel.

Labor costs typically represent more than 60 percent of a hospital's total expense budget. Thus unfavorably high staffing ratios, if not warranted by a commensurately high case mix, may be a gross indication of low productivity possibly contributing to distress. If information is available, it is advisable to investigate productivity at the departmental level by reviewing or conducting analyses that measure staff per departmental volume of output and direct and fully allocated cost per unit of output. Such analyses are similar to those performed in an operations review or operations improvement program conducted by a recognized consulting firm.

Unless justified by a hospital's location, more complex case mix, or more sophisticated personnel skill mix, high levels of salary and benefits expense per worker may indicate that employee compensation levels may be too high, or that there is excessive reliance on agency nurses or temporary personnel. During a period of declining utilization, salary and benefits expense is one of the categories of costs that can be most easily controlled, because a greater proportion of costs in this category is likely to be variable or semivariable. As with the case of average operating cost per case, high staffing levels are often the result of decreased utilization without commensurate reductions in staffing. In such instances, the development of management strategies for reducing staffing should be considered.

Another measure that should be investigated is the proportion of total costs represented by overhead (or administrative and general) functions in the hospital. High values for overhead expense as a proportion of operating expense suggest the need to examine the nature and magnitude of the general and administrative costs being incurred. Because this category of costs tends to be less variable in nature than the costs incurred in patient revenue centers, high values (which are often associated with a low occupancy rate) may indicate a facility that has not adjusted to a lower level of utilization, and one whose efficiency will be further impaired if utilization continues to decline.

Hospital Management

Maintaining the financial viability of a hospital requires competent, experienced, and innovative managers who are able to anticipate and react quickly to the earliest warning signals of distress. Although obtaining information on the capability of management is among the hardest tasks, the quality of a facility's senior management—including their past financial performance, age and experience, rate of turnover, and relationship with their board and medical staff—is among the most crucial determinants of future financial success.

A high rate of turnover in the senior management of a hospital is generally a negative development, possibly signaling poorly qualified personnel, insufficient experience, or internal conflicts with the board or medical staff, and definitely a cause of disruption in the continuity of management of the enterprise. A history of a lack of communication, absence of coordination, turf battles, personality conflicts, and other signs of poor relationships between two or more of the three management bodies in an institution—the board of trustees, executive management, and the medical staff—are other clear signs that a hospital may be vulnerable to distress.

Another warning signal is the absence or lack of use of strategic plans, mission statements, capital and operating budgets, physician recruiting and retention strategies, and similar long-range plans. Planning, budgeting, and otherwise anticipating the future; developing goals and priorities; and formulating strategies and courses of action to accomplish those objectives are some of the most critical responsibilities of management. The absence or disuse of internal processes of strategic and financial planning is a warning signal that a hospital lacks a mechanism for positioning itself for continued viability. The absence of an updated, unified strategic and financial plan in the areas of assessing market position and competition, evaluating the type and amount of needed future capital spending, and analyzing new business ventures and corporate restructurings or reorganizations is particularly unfavorable.

Medical and Nursing Staff

Another critical area to examine is the quality, continuity, and satisfaction of a hospital's medical staff. To the extent that such information is available, the investigation should consider the medical staff's range and mix of specialties, educational affiliations, number of board-designated physicians, average age, concentration of admissions from key admitters, turnover rates, and recruitment and retention programs. Similarly, the hospital's recent vacancy and turnover rates for nurses should be examined, as well as the reasons for excessive reliance on temporary or agency nurses.

Recognizing the Financial Statement Indicators of Distress

The last major step in the assessment of a hospital's potential for financial distress is an examination of significant trends in the hospital's financial performance. Analysis of the facility's levels of profitability and liquidity, its capital structure, and its creditworthiness and solvency will provide indicators of its short-term health and predictors of its future viability.

Profitability

Profitability refers to a hospital's ability to generate an excess of revenues over expenses. The ability to achieve consistent and adequate earnings or profits over the long run is critical to a hospital's financial viability. Insufficient levels of profitability may drain a hospital's working capital and impair its liquidity, forcing the facility to invade its reserves or fund balance in order to continue operations. More important, without sufficient levels of profitability, a hospital may be unable to accumulate the funds necessary for the replacement of its assets and will have difficulty accessing the public debt markets to raise capital. Ultimately, an unprofitable hospital will probably be unable to replenish its capital base, suffering a loss of market position and even greater financial distress.

Profits are a function of the prices charged by a hospital, the net revenue it collects, the volume of care provided, the efficiency of its patient care operations, and its ability to derive income from investments, philanthropy, public subsidies, and other sources not related to patient care.

An uncollectible or deductible ratio, which measures the proportion of billed charges that a hospital does not expect or is unable to collect, should be examined and disaggregated into the amounts due to contractual allowances, bad debts, and charity care. High or increasing values for this ratio should be investigated, because they may indicate one or more unfavorable developments: either an increase in contractual allowances and discounts (that is, an increase in the payment differential between charge-based and formula-based payers) or an increase in the amount of uncompensated care being provided by a hospital. Often, it may be useful to compare a hospital's net operating revenue per discharge and expense per discharge with those of peer hospitals in order to obtain a preliminary answer as to whether low profitability is the result of relatively high costs or insufficient revenues.

The two most frequently examined measures of profitability are a hospital's operating profit margin and the total profit margin. An operating profit margin, because it measures profitability with respect to the provision of patient care services, may be more revealing of internal or operational factors contributing to distress. A total profit margin, which includes sources of nonoperating revenue, such as investment income, private philanthropy, public subsidies, and other income not derived from hospital operations, may be a better measure of the overall likelihood of distress. A history of frequent losses from operations, and more important, frequent bottom-line losses, is cause for concern. The reasons for such losses should be explored thoroughly.

Another analysis of profitability should be made on the basis of the cash flow generated by the hospital (that is, its earnings before interest, taxes, depreciation, and amortization). This amount is a better measure of the funds truly at a hospital's disposal for capital expenditures or debt repayment.

Another important measure of profitability—return on equity—measures a hospital's earnings in relation to its equity (that is, its unrestricted fund balance). An insufficient return on its fund balance will cause a weakening hospital balance sheet by eroding the value of the hospital's equity. In an environment in which there is no volume growth, a hospital needs to earn a rate of return on its fund balance that is at least equal to the rate of inflation. If total volume is growing, the required rate of return on fund balances is (1 + the rate of inflation) multiplied by (1 + the rate of growth), with the inflation and growth rates expressed as decimals. Hence, 5 percent inflation and 3 percent growth would require a rate of return on its fund balance of (1.05) × (1.03), or 1.0815, equivalent to an 8.15 percent return on equity, in order to ensure that the hospital's equity would not be diluted in that year. For example, in an environment in which utilization is declining 3 percent a year, the required return would be (1.05) × (.97), or 1.0185, or 1.85 percent.

Although this return is not typically examined by concerned parties, it is a critical one for a hospital's board and management. Several years of insufficient profitability will create a substantially enhanced need for debt financing to support a hospital's balance sheet, at a time when profitability is weak.

Liquidity

In general, *liquidity* refers to a hospital's ability to meet its current obligations (that is, obligations due or becoming due within one year) using the hospital's cash and cash equivalents, plus its assets that are most easily convertible to cash. Measures of liquidity are critical indicators of short-term financial health, as well as useful predictors of long-term solvency. Poor or deteriorating levels of liquidity can impair a hospital's ability to make payments to its employees, vendors, suppliers, banks, lessors, and similar short-term creditors who, if they respond with adverse actions, can pose an immediate threat to the hospital's ability to operate on a day-to-day basis.

Liquidity Ratios

The five measures of liquidity most frequently investigated are the current ratio, acid test ratio, number of days in net accounts receivable, number of days in accounts payable (or average payment period), and number of days of cash on hand. A hospital's current ratio expresses its total current assets as a percentage of its total current liabilities; although it depends on the type of hospital, a current ratio of less than 1.50 is generally cause for further investigation, if not concern.

A hospital's current ratio may appear high as a result of the inclusion of relatively illiquid assets, such as accounts receivable and inventory, which may not be readily convertible into sources of funds. Consequently, the current ratio should be evaluated in conjunction with the facility's number of days in net accounts receivable. A large number of days in receivables, besides raising questions about the value of the receivables, may indicate that the current ratio overstates the hospital's liquidity.

An important alternative approach is to examine the acid test ratio, which considers only the hospital's most liquid current assets—namely, cash and marketable securities—in relation to its current liabilities. With the exception of facilities that may manage cash through a parent or separate entity, values for the acid test ratio that are less than 0.1 should be scrutinized. A related ratio is the number of days of cash on hand, which estimates the number of days that a hospital could continue to meet its cash expenses were no further revenue to be received. Again, notwithstanding hospitals engaging in centralized cash management, fewer than 10 days of cash on hand may signal an impending liquidity crisis. Finally, though generally not as important a cause for concern, maintaining large amounts of liquid assets compared with current liabilities may indicate excessively conservative financial management, to the extent that the hospital has forgone important strategic projects or higher-yielding investments in favor of unnecessary liquidity.

Working Capital Management Ratios

The number of days in net accounts receivable has an important bearing on short-term financial health, and both the level and the trend in this ratio should be examined. A large or increasing number of days in accounts receivable may indicate problems in the areas of accounting, patient billing, collections, medical records, or utilization management, and may raise questions about the collectibility of the revenues booked. The average payment period measures the average amount of time that elapses before current liabilities are paid. Although it varies by hospital, values in excess of 80 or 90 days for the average payment period should be investigated. An unmistakable trend of an increasing number of days in receivables coupled with increases in the hospital's average payment period is typically a warning signal of distress.

Capital Structure

A hospital's capital structure is often directly related to existing or future financial distress; for example, a relatively high degree of financial leverage—that is, a large amount of long-term debt in relation to the hospital's assets or capitalization—may saddle a hospital with high debt service costs, increasing the hospital's vulnerability to financial distress should its utilization or profitability decline. A large burden of debt may also impair a hospital's ability to incur additional long-term debt and gain access to other sources of outside funding or financing needed for growth and expansion. Consequently, specific ratios measuring capital structure are often examined in order to gauge a hospital's short- and long-term financial health and viability.

Financial Leverage

Four key measures of financial leverage that typically are examined are the ratio of a hospital's long-term debt to (1) its total assets, (2) its net fixed assets, (3) its equity or fund balance, and (4) its total capitalization. Each ratio measures the proportion of the hospital's assets, equity, or capitalization that was financed through the use of long-term debt as opposed to other sources, such as retained earnings, philanthropy, or other equity. Less frequently, the ratio of a hospital's total (current and long-term) debt to its beds in service is calculated.

Employing too much financial leverage places a hospital at a greater risk when facing unexpected, financially stressful events; the fixed expenses (primarily, the debt service costs) associated with such debt cannot be avoided in the short run, leaving the hospital with a smaller cushion than hospitals with lower leverage. Relatively high values for long-term debt as a proportion of total assets, net fixed assets, or capitalization often imply that the facility has a diminished capacity to assume additional debt, which may seriously impair its long-term ability to raise capital for the renovation and replacement of existing plant and equipment and which, in turn, may directly decrease the hospital's position in its service area. Although there is substantial variation among hospitals, generally speaking, long-term debt that exceeds 75 percent of total assets, 100 percent of capitalization, or 125 percent of net fixed assets is cause for further investigation.

Asset Age and Capital Intensity

The average age of plant, property, and equipment, or the average accounting age of the hospital's capital assets, is an approximation of the actual age of the hospital's buildings, fixtures, and major movable equipment. Higher values are associated with older physical plants, indicating that the attractiveness of the facility to patients and physicians may have declined.

In older hospitals, less time likely remains before replacement or renovation of assets is necessary, compounding the stress placed on the organization.

The degree of a hospital's capital intensity is typically measured by the amount of net fixed assets (property, plant, and equipment) per bed. Lower values indicate a smaller investment in the fixed-capital assets of property, plant, and major movable equipment relative to the hospital's size. Lower values are generally characteristic of smaller facilities, older facilities, and facilities that provide a narrower scope of services. Not surprisingly, a lower degree of capital intensity may be associated with a deteriorating physical plant, an eroding capital base, the lack of sufficient equipment, and lower patient amenity levels, all of which diminish the attractiveness of the hospital to physicians and patients. On the other hand, a high level of capital intensity may be unnecessary to remain competitive; it may, instead, signal a large burden of debt, high financial leverage, and high operating leverage, all of which can leave a hospital vulnerable to distress in the event of utilization declines or other unexpected, adverse developments.

Another indication of an excessive degree of capital intensity and/or an excessive reliance on debt financing is a high ratio of capital-related costs (primarily, depreciation and interest) to operating costs. Although there is wide variation among hospitals, capital-related costs that exceed 15 percent of operating costs represent a substantial fixed-cost burden and may make it difficult for a hospital to provide care at an efficient cost, and also leave it vulnerable to distress should the hospital experience declines in volume. The methodology recently adopted by the Medicare program, which pays for capital costs on a per-case, prospective basis, will likely subject high-capital-cost hospitals to a greater risk of lower Medicare reimbursement than under the previous cost-based system.

Creditworthiness and Solvency

Three frequently relied-on indicators of creditworthiness are a hospital's debt service coverage ratio, debt service as a proportion of net revenue, and ratio of cash flow to total debt. All these ratios are relied on heavily by financing authorities, underwriters, bond insurers, and rating agencies in evaluating a hospital's ability to promptly pay interest and repay the principal associated with its long-term indebtedness.

A debt service coverage ratio that falls below the standards relied on by the credit-rating agencies is often the key factor in the assignment of a low credit rating to the debt issue, and is highly predictive of the downgrading of an issue. Financing authorities and municipal bond insurers typically establish minimum debt service coverage requirements. Failing to maintain the minimum level typically constitutes a technical default by the hospital on the loan agreement. Banks and other financial institutions view low and declining values for these ratios as one of the clearest signals of financial distress, even though it is often predated by less visible signs of deterioration in market position, utilization, profitability, or other categories of performance.

A debt service coverage ratio measures the relationship between the funds available in one year for the payment of debt service (net income, depreciation, and interest) to that year's principal and interest payments. Although it depends in large part on the particular hospital, a ratio of less than 1.25 times suggests possible distress, particularly if a hospital is in the early years of a long-term debt repayment cycle. The ratio of cash flow to total debt measures the proportion of a hospital's total (current and long-term) debt obligations that could be met within one year; values of less than 10 percent should be investigated.

Conclusion

Every hospital has a large number of stakeholders who have a common vested interest in ensuring that their institution remains financially viable and whose interests are served by detecting as soon as possible any warning signs that their hospital's financial health is threatened. The early identification of potential financial distress requires comprehensive investigation and assessment of numerous factors and myriad areas of hospital performance. Because of the wide diversity among hospitals, a recommended approach begins with a comparative analysis of a subject hospital's performance with that of similarly situated hospitals representing a carefully selected peer group. Specific performance areas that should be investigated include factors related to the hospital's external environment (such as its market position, service offering, payer mix, reimbursement and regulatory climate, and service-area demographics), as well as its internal operations (such as management prowess, medical staff relations, staffing productivity, and clinical efficiency). At the same time, the process must include a thorough examination of the facility's past and current financial performance, gained through an analysis of the income statement and balance sheet ratios describing its profitability, liquidity, capital structure, creditworthiness, and solvency. A careful investigation of these areas should also yield many clues to the underlying reasons for distress. Identifying the symptoms of financial distress and understanding the reasons for them are the vital first steps toward the formulation and implementation of a corrective plan of action that will put the financially distressed hospital on the path to recovery.

Notes and References

1. One prominent author has defined *distress* as the "loss of ability to control a hospital's destiny," such as when the board and management of a hospital no

longer have viable choices to proactively manage and strategically position the institution. Unland, J. J. *Predicting and Preventing Hospital Decline.* Chicago: The Health Management Research Institute, 1991, p. 17.

2. McCue, M. J., Pillari, G. D., and Renn, S. C. Factors affecting credit rating downgrades of hospital revenue bonds. *Inquiry* 27(3):242–54, Fall 1990.

3. Standard & Poor's Corporation. *Debt Ratings Criteria: Municipal Overview.* New York City: Standard & Poor's Corp., 1989. *See also* the proceedings of *Healthcare Ratings: A Standard & Poor's Seminar.* Indian Wells, CA, 18-19 Apr. 1990 (New York City: Standard & Poor's Corp., 1990).

4. See, for example, Lillie-Blanton, M. A., Felt, S. E., and Renn, S. C. Rural and urban hospital closures, 1985–1988: operating and environmental characteristics that affect risk. *Inquiry* 29(3):332–44, Fall 1992; Hadley, J., *Hospital Closures in the 1980s: A Preliminary Analysis of Data from the American Hospital Association's Annual Survey of Hospitals.* Washington, DC: Prospective Payment Assessment Commission, May 1989; and Samuels, S., Noer, J., Chen, S., Li, W., Coleman, J., and Choi, C. *The Impact of Market Factors on Hospital Closures.* Chicago: American Hospital Association, May 1990.

5. For an overview, see, for example, Prospective Payment Assessment Commission. *Medicare and the American Health Care System: Report to the Congress, June 1992.* Washington, DC: Prospective Payment Assessment Commission, 1992, pp. 37–47.

6. Author's calculations based on data from the Prospective Payment Assessment Commission. *Medicare and the American Health Care System: Report to the Congress, June 1992,* p. 48.

7. Author's calculations based on data from the Prospective Payment Assessment Commission. *Medicare and the American Health Care System: Report to the Congress, June 1992,* p. 53.

8. Prospective Payment Assessment Commission. *Medicaid Hospital Payment, Congressional Report C-9-02.* Washington, DC: Prospective Payment Assessment Commission, Oct. 1, 1991, p. 59.

9. Group Health Association of America. *Patterns in HMO Enrollment.* Washington, DC: GHAA, June 1991.

10. Porter, M. J., and Ball, P. A. *The InterStudy Competitive Edge* 2(1):8, 1992.

11. InterStudy. *Managed Care: A Decade in Review.* Excelsior, MN: InterStudy, July 1991, p. 1; Health Care Investment Analysts, Inc., *The HMO Performance Almanac.* Baltimore: HCIA, 1992, p. 4.

12. *Health Care Ratings: A Standard & Poor's Seminar.* The institution referred to in the text is Choate-Symmes Hospital in Massachusetts.

13. Unpublished data from Health Care Investment Analysts, Inc., Baltimore, MD.

14. McCue and others.

15. Lillie-Blanton and others.

Chapter 3

Strategic Repositioning

Mark E. Grube

Hospitals in turnaround situations have traditionally focused on operations and near-term cash flow rather than strategic repositioning for the long term. This emphasis is understandable in that the time frame for strategic repositioning can extend perhaps beyond the organization's imaginable future. The organization in a turnaround situation is typically more concerned with meeting its next interest payment or payroll. Clearly, these immediate obligations require attention, but it is also vitally important that the organization consider how it will succeed over a more extended period of time. Cost and cash flow improvements are not endless, so the turnaround hospital needs to be careful that productivity enhancement efforts do not handicap it by eliminating programs, services, or businesses that might be critical to its future success.

This chapter addresses strategic repositioning with an emphasis on market, programmatic, and related business development. Specifically, it is designed to assist health care providers in their efforts to identify market needs and opportunities and, more broadly, to evaluate whether these needs and opportunities would be most effectively addressed by the organization on a stand-alone basis or through affiliation or integration with other providers. Three specific topics are covered:

- Target market development
- Business and service development
- Independence versus system affiliation

Certainly, each of these areas is broad enough to merit an independent discussion. The goal here is not to engage in a detailed review of each topic but, rather, to provide the reader with a direction and tools for sorting through the key issues. Of course, strategic repositioning also involves longer-term operations improvement and organization redesign—issues addressed in other chapters of this book.

Target Market Development

Target market development involves defining the relevant market, analyzing demand drivers, and establishing development priorities and strategies for addressing market opportunities.

Defining the Market

Strategic repositioning should begin with an understanding of the market served by an organization and the dynamics inherent in that market. For hospitals, market definition is complex. The market of a hospital typically includes a variety of constituencies, including the community or general population, physicians, other health care providers, and purchasers of care, including insurers and/or employers. A reasonable place to begin is with an analysis of the market's relevant geographic service range: those areas that are either currently served by the hospital or that represent realistic development opportunities.

In defining the relevant geographic market, several factors deserve consideration:

- *Patient origin.* The proportion of a hospital's patients who reside in a specific ZIP code, city, or county
- *Market share.* The proportion of patients who utilize the hospital for service relative to the entire patient population
- *Out-migration.* The extent to which the resident population tends to utilize health care services in other geographic markets
- *Natural barriers.* Lakes, rivers, and other natural features that represent real or psychological boundaries
- *Transportation infrastructure and trade patterns.* Highway and road systems, mass transit systems, and traditional population travel patterns to retail and other businesses that enhance or impair a hospital's access to specific geographic markets

Following analysis of these characteristics, it is often useful to cluster the ZIP codes or cities and towns into larger, more meaningful groups. The scope of the relevant geographic market should be realistic. A basic community hospital in a highly competitive market will have great difficulty in accessing patients in distant geographic areas, and therefore should put little or no effort into evaluating opportunity in those markets. (An example of a geographic market clustering is presented in figure 3-1.) With these definitions in mind, efforts can begin to evaluate the demand drivers present in each market and their related strategic implications.

Understanding the Market Demand Drivers

Determining health care service demand in a specific geographic area is a relatively straightforward process. It can begin with an analysis of disease incidence or health provider use rates (or estimations) for the defined population. However, establishing market development targets for a hospital in a turnaround situation requires not only definition of market size, but also

Figure 3-1. Geographic Sector Definition, Community Memorial Hospital

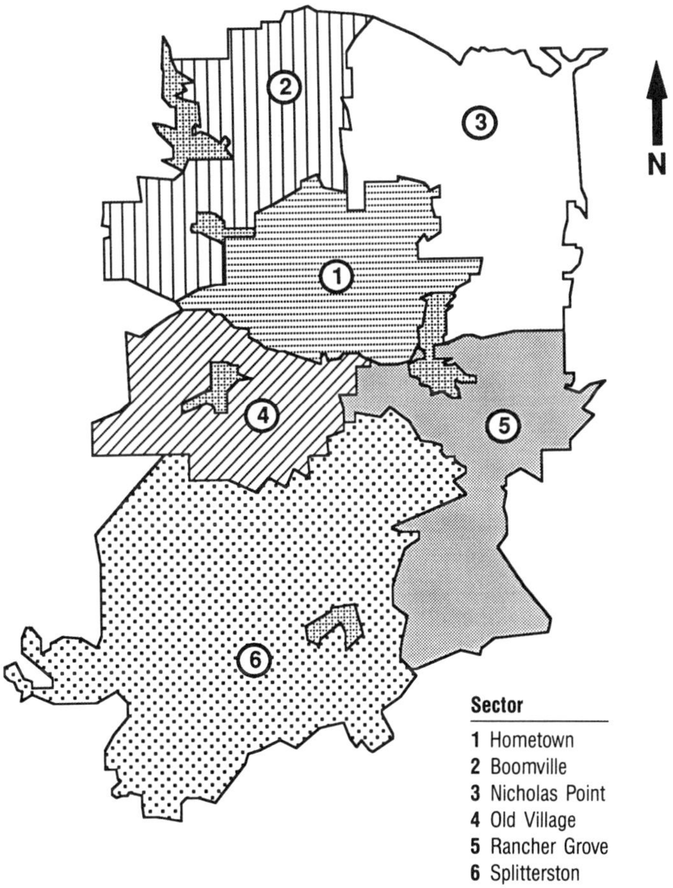

an understanding of the demand drivers or use-pattern influences. Understanding demand drivers is critical for establishing strategies for addressing market opportunity.

In the health care industry, demand drivers are unique in virtually every market across the country. Moreover, these drivers are dynamic; the key determinants of health resource consumption patterns within a given market are likely to change over time. Therefore, strategic repositioning requires an understanding of both current and anticipated market characteristics. Specifically, target market identification should evaluate demographic and socioeconomic characteristics, physician resources, competition, and the purchasers of care, including the government, indemnity insurers, managed care organizations, and employers.

Demographic and Socioeconomic Characteristics

Realized and latent health service demand is a function of the demographic characteristics of a geographic area, primarily population size, projected population growth, and population age and sex distribution. Socioeconomic characteristics are typically good indicators of how this demand for health service will be reimbursed: through some form of private insurance, governmental program, or an individual's own financial resources (or lack thereof).

It might appear obvious that the most attractive development opportunities are in large, growing markets with well-insured population bases; however, experience suggests that hospitals too often focus development efforts on rapidly growing, affluent markets without placing enough weight on the actual size of the population. A troubled hospital may therefore derive substantial benefit from targeting markets that are large and well insured, but not necessarily affluent.

Physician Resources

Traditionally, physicians have been the primary decision makers in determining where their patients receive health care services. Although managed care plans are increasingly directing or influencing point-of-service decisions, as of 1993 the physician continues to play a primary role. Accordingly, target market development should clearly evaluate the potential for placement of additional "friendly" physicians in geographic areas of opportunity and/or the ability to attract existing area physicians to the institution.

Physician Recruitment

Identifying opportunities to expand physician resources in a given market involves comparing specialty-specific physician need to the current physician supply. Several widely used physician-to-population standards can be applied to determine need within a market. Recent research into physician supply issues suggests that in many markets there is a need for further development of primary care physician resources.[1] Primary care physicians are particularly important; not only do they directly generate activity at a hospital, but they also are the primary referral base for the hospital's specialists.

Many hospitals today find that the most effective strategy for physician recruitment is to work with the existing medical staff to bring on partners and, in turn, expand their own practice base. Although federal legislation increasingly limits what a hospital can do in recruiting physicians, presenting practitioners with evidence of clear market opportunity can be extremely effective in medical staff development efforts.

Conversion of Existing Physician Practice

Changing the practice patterns of physicians currently in the defined target market is a more difficult process. Physicians become accustomed to practicing in a given institution(s) and develop relationships with nursing and other hospital staff that can be difficult to supplant. Thus, the effort to change physician practice patterns cannot be generic, but must respond to the individual needs of each physician or group. This requires a great deal of energy. A strategy must be tailored for each individual, beginning with a one-on-one conversation to determine precisely what it would take to attract that physician or group and whether the hospital is able to respond effectively.

An important consideration for most physicians and groups is the ability to readily access specific hospital services (for example, beds, surgery, select diagnostic areas). Given that most hospitals in turnaround situations maintain significant excess capacity, marketing improved accessibility can be an effective strategy for these institutions. This is an example of what might appeal to an individual physician or group. Other opportunities might include acquisition of a specific piece of equipment or technology, facilitating sharing of on-call coverage, providing practice management support, or improving access to specialists for consultation. There is likely to be skepticism among physicians as to the ability of a hospital in a turnaround situation to follow through on commitments (for example, new technology, practice support). As a result, a hospital needs to present a specific program for its turnaround to win the confidence of the physicians already on staff (whose confidence in the institution may be wavering) as well as potential new staff members.

Market Share

The hospital's position within a given geographic market is also a critical variable in identifying opportunity. Markets in which certain health care providers enjoy a strategic advantage based on physical presence and/or entrenched service utilization patterns are clearly less attractive than those in which these characteristics are less prevalent. These providers may include not only other hospitals, but also physician groups and freestanding diagnostic and treatment centers.

Creating a good working map of the area that shows the locations of relevant providers is a useful starting point for targeting potential market share. Figure 3-2 presents an example of such a map. Visual inspection can sometimes identify pockets of opportunity, where no single provider dominates the market. For greater precision, many state hospital associations maintain sophisticated data bases that can be used to measure market penetration levels in terms of inpatient admissions on a provider- and geography-specific (typically ZIP code) basis.

Figure 3-2. Location of Key Providers near Community Memorial Hospital

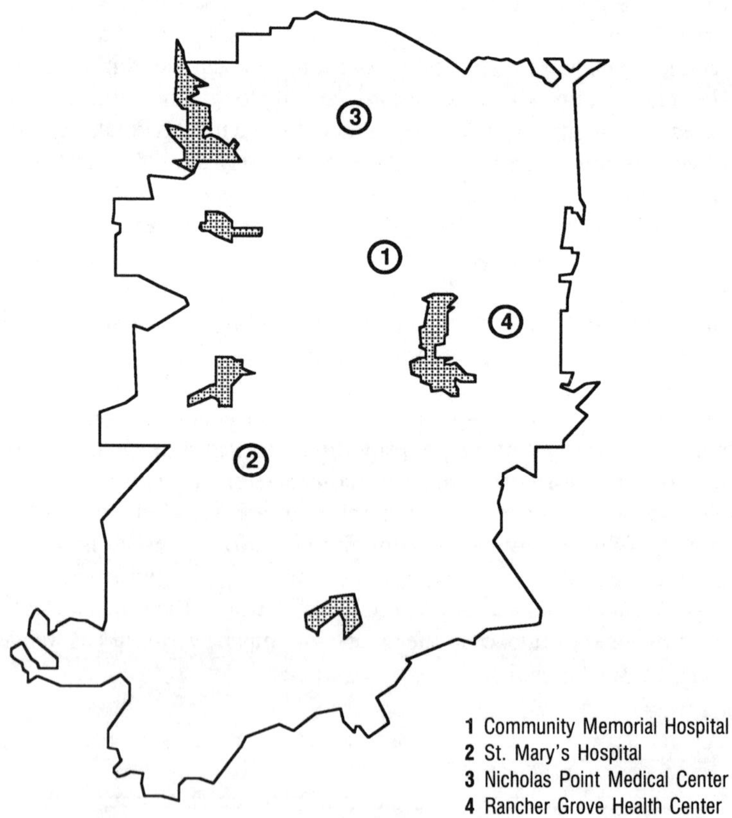

Managed Care

Managed care organizations, including health maintenance organizations (HMOs) and preferred provider organizations (PPOs), are evolving into a key influence on point-of-service decisions in many markets. Specifically, these organizations establish contracts with health care providers at a predetermined capitated or fixed rate or on a discounted fee-for-service basis, and then employ various utilization management tools or incentives to influence hospital utilization patterns for both patients and physicians. In areas where managed care organizations control a substantial portion of the insured population, not only can effective managed care contracting be a mechanism for building a hospital's activity base, but it can also be critical to the institution's long-term survival.

For many hospitals, participating in the managed care market has included a make-versus-buy decision; that is, determining the level of strategic advantage derived from developing and sponsoring a managed care product versus working with existing HMOs and PPOs. Because hospitals in turnaround situations are unlikely to be able to dedicate or develop the resources necessary to directly enter the managed care market in the near term, this discussion will focus on working with existing organizations. Effective managed care contracting requires hospitals to:

- Understand the attributes of the local insurance market
- Establish goals and objectives in managed care
- Respond to the needs and incentives of the managed care organizations
- Effectively manage the risks associated with the individual contracts

The Local Insurance Market

The current and anticipated future level of managed care organization penetration, both collectively and individually, determines the success of an effective managed care strategy. If managed care organizations neither maintain nor are expected to develop a substantial enrollment base in a market, it is inappropriate to focus a great deal of attention on the managed care market. Conversely, significant current and/or future enrollment bases can represent a substantial contracting opportunity.

A solid fact base on managed care enrollment by geographic area can be difficult to obtain due to state-by-state variations in the reporting requirements to the insurance commission. Reasonable proxies can be developed through discussions with the benefits managers of area employers. Again, the goal is to determine which organizations control significant populations and thus could generate incremental business for the organization.

Managed Care Business Goals and Objectives

Clear articulation of a hospital's managed care business goals and objectives is important to ensure effective managed care contracting. Contracting with a managed care organization is likely to result in the utilization of two patient populations at an individual institution: patients who would have used the organization in any event and, as a result, represent business converted from one insurer to another; and new patients (or incremental business) who would likely have been serviced by another organization. Thus, managed care contracting strategies must include a defensive strategy to protect the existing business base and an offensive strategy to secure new patient populations.

The Needs and Incentives of Managed Care Organizations

Most managed care organizations operate under a profit motive. Accordingly, their goals are to offer a marketable product that will allow them to earn a profit on the difference between their collected premium dollars and their operating costs and disbursements to contracting provider organizations. Marketable products offer the employer value through unique combinations of cost, quality, and access. Because quality has traditionally been difficult to measure across provider organizations, in recent years most of the emphasis has been on cost and access; however, both purchasers of care and providers of care are currently focusing a great deal of effort on developing outcome-based quality measurement tools. Future managed care contracting is likely to focus on value—the combination of cost and quality.

Understanding an organization's relative strengths and weaknesses versus those of other providers in terms of cost, quality, and access will help market the organization to managed care plans most effectively. It will also help define strategies to be pursued to enhance leverage in negotiations by identifying weaknesses to be addressed through future strategic initiatives.

Managed Contract Risks

The specific risks that must be managed in a contract with a managed care organization will obviously depend on the nature of the contract. Generally, such contracts pose elements of production, utilization, and actuarial risk, and effective contracting requires diligent management of these risk categories.

Production risk simply means being able to generate a margin of return under the terms of the contract. For example, if the contract involves a discount of 25 percent from gross charges, the hospital must be assured that it can make a profit at this price level. Although this risk seems relatively simple to define, many hospitals do not have a complete and accurate understanding of their costs and therefore have difficulty defining production risk.

Utilization risk represents the degree to which the financial performance of the contract depends on the level of service utilization. If under the agreed-on reimbursement terms the hospital will break even on 1,000 admissions and lose or earn money on utilization below or above that level, the hospital has assumed utilization risk.

Actuarial risk is most often associated with capitation contracts, by which a provider agrees to cover the hospital service needs of a managed care population for a preset price per member. In such cases, the provider is not only likely to absorb production and utilization risk, but also is vulnerable to fluctuations in the health status of the capitated population.

Other Purchasers of Care

Opportunities may also exist within the market to address the needs of other purchasers of care, including the government, indemnity insurers, and major employers. Again, the size of the local population represented by each of these purchasers will determine the need to establish specific strategies to address these groups. A broad array of secondary information sources is available to assist in identifying the major potential opportunities. Generally, direct discussions with the relevant groups are likely to be the most effective means for identifying their specific needs and developing responsive strategies.

Establishing Target Market Development Priorities

For hospitals in turnaround situations, the difficulty often lies not in identifying market development opportunities, but in establishing priorities and focusing resources on those opportunities that represent the strongest development potential for the organization. Preparing a target market opportunity evaluation matrix can be a useful mechanism for screening relevant markets, establishing priorities, and charting a preliminary direction as to the most effective means of addressing the target area.

Figure 3-3 presents a hypothetical target market opportunity evaluation matrix for Community Memorial Hospital, a fictional organization. The evaluation criteria represent each of the market attributes described above: market size, physician resources, market share, and purchasers of care. In this example, two of the six markets profiled—Boomville and Splitterston—appear to represent strong development opportunities. Boomville is a moderate-sized community with strong projected growth and limited physician resources. Community Memorial Hospital has established a relatively strong presence in Boomville. An appropriate development strategy in this market may be to expand the base of primary care physicians, either directly or in conjunction with existing physicians on the medical staff. Splitterston represents a large market in which no single institution has established dominance.

Figure 3-3. Target Market Opportunity Evaluation Matrix for Community Memorial Hospital

	Market Size			Physician Need			
Market	Adjusted Patient Days	5-Year Projected Population Growth	Percent of Home Health Income <$10,000	Primary Care	Specialty	Market Share, Other Area Providers Combined	Managed Care Presence
Hometown	72,000	−1.0%	4.8%	2	0	14%	Riverfront HMO—5% Hometown Health—15%
Boomville	38,000	4.5%	3.0%	10	3	64%	Riverfront HMO—3% Hometown Health—5%
Nicholas Point	26,000	−2.0%	8.0%	0	0	71%	Riverfront HMO—12% Hometown Health—8%
Old Village	16,000	−3.0%	7.0%	3	1	56%	Riverfront HMO—0% Hometown Health—4%
Rancher Grove	8,000	1.0%	5.0%	2	0	44%	Riverfront HMO—0% Hometown Health—0%
Splitterston	54,000	0.4%	6.0%	5	2	68%	Riverfront HMO—18% Hometown Health—2%

Strategies for expanding market presence in Splitterston might best include trying to increase the activity levels of area physicians at Community Memorial Hospital and aggressive contracting with the dominant managed care provider—Riverfront HMO.

Unfortunately, not all situations present such concrete development opportunities, but applying this systematic approach to market evaluation should be useful in assessing the current market situation.

Business and Service Development

Concurrent with target market identification, hospitals in turnaround situations often also need to reevaluate their business definition and service mix. (For clarity, it is appropriate to define the difference between business and service mix. *Business mix* refers to the range of operating units within a health care organization. *Service mix* refers to the range of programs or products offered within an operating unit. Figures 3-4 and 3-5 provide illustrative examples of business and service mix.) This evaluation might prompt the organization to expand its traditional focus into new business lines, abandon other business lines, concentrate development efforts within select business units, or pursue a combination of all of these. Essentially, the evaluation spans the diversification and service portfolio management strategies discussed below.

Diversification Strategies

Among health care organizations and general businesses alike, diversification strategies tend to fall into two broad categories: conglomerate and concentric. *Conglomerate diversification* generally involves establishing business activity in traditionally unrelated industry segments. For example, a hospital that decides to go into the fast-food business is pursuing a conglomerate diversification strategy. *Concentric diversification* involves establishing business activity in closely related but traditionally disparate activities. Concentric diversification often evolves through vertical integration, such as when an HMO acquires or develops its own hospital.

Conglomerate diversification strategies have met with limited success in both general industry and the hospital industry. It may be speculated that this weak performance of conglomerate diversification is indicative of the lack of value created through linkage of unrelated businesses. Because most hospitals in the United States are not-for-profit organizations, few governance boards are likely to support the extension of hospital activity into businesses unrelated to health care. For these reasons, this discussion focuses on concentric diversification strategies.

Figure 3-4. Business Mix (Example)

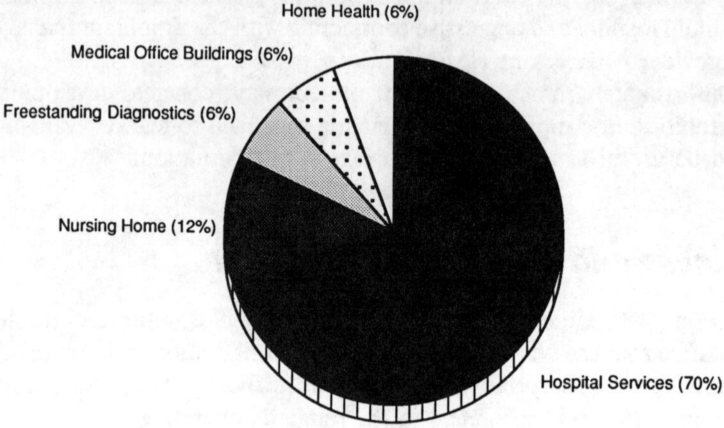

Figure 3-5. Hospital Service Mix (Example)

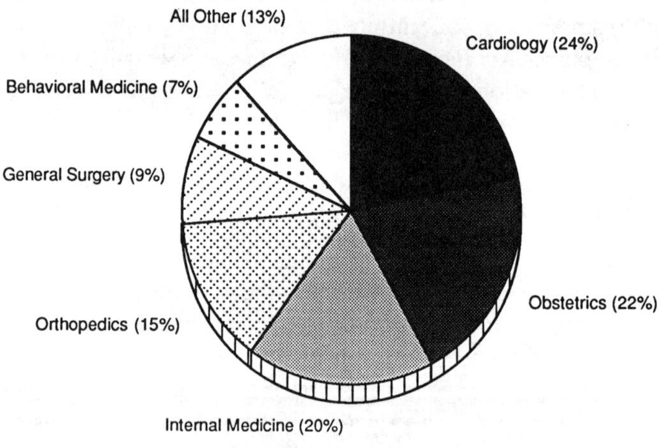

During the 1980s, many hospitals redefined their businesses to move beyond acute inpatient care and offer complete health care and even integrated health care delivery systems. This important redefinition provided the impetus for the extension of hospital activities into new health care businesses, such as freestanding diagnostic centers, urgent care centers, managed care organizations, long-term care, and home health. The results of these efforts have been mixed.[2]

For turnaround hospitals and health care providers, the challenges of entering a new business line are formidable. New business development requires close managerial attention and often substantial capital support during the start-up phase. Turnaround organizations would do better to concentrate on evaluating their existing lines as enhancement, maintenance, or retrenchment businesses and then take appropriate action to support the strategy associated with the classification. Several criteria can be applied to classify business lines into these categories:

- Proportion of organizational revenues
- Relationship to organizational mission and the core business(es)
- Historical financial performance
- Competitive position
- Managerial resource requirements
- Anticipated future capital requirements
- Potential divestment value
- Near- and long-term industry and business outlook

In certain situations, the organization may recognize that although a business line is financially rewarding and has a relatively bright outlook, it represents a relatively small portion of the organization's overall business activity. In this case, the institution might best be served by selling that unit and redirecting capital to other activities. In other situations the importance of organizational mission may overwhelm economic considerations. Regardless of the outcome, reassessing business mix is vitally important in times of organizational distress.

Service Portfolio Management Strategies

Assuming an organization has decided to continue its activity in the hospital industry following the diversification strategy assessment, specific consideration needs to be given to the hospital's service portfolio. Many hospitals have enjoyed considerable success by concentrating development efforts on a discrete set of programs and services. For some organizations, this has involved the development of regional referral centers in tertiary services; for others, it has involved establishing prominence in ambulatory care or primary care services. Whatever the specific services involved, the concept is the same—making a conscious decision to direct organizational resources and attention to a small group of activities.

Service Development Priorities

As in business diversification strategy evaluation, service portfolio analysis should begin by defining the service units and applying criteria to classify programs as enhancement, maintenance, or retrenchment categories. In hospitals, a logical method of segmentation is to define services along clinical lines (internal medicine, cardiology, obstetrics, neurosurgery, and so on) and/or in terms of the market served (for example, women's and geriatric programs). The level of service segmentation appropriate in an individual hospital largely depends on the complexity of the organization. For example, an appropriate service segmentation for a university teaching hospital might involve identification of 25 to 30 discrete programs and services. A rural community hospital may appropriately contain only 5 to 10 service units.

Once the business has been segmented into discrete service groupings, the next step is to identify and apply screening criteria. A useful tool to help sort through hospital programs and services is an opportunity evaluation chart that ranks each program against measures of market opportunity and hospital capabilities. In addition to existing services, programs not currently available at the hospital may also be evaluated.

Measures of market opportunity might include:

- Market size
- Projected market growth
- Payer mix
- Contribution margin
- Competition
- Implementation timing
- Capital requirements

Measures of hospital capability might include:

- Current market share
- Existing physician resources
- Other clinical resources
- Physical plant support

Figure 3-6 is a hypothetical opportunity evaluation matrix for Community Memorial Hospital. (This matrix is purely an example and, without application of relevant information on an individual market and hospital, cannot be depended on to direct service line development decisions.) Essentially, the objective is to structure the hospital's service mix in a manner that matches hospital capability to market opportunity. In a perfectly balanced portfolio, all programs and services would fall along a 45-degree line drawn from the intersection of the horizontal and vertical axes. Programs positioned above and relatively distant from the 45-degree line represent the strongest development opportunity. Programs and services below and relatively distant from the line may represent retrenchment candidates.

For Community Memorial Hospital, the programs of greatest development opportunity include cardiology, internal medicine, and obstetrics. The

Figure 3-6. Community Memorial Hospital Program Opportunity Evaluation

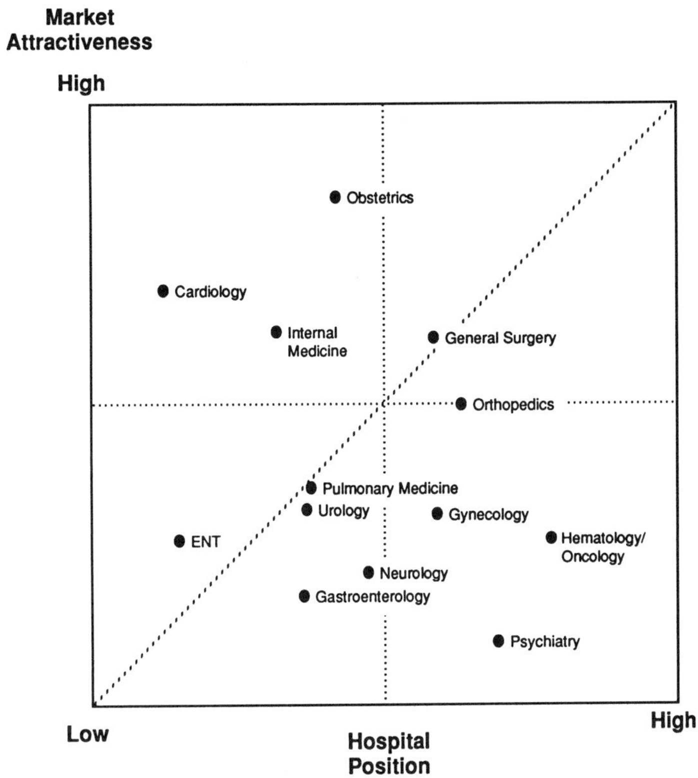

retrenchment candidates include psychiatry and rehabilitation services. In making final program development decisions, the organization must also consider mission issues and the importance of the program to its overall strategy and/or other programs and services. For example, if obstetrics were positioned in a retrenchment category, the organization may still not wish to divest the program, considering its importance in managed care contracting and its role in the hospital's mission.

In turnaround situations, greater weight should be placed on capital and implementation time requirements. Turnaround hospitals often do not have the capital or time necessary to launch new programs or significantly modify services. Again, it is important to stress the prudence of focusing on a small group of such services. Given the managerial attention required to refine service mix, typically no more than three or four services can be effectively reconfigured.

Service Development and/or Refinement Action Plans

Once a hospital has established the three or four programs that are candidates for development or refinement, identification of the specific modifications to be pursued can begin. Two basic approaches—the key manager approach and the task group approach—are generally employed by hospitals today. Both may be supported by outside expertise.

In the key manager approach, an individual is assigned responsibility for development of an action plan for a specific service. The task group approach assigns the same responsibility to a group of individuals, usually including executive management, department heads, physicians, and other clinicians as appropriate. In either case, the development plan should define:

- Development or refinement objectives
- Financial and/or volume goals
- Key market, technology, operational, and organizational issues to be addressed
- Specific initiatives and activities to be pursued
- Operating and capital requirements associated with the initiatives and activities
- Implementation responsibilities, timing, and monitoring processes

The service action planning process should take no longer than three or four months to complete in a task group setting, and even less time through the key manager approach. This process may seem somewhat formal, but because these services will be critical to sustaining the organization in the future, it is important that some structure be imposed in their development. Establishing a monitoring process once the action plan is defined will facilitate mid-course corrections and adjustments in response to changing market and internal conditions.

Independence versus System Affiliation

Perhaps the most important strategic decision for a hospital in a turnaround situation is whether to remain an independent organization or to pursue some form of affiliation with another health care organization(s). Over the past decade, the growth of health care systems has been substantial (see figure 3-7). In 1980, approximately 14 percent of U.S. hospitals were part of a health care system, compared to 54 percent in 1990. This growth is largely attributable to changes in the economic conditions within the industry and the advantages that systems are perceived to offer in terms of market, operation, and organizational positioning. For these reasons, turnaround hospitals and strong health care providers alike are pursuing various affiliation linkages.

Figure 3-7. National Trends in Hospital Systems Development

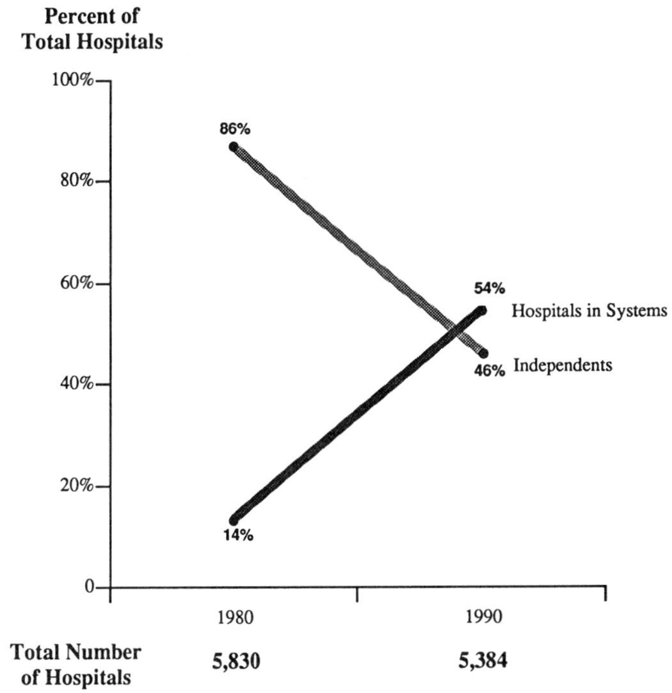

Sources: *American Hospital Association Hospital Statistics: A Comprehensive Summary of U.S. Hospitals.* 1991–92 ed. Chicago: AHA, 1992. *American Hospital Association Guide to the Health Care Field: Hospitals, Health Care Systems, Health Care Organizations, Agencies, and Providers.* 1991 ed. Chicago: AHA, 1991. Conversation with AHA Multi-Hospital System Data Analyst, December 1991.

Determining whether system affiliation is appropriate for an organization requires:

- Reassessment of role and mission
- A frank appraisal of the hospital's ability to effectively respond to the market as an independent entity
- Definition of organizational objectives
- Examination of alternative forms of affiliation
- Identification and evaluation of potential partners

Role and Mission Reassessment

The role and mission of most community and religious-sponsored hospitals in the United States is to provide access to high-quality health care services for their defined service areas. For most organizations, the question is not whether this role and mission is still appropriate but, rather, how it can best be accomplished. Specifically, the relevant strategic issue is whether community needs are best served by the organization as an independent entity or as part of a system. Given the excess capacity throughout the industry today, the turnaround hospital must face the tougher question: Will the hospital's survival, either alone or through affiliation, really benefit the community?

The answer to this question eventually centers on the definition of service area needs and the critical success requirements for the organization in the current and anticipated future market environment. Clearly, these issues are most appropriately addressed at the board and possibly executive management level.

Market Needs Appraisal

Perhaps the most effective way to perform an unbiased assessment of market needs is the "man from Mars" approach. Starting with a blank sheet of paper, the exercise begins by putting aside the existing provider structure and postulating an ideal health service delivery system in the current and anticipated future market. The ideal structure should address:

- Projected health care service demand
- Effective access to various levels of care
- Cost efficiency
- Quality of care
- Relationships between providers throughout a vertical care continuum

Once this ideal structure has been defined, it should be possible to identify the attributes and critical success factors for providers, with particular emphasis on scale, scope, and quality. Determining how the organization moves from its current configuration to this ideal delivery structure is the essence of health care provider strategy development.

Organizational Objectives

Articulation of broad organizational objectives provides a context in which to evaluate whether the hospital would be most effective in meeting community needs independently or in affiliation. The objectives should identify goals related to the hospital's:

- Market penetration levels
- Business and service mix
- Physicians and other clinical personnel
- Operations
- Financial condition

With these objectives in mind, the hospital's board and executive management should execute an unemotional assessment of the organization's ability to meet the objectives independently. If it is determined that affiliation alternatives should be explored, the hospital should begin to explore the nature of the affiliation and analyze its potential partners.

Affiliation Alternatives

Over the years, provider affiliations have encompassed a broad range of relationships, from relatively loose ties to full consolidation. Identifying which affiliation alternative is most appropriate for an organization involves assessing the level of benefit derived from each type of relationship against the strategic objectives. There are countless potential forms of affiliation; for purposes of this discussion they have been grouped into five categories:

- Group purchasing arrangements
- Contracting networks
- Programmatic and support service affiliations
- Management relationships
- Consolidation

Group Purchasing Arrangements

Group purchasing arrangements are simply agreements among providers to jointly acquire products and services from resource vendors. The arrangements offer strategic advantage through the negotiating leverage that is gained by ordering in bulk quantity. Group purchasing arrangements are widespread throughout the country and are often sponsored by state and local provider associations.[3] Although effective, these arrangements are, by definition, extremely limited in scope and thus do not offer substantial benefit against most of an organization's strategic objectives.

Contracting Networks

Contracting networks are agreements among providers to jointly contract with managed care organizations, employers, and other purchasers of care for the provision of health care services. In addition to contracting with existing managed care organizations, many networks establish their own managed care products. The primary benefits derived for member organizations include the development of a broader service distribution network and service scope than any single organization can provide and the increased contract negotiating leverage that is derived through the massing of providers.

Contracting networks are also widely developed throughout the country, although they vary considerably in the level of contract exclusivity among their member organizations. Many hospitals are a part of several provider networks. Although contracting networks form the nucleus for more highly developed future relationships, in and of themselves they typically offer benefit for only a relatively limited set of an organization's market and programmatic objectives.

Programmatic and Support Service Relationships

Programmatic relationships between providers involve linkages to support the joint delivery of a single service or multiple services. Typically, *programmatic relationships* are arrangements between a tertiary or specialty care provider and a community-based institution. An example of such an arrangement is a cancer program affiliation by which physicians from the tertiary provider deliver some services in the local community and direct care for more complex activity to a referral center. The community provider organization benefits by improving access to specialty resources in the local market. The tertiary care provider benefits by strengthening the referral base necessary to support sophisticated capabilities. An example of a support service arrangement is the sponsorship of a single laundry service by multiple institutions. Most support service arrangements require relatively close geographic proximity among the providers to be effective.

Programmatic and support service relationships have become popular in many parts of the country, particularly in the clinical areas of oncology, cardiac care, and behavioral medicine (for example, psychiatry and substance abuse services) and support services including laundry, billing, and data processing. These relationships are effective in improving the quality of care delivered within a local market and, sometimes, in reducing operating redundancies across providers. The strategic benefit of programmatic and support service affiliations is limited to the specific programs and services encompassed by the relationship.

Management Relationships

A *management relationship* is an agreement by one institution to provide a defined range of managerial support services for another. The range of managerial relationships can involve a single executive (usually the chief executive officer) or an entire management function. The theory supporting the management relationship is that the contractee will benefit through access to a level of expertise that it ordinarily may not be able to support, and the contractor will benefit through being able to offer a broader range of opportunity to its organizational executives.

During the late 1970s and early 1980s, managerial relationships were a popular affiliation form, particularly for rural institutions. However, since that time, the number of such relationships has declined, presumably reflecting either the ineffectiveness of the relationship for one or both contracting organizations or the greater appeal of other strategic relationships.

Consolidation

Consolidation involves the integration of health care providers into a common organizational form. Consolidation can occur through the merger of two or more parties or through the direct acquisition of an organization. A broad array of organizational forms has been utilized in consolidation activities, varying primarily according to the level of control or influence the previously independent entities retain in the decision-making processes of the combined organization. In a true consolidation one or multiple parties necessarily relinquish some level of autonomy.

As previously discussed, consolidation activity in the health care industry has picked up over the past several years. Due to the broad scope of consolidation and the ability to redirect more significant resources, consolidation offers the broadest potential strategic advantage across organizational objectives. Its principal disadvantage lies in the level of control the previously independent organizations must yield to one another. Accordingly, much of the discussion between consolidating entities involves proscribing limits to the use of previously independent assets. A major drawback to a consolidation as opposed to other affiliation strategies is the burden of overcoming antitrust challenges. This is particularly the case in communities with small numbers of providers.

Affiliation Forms

From the preceding discussion, it is apparent that most forms of affiliation are successful in addressing only a limited set of strategic objectives. The appropriate affiliation relationship for an individual organization is one that most directly addresses its highest-priority objectives.

As in the target market development and business and service development, an affiliation model evaluation matrix can be a useful mechanism for assessing which affiliation model presents the greatest opportunity for an individual organization. Figure 3-8 is an example matrix for Community Memorial Hospital. The matrix is designed to evaluate how well each form of affiliation meets specific strategic objectives. As the figure indicates, Community Memorial Hospital has broad-based organizational needs that can only be realistically fulfilled through some form of consolidation with another provider. Organizations with more narrowly defined needs may well fulfill their strategic objectives through a more limited relationship.

Identification and Evaluation of Potential Partners

Once the affiliation arrangement of choice is defined, a process for identifying and evaluating potential partners should be initiated. The individual organizations considered will, of course, vary depending on the type of relationship desired. However, the initial list of candidates should be relatively broad.

Figure 3-8. Affiliation Alternatives (Example)

Low *Spectrum of Organizational Consolidation* High

Critical Success Factors	Purchasing Groups	Networks	Managed Organization	Merger/ Consolidation
Market:				
Market Synergy	○	◒	◒	◒
Enhance Image	○	◒	◒	◒
Position for Managed Care	○	●	◒	◒
Program/Physician Development:				
Existing Physician Referral Patterns	○	○	○	◒
Support Programmatic Development	○	○	◒	●
Ability to Recruit/Sustain Physician Loyalties	○	○	◒	◒
Provide Depth of Specialists	○	◒	◒	◒
Operations:				
Resize Organization	○	○	◒	●
Maintain Efficient Operations	○	○	◒	◒
Realize Economies of Scale	◒	◒	◒	●
Financial:				
Provide Capital as Necessary	○	◒	○	●
Maintain Fiscal Viability	○	○	○	●
Leadership:				
Access to Specialized Expertise	○	○	◒	●
Management Capability to Effect Change	○	○	◒	●

Key: ● Typical Advantage ◒ Occasional Advantage ○ No Advantage

For a consolidation, the evaluation process obviously merits considerable effort. In addition to the strategic objectives, issues related to interorganizational compatibility such as mission and culture need to be considered carefully. Finally, a strategy should also be devised for approaching and entering into discussions with the potential partner(s). Consolidation is rarely a simple process, but the obstacles and barriers are often easily identified. It is therefore imperative to periodically revisit the rationale that defined the need to pursue consolidation.

Conclusion

Although the hospital in a turnaround situation is generally most concerned with its immediate cash flow condition, if it is to survive, it must focus some of its resources on developing ways to reposition itself for the long term. The first step in the repositioning process is to define the hospital's geographic market, understand the demands that drive that market, and target and prioritize the hospital's servicing opportunities within its market. At the same time, the turnaround hospital needs to reassess and possibly redefine its business lines and the programs and services it offers. Typically, an appropriate strategy is to focus on a small group of services for reconfiguration and improvement of operations. The next major strategic issue to address is whether to remain independent or to affiliate with some other health care provider. The turnaround hospital completely immersed in today's cash flow concerns may find that its short-term solutions will circumvent its long-term success.

References

1. Politzer, R. M., Harris, D. L., Gaston, M. H., and Mullan, F. Primary care physician supply and the medically underserved. *Journal of the American Medical Association* 266:104, July 3, 1991.
2. Sabatino, F. Home health, diagnostic centers were financial winners in 1990. *Hospitals* 65(1):27–29, Jan. 5, 1991.
3. Group purchasing will grow, industry to consolidate. *Health Industry Today* 54:6, June 1991.

Chapter 4

The Turnaround Process: Management, Board, and Cultural Changes

Sandra Shelley and Lauren Jones

Sustaining the results of a hospital turnaround process has as much to do with organizational strategy as it does with financial prowess. In a financial crisis, hospital executives often take a short-term perspective of the process. But, as pointed out in chapter 3, in order to maintain the benefits from a turnaround, the hospital has to at the same time reposition itself for the future in terms of long-term operations improvement. This process must also involve fundamental organizational change – change in the way people think and behave, change in the work that is done and the processes for doing it, and change in the policies, procedures, and structures that organize and deploy resources.

The nonfinancial aspects of the turnaround process are essential elements of an organizational strategy to complete and sustain a hospital turnaround by:

- Creating an organizational vision that transcends the initial cost-cutting measures
- Identifying organizational values that facilitate the turnaround process
- Defining a culture built on continuous improvement and efficiency
- Redefining policies, procedures, and practices to capitalize on the basic desire of people to do a good job
- Structuring the organization to perform more effectively

Although in this chapter organizational concepts, tools, and techniques are discussed in the context of a turnaround process, they are also applicable to other situations that require large-scale change.

Portions of this chapter are copyrighted by Lauren Jones, 1992. The authors also use, with permission, concepts first presented in J. Nackle and S. Shelley, Leadership for patient care. *Journal of the Society for Health Systems* 2(3):5–12, 1991.

Organizational Strategy for a Turnaround Process

Health care organizations consist of people, and thus a knowledge of human nature contributes to a knowledge of the way hospitals operate. When some health care executives think of organizational strategy, they think only of organizational structure and, from this myopic perspective, view organizational change as the movement of lines and boxes on an organizational chart. The executive orchestrating a hospital turnaround must recognize that organizational dynamics—how people within the organization behave—is as important as organizational structure.

Figure 4-1 depicts the constituent dimensions of a comprehensive organizational strategy. Organizational strategy is composed of process and architectural components, each further subdivided into two dominant dimensions. The process component includes a behavioral dimension and a cultural dimension. The architectural component is separated into procedural and structural dimensions.

Even though individual and group behavior is the basis of almost every activity that takes place in health care organizations, how people think and act are business dynamics underappreciated by most hospital executives. Understanding *intrapersonal behavior* (what individuals think of themselves and their work) is central to an awareness of *interpersonal behavior* (how individuals work with other people).

Figure 4-1. Dimensions of Organizational Strategy

Processes	Intrapersonal and Interpersonal Behavior	Culture
Architecture	Policies and Procedures	Structure

Organizational *culture* embodies individual and group behavior in a collective value system that gives the organization its unique identity. Culture can be thought of as behavior persistent over time, such that it becomes an important determinant of future behavior. Because it is intangible, culture is easy to dismiss in making business decisions; yet the pervasive impact of culture on every aspect of the business enterprise makes it a most important factor for sustaining a turnaround process.

Culture is made explicit through the codification of norms and values into *policies* and *procedures.* Policies and procedures concretely detail appropriate and inappropriate activity in the work setting and thus are powerful tools for shaping organizational behavior. Similarly, organizational *structure* has a potent influence on how people act in the work setting. The way people are positioned within a system greatly influences their communication, decisions, productivity, and ultimate sense of personal responsibility for the success of the organization.

The *architectural components* of an organizational strategy are concrete, controlled, and quantifiable. In this sense they can be thought of as "left-brain" functions. Because structure, policies, and procedures possess certain concrete qualities, they are often erroneously thought of as the sole elements of an organizational strategy. But attention to these left-brain attributes of the organization must be balanced with attention to the "right-brain" attributes, the *process components.* The remainder of this chapter is devoted to a more in-depth consideration of all four dimensions of a well-balanced organizational strategy for a successful hospital turnaround.

Executive Leadership Behavior for a Turnaround with Staying Power

In today's health care environment, strong leadership has become the cornerstone of success. Orchestrating a turnaround is a formidable challenge for even the most sophisticated and capable health care executives, and only strong leaders can guide their organizations through troubled times to attain advantage in their market areas. Several leadership qualities are critical to a successful turnaround, and hospital executives can take various actions to demonstrate their leadership position.

Vision is foremost. Employees at all levels—chief executive officer (CEO), middle managers, line supervisors, and other associates—must understand and share a core vision that embraces a common philosophy, a clear mission statement, a contemporary strategy for goal achievement, and a supportive environment for program implementation. The organization's vision is a blueprint for its future. There is a difference, though, between *visionary thinking,* which is focused on the analysis of facts and trends, and *wishful thinking,* which can be egocentric and capricious. A vision should serve to galvanize and focus people's thoughts about both the present and the future of the organization.

An effective organizational strategy begins with leaders who can translate their ideas into a vision that is meaningful to their constituencies. Once hospital leaders have developed a strategic vision, it must be communicated to the board of trustees and to every single employee in the organization. Every member of the organization should be able to articulate the direction of the organization and his or her role in achieving its vision. In a turnaround situation, a cogent vision of organizational effectiveness is particularly important to transcend the focus on short-term financial tactics.

Beyond fiscal concerns, a sense of excellence, trust, and teamwork is invaluable in a turnaround situation. Health care workers must understand their responsibilities not only in terms of tasks and activities, but, more important, in terms of high-quality customer outcomes. Direct patient care providers should understand how their responsibilities interact with others in the organization. Those employees who indirectly support patients must also be familiar with the standards of care and service to which the institution is committed. They, too, must be concerned about customer satisfaction, though their customers may be other hospital departments or individual employees.

The therapeutic process is predicated on a sense of trust. Therefore, a cogent vision is built upon a "trust culture." Often, the turnaround process can threaten employee morale and security. To preserve the essential sense of trust among both providers and recipients of patient care services, employees must feel safe, secure, and supported in their own work environment.

With the rapid pace of scientific discovery and product innovation, the useful life of information about disease processes, medical protocols, and technology is often less than five years. The resulting proliferation of specialists and the increasingly complex social, ethical, legal, and financial aspects of health care have given new meaning to the term *interdisciplinary.* More so today than in the past, patient care is a highly interdependent activity. It involves a variety of clinical disciplines and a host of other business, religious, political, and technical experts. Any strategic vision for a turnaround must therefore involve the concept of teamwork.

Contemporary leaders are adopting participative management styles to enhance decision making, promote commitment and enthusiasm, encourage flexibility and openness to change, and foster entrepreneurial behavior among their employees. Executives of organizations in financial crisis especially must think beyond the strictly financial dimensions of the turnaround process and inspire employees to join them in creating a robust vision of the effective organization of the future.

The ability to create an environment driven by innovation is another invaluable leadership characteristic. Tradition-bound thinking and behavior, and the organization of most hospitals into strict functional departments, creates a bureaucratic work environment in which employees are expected to follow directions, conform to policy and procedure, and adapt to their surroundings. In contrast, if leaders of a hospital turnaround are to sustain the outcomes of the process, they must create an environment in which innovation is an expected employee behavior, there is a passion for asking questions and encouragement for looking at situations from varying perspectives, and there is support for trying different approaches to problem solving. In innovative organizations there is a pervasive sense of optimism that things can always be done better. Employees embrace problems as challenges to be met rather than obstacles to be overcome.

Innovation requires health care executives who are comfortable with change. Being a change agent means taking some risks—not random and uncalculated risks but, rather, reasonable decisions based on new concepts in both management and patient care delivery. Leaders of a turnaround process can control risk through a parallel process of "buy-in" and "tie-in." By getting employees to buy into an idea beforehand, the staff develops a sense of personal investment in the idea. Leaders can also cultivate a collective sense of responsibility by having staff tied into the outcomes of change through the performance appraisal process, incentive structure, and promotion system. Employees should see their jobs as having two primary outcomes: (1) getting the current job done today, and (2) improving that job for tomorrow.

In a hospital turnaround, relationships between providers and payers, the board and the CEO, management and employees, hospital executives and community members, and patients and care givers require a great deal of attention by an executive who is highly skilled in the human dynamics of relationships and organizational culture and how both these factors can inhibit or enhance organizational efficiency. An organization's culture has roots in the institution's traditions and long-standing modes of operation, including historical relationships among constituents. These traditional interdepartmental, nurse–physician, employee–supervisor, and patient–provider relationships can bind employees to an antiquated model of service delivery, which may hamper or limit short-term or continuous improvement efforts. Leaders must be fluent in the theories and tactics of change management. They must demonstrate finesse in their ability to unlock established dysfunctional relationships without destroying the human relationships that are so important to the health care enterprise.

Relationships can be thought of as the infrastructure of the health care delivery system. Leadership in a hospital turnaround entails recognizing the importance of relationships, both inside and outside the organization, and leveraging those relationships to create a commitment to and momentum for the turnaround process. A successful turnaround does not happen in a vacuum. Hospital executives must assume visible leadership positions and orchestrate the process of change. Although many management skills and executive attributes are necessary in guiding a turnaround process, vision, innovation, and relationship-building skills are the most vital for a turnaround with staying power.

The Impact of Culture on a Turnaround Process

Culture is the collective behavior of an organization, comprising the individual and interpersonal behaviors of all its members. Executives in a turnaround process must understand the present culture to determine what must change for improved performance of the organization. But it is extremely difficult to objectively assess one's own culture. Executives are best served by objective survey instruments that assess organizational cultures by identifying key organizational values. These values can then be compared and contrasted among different groups within the hospital: board members, executives, middle management, staff, and physicians. One group's perceptions may differ sharply from another's, creating a cultural dissonance within the organization. For example, the executive team may identify the hospital as an organization without major problems, whereas the physicians may question the competency of the staff and the staff indicate a desire for more autonomy and decision-making power. In addition to identifying cultural dissonance, a cultural survey provides a benchmark from which to monitor the progress of organizational change throughout the turnaround process.

Identifying existing organizational values enables leaders to analyze organizational behaviors that express those values. The hospital executive can then predict behaviors that might hinder the turnaround process. For example, a cultural survey at a large medical center revealed that employees believed "you can do anything here and still not get fired." This organization apparently rewarded tenure instead of competence. Employees who were not doing their jobs received the same salary increases as those who exceeded their performance objectives. When the CEO announced that all employees would be accountable for helping to achieve the goals related to the turnaround, employees exhibited a predictable and understandable lack of enthusiasm.

The values that constitute the culture of an organization can be broken down into specific behaviors that express those values. For example, if creativity is an organizational value, subsequent behaviors might include risk taking, questioning systems, gainsharing, and so on. Initially, executive teams must reach consensus on the values that will be required to attain the hospital's future vision. The specific behaviors necessary to substantiate these values are best determined in conjunction with middle managers, staff, and other important constituents. The behaviors that elucidate core values must then become the performance expectations for all associates. Clear-cut performance expectations allow associates to decide whether the organization is a "good fit" for them. They also permit coaching opportunities for associates who are technically proficient but exhibit inappropriate attitude or lack team involvement.

In her book *Danger in the Comfort Zone,*[1] Judith Bardwick calls tenured and underperforming employees "entitled." She contends that only fear will shake these employees out of their stupor. In contrast, many health care executives have adopted total quality management (TQM), which emphasizes driving fear out of the organization. The key to handling the apparent dichotomy of these two philosophies is to make performance expectations clear, provide coaching for employees so they can meet or exceed performance expectations, and establish meaningful incentives and rewards for meeting them. The clearer the direction of the organization and the behaviors expected to reach the vision, the more consistent the collective behaviors (culture) of the hospital.

Conceptually, it is easy to understand that shaping an organizational culture requires a great deal of time. Unfortunately, most hospital executives value *doing,* not *thinking.* In his book *The Fifth Discipline,*[2] Peter Senge discusses the vulnerability of organizations that undervalue thinking. Senge describes the importance of creating learning organizations – organizations that are inhabited by creative, invested employees who anticipate change and take ownership in the change process.

Health care executives should address the following questions to assess how well their current culture empowers employees to think and creatively participate in the success of the organization:

- How are questions viewed in the hospital?
- Do managers interpret questions as challenges?
- How are mistakes handled?
- Are multiple solutions offered in problem solving?
- Do managers rush from questions to solutions?
- Is there opportunity to reflect on the questions and the proposed solutions?
- Does the organizational structure support open communication?
- Is interdepartmental communication encouraged?
- Can staff talk with other managers?
- Can executives talk with staff outside their areas of responsibility?

Developing a true learning organization requires employees who are autonomous and empowered, a work condition that not all employees value. In a 1983 survey of health care workers, half valued autonomy, a finding that has been substantiated in further research.[3] How can leaders coach employees to become autonomous and empowered? The key is to understand empowerment and to devise strategies that enable employees to be successful. A culture that emphasizes employee empowerment is the foundation of an organization committed to continuous improvement. Sustaining the effects of a turnaround requires ongoing analysis and constant refinement of performance standards, organizational processes, relationship factors, and outcomes. Executives responsible for a turnaround process must grapple with the fact that, even in the face of evidence that current practices are ineffective, hospitals tend to cling to their old ways of doing things. In a culture embracing continuous improvement, every day everyone asks why they do what they do, and whether they should do it that way again tomorrow. Making quality everyone's job is basic to an organizational attitude of cost-effectiveness and continuous improvement.

The CEO in a turnaround situation must take the lead in balancing the necessary cost cuts with the organization's commitment to quality, starting by establishing an expectation with the board that he or she will be held to certain quality standards. The board in turn must monitor results on an ongoing basis and be ready to take action as necessary. The CEO must also communicate the quality standards, board expectations, and periodic assessments to all other employees. Through this process the organization's quality goals will not get lost in the sometimes urgent need to cut costs.

Insight into the values and behaviors that underlie organizational processes gives the hospital executive a powerful tool to get at the root causes of inefficiencies. Turnarounds have the best likelihood for success when, in addition to cost objectives, hospital leaders fully understand the cultural dimensions that inhibit or enhance the improvement process.

Human Resource Practices and Policies That Support a Turnaround

Today's business literature is replete with references to emerging humanistic management theory. Peter Senge, Chris Argyris, and other authors have made persuasive arguments that the people who constitute U.S. organizations are the most influential force shaping the future of American business.[4,5] The common theme among these theorists is that successful organizations of the future will have the ability to capitalize on the creativity of the work force and the genuine desire of most people to do a good job. For most, this notion has an intuitive appeal, but it also marks a radical departure from the more prevalent method of forcing employees to conform to the prefabricated mold of traditional bureaucracies.

Executives are changing the way they think about the people they employ. The dominant paradigm of "managing human resources" is shifting to one of "leveraging human assets." Human *resource* management implies that people are no more important than any other commodity acquired and expended in the business enterprise. Conversely, human *assets* are precious sources of equity that can be leveraged for the continued growth and viability of the organization. Because the core business of the hospital is caring for people, this emphasis on human assets is particularly apt.

Executives who mistakenly think of a turnaround as an event rather than a process see their role as making a series of decisions rather than managing a continuous change process. In addition to raising volumes and maximizing prices and reimbursement, traditional turnaround tactics have been narrowly focused on reducing costs by doing the same things faster and with fewer people. Although these approaches have been effective for actualizing a certain portion of the cost-saving opportunities inherent in hospital operations, compressing the same amount of work into a tighter time frame with fewer resources places stress on the organization. When this is the only strategy to contain costs, *stress* often becomes *distress* and remaining resources are quickly exhausted. To maintain its customary level of work output, the organization must reinvest additional resources back into the system. This phenomenon is referred to as the "creep effect" of escalating costs and is recognized by the deleterious cycle of short-term cost cutting followed by rising costs.

Traditional productivity and across-the-board cost-cutting measures are extremely important to the momentum of a hospital turnaround process, particularly in its initial phases. But these traditional strategies have a certain threshold of efficiency. More far-reaching and sustainable cost improvements require an accompanying approach that transforms the organizational culture to emphasize doing the right thing, in the right way, at the right time. This emphasis puts people right at the core of the turnaround process—people who are doing the work of improving their own work processes.

Challenging the leadership paradigms that govern human resource practices and policies requires fundamental change. In traditional American business settings, human resource practices and policies have focused on the command and control of workers and work activities. The historic priorities of management have been:

- Adherence to productivity and financial targets
- Tight command over employee schedules and work habits
- Rigid control of work processes through numerous policies and procedures

This proclivity toward control is compounded in a turnaround situation by the human tendency to exercise more control during times of uncertainty. Tighter control precludes the spontaneous and innovative actions that allow organizations to thrive. Organizations that successfully weather tough times:

- Accommodate diversity rather than conformity
- Use information as a form of empowerment rather than control
- Educate workers to make decisions rather than follow directions
- Grant authority based on the problems to be solved rather than the organizational hierarchy

Restructuring the Effective Organization

Leadership in health care has too long been viewed as a matter of control, analysis, discipline, and logic. Today's diverse business and health care environment dictates a different leadership paradigm. If change is managed in an innovative way, the turnaround process can serve as a catalyst for fundamentally restructuring the organization.

Creatively restructuring an institution requires a keen understanding of the people it comprises. The first consideration should be the education of many of those in health care. The course work leading to clinical or administrative practice is steeped in the empirical sciences. Most learning in the basic and the applied sciences is by rote memorization. Even in paraprofessional and support positions, the focus of job training is mastering repetitive tasks, policies, and procedures. The work patterns and career paths of health care workers tend to follow narrow lines, often determined by the choice of an entry-level occupation. In addition, most people in health care work in structured institutions, organized along strict functional department lines. These traditional educational processes, work practices, and organizational structures have created an array of discrete practitioners who:

- Have little knowledge of each other's work
- Focus on performing increasingly complex technical tasks
- Develop departmental loyalties rather than customer or institutional loyalties

Hospitals must integrate their services to survive in today's competitive, hyperacute, and customer-sensitive environment. Most hospital processes now involve a complex set of activities that cut across functional disciplines. Improved performance requires the efforts of an interdependent group of practitioners who are focused on systemic processes that maximize efficiency, reduce response time, and deliver integrated customer service. This contemporary view of work units, in contrast to the traditional, functional compartmentalization of work groups, presents an interesting dilemma that must be addressed.

The cost reductions necessary for a hospital turnaround involve a considerable amount of change. The savvy hospital executive will recognize this as an opportunity to restructure the organization to be more flexible, proactive, and customer-focused. Choosing the appropriate structure to accomplish this presents a significant challenge. Successful, dynamic institutions typically have developed organizational structures that emphasize key business processes rather than occupational specialties and that align workers to satisfy customer requirements rather than departmental requirements.

Hospital executives who view a turnaround as the beginning of a continuous process must encourage employees to examine their work processes from the perspective of the customers they serve. Because most hospital activities focus on functional tasks rather than customer expectations, this view will require a departure from many conventional practices. A first task in moving from a functional to a systems orientation is to identify major clinical and business processes critical to the success of the organization. These clinical and business processes become the focus for analysis, problem solving, and action. Clustering people around key business processes rather than occupational groupings enables them to think beyond their individual jobs and see the bigger picture. The method for fostering system thinking and behavior—whether restructuring, committee work, or new communication channels—is less important than the fact that it occurs. Moving from a functional to a systems orientation will challenge traditional role definitions, reporting relationships, geographic allocation of services, and management of resources.

The turnaround process presents an opportunity to cultivate new attitudes about organizational structure and roles. It gives an executive the opportunity to establish a mind-set that reporting relationships, communication channels, and project teams are flexible. When employees embrace this mind-set, work groups can then be formed and reformed around significant issues affecting the organization rather than around occupational affiliations or structured reporting lines.

The restructuring that is a natural consequence of a turnaround process presents a unique opportunity for the hospital to realign the entrenched boundaries that dominate employee actions. Executives must challenge the prevailing attitude that people in a particular occupation must report to individuals of a like occupation (accountants to an accountant, nurses to a nurse, pharmacists to a pharmacist). This paradigm of occupational grouping also underlies the customary practice of promoting to management the best practitioners in a given occupation, in many instances without proper attention to the different skill sets required for clinical practice and management. Helping people adopt these new work orientations facilitates a more integrated and systemic response to organizational issues. Figure 4-2 depicts some of the more contemporary responsibilities and skills equated with management roles in innovative, quality-oriented organizations.

Many of the circumstances that contribute to a turnaround situation involve inefficient hospital operations. So often, hospital practices, policies, and procedures are designed to satisfy departmental, accreditation, and professional requirements rather than customer preferences. As a consequence, many hospital activities add little value to patient outcomes. In addition, many hospitals emphasize technical competence to the extent that the act of performing a task or procedure is more important than its impact on the customer. Thus, many people working in hospitals view their jobs as completing tasks and procedures rather than taking care of customers.

Figure 4-2. Organizational Template for Role Restructuring

Role	Responsibilities
Chief Executive Officer	• Oversee ability to achieve stakeholder needs (e.g., community, business, affiliates, medical staff, insurers) • Shape and champion organizational direction and priorities • Oversee strategy execution
Executive Officer	• Oversee integrity of organization (i.e., maintain system harmony) • Distribute resources in efficacious manner • Interpret and refine organizational direction and priorities
Service System Director	• Coordinate all components of major service systems • Span boundaries to link organizational units around substantive issues • Implement continuous improvement of service system • Develop and maintain customer relationships
Work Unit Manager	• Manage activities related to major process of service unit; 24-hour accountability for people, fiscal, and physical resources • Maintain functional currency on system processes • Identify and resolve impediments to production of products or services • Measure and ensure customer satisfaction

To focus employees on satisfying customers, all those involved in a service delivery system must be held accountable for customer outcomes. Creating an organizational atmosphere where work is determined by customer requirement rather than departmental requirement can be facilitated in several ways. Where possible, executives must look for creative ways to position employees closer to the point of service delivery through direct-line accountability. Where line accountability is impractical, feedback from those who are accountable for service can be incorporated into the performance appraisals of those who support service delivery. Finally, employees can be empowered to provide better service by replacing policies and procedures that dictate tasks with decision support tools that facilitate customer-based decisions.

Conclusion

Orchestrating a turnaround process and sustaining its benefits requires implementation of a comprehensive organizational strategy. A comprehensive strategy includes changes in the nonfinancial aspects of the organization as well: behavior, culture, policies and procedures, and structure. A hospital turnaround must be conceptualized as a process, not an event. Executives must see their role as more than executing a series of cost cuts. Effective leadership in a turnaround begins with a clear vision that focuses the entire organization on continuous improvement. Traditional policies, practices, and structures that insist on compliance and stifle innovation must be challenged. The hallmark of a successful turnaround is a culture where employees embrace change as a challenge to be met rather than an obstacle to be overcome.

References

1. Bardwick, J. *Danger in the Comfort Zone: Why America's Job Holders Must Renounce Entitlement and Earn Their Keep.* New York City: AMACOM, 1991.
2. Senge, P. M. *The Fifth Discipline: The Art and Practice of the Learning Organization.* New York City: Doubleday, 1990.
3. Jones, L. The professionalization of nursing. Dissertation, Union Graduate School, Cincinnati, 1983.
4. See especially Argyris, C., and Schon, D. *Organizational Learning: A Theory-in-Action Perspective.* Reading, MA: Addison-Wesley, 1978.
5. Senge.

Chapter 5

Revenue and Cash Management Strategies

Bonnie Brickell and Loree Lewan Hanas

Having set the stage for changes in the nonfinancial aspects of the organization—its leadership, culture, structure, and so on, a comprehensive turnaround strategy must then address the specifics of the hospital's financial performance. Cash flow and days of net revenue in accounts receivable are two important measures of a hospital's financial position. With the inception of the Medicare prospective payment system in 1983 and the subsequent move from cost-based payment mechanisms, revenue enhancement strategies and mechanisms for effective collection of accounts receivable have become increasingly important. For the distressed hospital, these strategies and mechanisms are often a critical component in achieving a successful turnaround.

Total days net revenue in accounts receivable, probably the best indicator of a hospital's cash flow, has varied substantially in recent years by hospital bed size.[1] According to AHA's HAS/Monitrend II data for November 1991, average days of net revenue in accounts receivable for all hospitals was 73, which represents, according to the Healthcare Financial Management Association, a 15 percent or a one-day increase over 1987.

Although the elimination of the periodic interim payment (PIP) program for Medicare in July 1987 had the most significant immediate impact for most hospitals, many factors have negatively influenced hospitals' ability to maintain cash flow. Continuing cuts in Medicare and Medicaid reimbursement have hampered cash flow. Additionally, regulatory changes such as outpatient bundling have eliminated many avenues for enhancing reimbursement.

As health care costs have risen, employers have shifted more of the financial burden of health care benefits to their employees. There has been a steady increase in deductibles and coinsurances. Seventy percent of all insureds had 100 percent coverage in 1980; that number dropped to 37 percent by 1988.

In addition to increased patient liability, the complexity of insurance plan types and options has confused many hospital admitting departments. Many hospitals are not aggressively pursuing up-front collections and are waiting until third-party payment or denial to begin collection procedures. Collection problems increase as accounts age. U.S. Department of Commerce figures show that accounts receivable older than 120 days lose more than 20 percent of their value.[2] Not surprisingly, levels of bad debt have been rising steadily, with a negative impact on cash flow.

The increasing amount of bad debt being written off by hospitals represents millions of dollars that hospitals will never see. According to the Hospital Accounts Receivable Analysis (HARA), hospitals reported average bad debt of 4.3 percent of gross revenues for the first quarter of 1991, compared with average bad debt of 3.7 percent of gross revenues for the first quarter of 1988. In 1990 alone, hospitals wrote off $11.3 billion as bad debt, the HARA report said.[3]

In addition, many hospitals do not realize how much self-pay revenues their facilities are generating. Most hospital executives believe self-pay revenues represent 6 to 9 percent of net revenues, but research has shown that most hospitals are generating 15 to 20 percent of their net revenues from self-pay patients. The higher self-pay percentage relates to patient liability remaining after third-party payment. Most hospital information systems are still geared for calculating revenue based on the primary financial class, which ignores the significant drop in insureds with 100 percent coverage. About half of the total self-pay percentages of net revenue (7.5 to 10 percent) are being written off as bad debt.[4]

There has been similarly dramatic growth in the underinsured/uninsured population. Recent estimates reveal that between 31 and 37 million persons in the United States do not have insurance coverage.[5] Uncompensated care costs are rising faster than overall hospital costs, and government subsidies are failing to keep pace. In addition, the unpaid care problem is no longer being shouldered by one specific group. The facilities seeing the greatest increases in expenditures are those not traditionally associated with uncompensated care—small, nonteaching, nondisproportionate care, and suburban hospitals.[6]

Although outpatient accounts constitute a larger percentage of total accounts in number, they account for only 24 percent of revenue.[7] It takes a similar amount of effort to collect an outpatient account as it does to collect an inpatient account, but the overall yield is much less. Hospitals' approach to collecting outpatient accounts has often been characterized either as passive and unfocused or as aggressive but with early write-offs to external agencies. Accordingly, outpatient accounts receivable are generally much older than inpatient accounts, and collection agency recoveries of outpatient write-offs are higher than recoveries of inpatient write-offs. Thus, the shift from inpatient to outpatient care has created additional stresses on hospital collections and cash flow.

Meanwhile, enrollment in managed care plans has skyrocketed. By the end of December 1990, the nation's 556 health maintenance organizations (HMOs) and 802 preferred provider organizations (PPOs) boasted 99.1 million members. From 1982 through 1990, enrollment increased by 86.5 million.[8] More managed care translates into increased discounting by hospitals and additional stresses on cash flow.

With all these factors hampering their ability to maintain cash flow, hospitals have been forced to place more emphasis on reducing accounts receivable to improve cash flow. Hospitals' investment in accounts receivable constitutes a very large percentage of a hospital's total assets—as high as 60 to 70 percent of the total current asset investment in many cases.[9]

Financing this heavy investment in receivables entails significant costs for health care providers. Holding large values of receivables involves either short-term borrowing costs (an option not available for many financially distressed hospitals) or lost investment returns from otherwise available equity capital.[10]

Effective receivables management can also accelerate and increase organizational cash flow. Some estimates indicate that, on average, a reduction of just five days in receivables could provide a one-time increase in operating cash flow of 20 percent. Permanent increases in cash flow are also possible through improvements in billing and collection practices. Improvements in collection practices could also greatly reduce revenue deductions for bad debts, thereby increasing cash flow.[11]

The business office accounts for a major portion of hospitals' administrative and financial expenses. For example, Monitrend data for the three months ending November 1990 show that, on average, the patient accounting and admitting functions account for more than 22 percent of the general administrative and fiscal budgets of hospitals.[12] Thus, in the effort to improve their financial health, hospitals face the dual challenge of bringing down days in receivables while controlling business office costs.[13]

Considering their limited abilities to reduce costs and considering the stresses on cash flow outlined above, hospitals must identify new sources of revenue among services they already provide, without affecting the cost side of the equation. Revenue enhancement strategies available to hospitals in financially distressed situations involve medical records and business office activities that occur after service delivery, but that significantly affect the amount of revenue generated by patient services.

Among these revenue enhancement strategies are:

- *Medical record processes,* specifically optimizing diagnosis-related group (DRG) reimbursement through effective ICD-9-CM coding and optimizing outpatient ambulatory surgery reimbursement through effective CPT-4 coding

- *Current Procedural Terminology (CPT)-4/Charge Description Master (CDM) maintenance,* specifically optimizing outpatient reimbursement by complete and comprehensive CPT-4 and HCFA Common Procedural Coding System (HCPCS) coding on the CDM
- *Pricing practices,* specifically improving hospital net revenue through more effective pricing of services provided to patients

The remainder of this chapter describes several proven strategies for enhancing revenue and improving cash flow.

Criteria for Evaluating Revenue Enhancement Opportunities

There are many methodologies and indicators for evaluating and identifying revenue enhancement opportunities. The criteria and factors considered should be viewed in conjunction with other performance measures to ensure that the most promising opportunity is identified and that the amount of opportunity is reasonably measured. A single statistic, such as the number of days in accounts receivable, should not be used as the sole indicator of potential revenue enhancement opportunities. The composition of the receivables in terms of payer mix, financial class, age, hospital size, account type, and patient type and geographic location, case mix, and economic stability of the surrounding community all affect the opportunity for revenue enhancement. Indicators and methodologies should also take into account particular circumstances surrounding the hospital's market as well as its size.

Accounts Receivable

Gross days of revenue in accounts receivable have averaged between 67 and 79 during the past several years for hospitals across the nation.[14] The opportunity for a hospital to generate improved cash flow usually increases as days in accounts receivable increase, though merely reducing the days in accounts receivable does not guarantee increased cash flow or revenue collection. If the days in accounts receivable are high due to a large percentage of old, potentially uncollectible accounts, the probability of turning the accounts into cash is minimal.

An evaluation of the aging categories, by financial class, will be particularly helpful in identifying revenue enhancement opportunities. The larger the percentage of newer accounts, the less likely a substantial one-time increase in cash flow and interest savings. As a rule of thumb, accounts receivable should be reviewed in terms of four aging categories: accounts less than 90 days old, accounts between 90 and 180 days old, accounts over 180 days old, and accounts over 1 year old. A hospital with efficient and effective billing and collection practices should have aging percentages close to the following:

- Fewer than 90 days—75%
- Between 90 and 180 days—15%
- Between 181 and 360 days—7%
- More than 360 days—3%

For financial classes or payers deviating from these percentages, follow-up activities could be focused to expedite payment and enhance revenue. A review of payment patterns and reimbursement trends is necessary to ensure that additional follow-up efforts are focused properly, though follow-up efforts alone will not necessarily result in increased cash. If a hospital employs additional personnel to call on accounts in the early stages of processing in the hope of expediting payment, but fails to provide direction regarding timing or number of attempts, follow-up efforts may be futile. Some payers by policy do not respond to follow-ups within a certain time frame or until an account reaches a specified age.

Medical Records

Reviewing the number of days of revenue associated with "discharged but not final billed" (DNFB) or suspense accounts presents an area of opportunity for a hospital to achieve a one-time increase in cash flow and reduction in interest expense for the revenue tied up in this area. If the days in DNFB are greater than 10, there may be an opportunity for interest reduction and potential revenue enhancement. A representative sample of accounts should be reviewed to evaluate the processes affecting unbilled accounts, such as the timing of coding, verifying benefits, completing attestations, and completing or resolving other missing or incorrect data elements.

The sample of unbilled accounts should be reviewed and documented in detail to determine the reasons for delay. The reasons for delay should be tracked and summarized by financial class, patient type, and physician. These data should be manipulated and analyzed to identify trends and patterns for which changes can be implemented to expedite account processing and enhance revenue. Any backlogs must be eliminated for efficient billing and collections.

Other Financial Operations

Other useful financial indicators in evaluating potential revenue enhancement opportunities include:

- Bad debt percentage
- Contractual allowance percentages

- The difference between expected and actual reimbursement
- Profit margins/financial indicators of other area hospitals

Bad debt percentages should be monitored regularly. Even small increases—as little as a quarter or half percent—may dramatically affect the hospital's bottom line. A hospital may want to perform a review of accounts written off to bad debt and accounts referred to a collection agency. If a collection agency is recovering more than 18 to 20 percent of accounts turned over to it, the hospital's follow-up efforts are inadequate. Referrals to collection agencies should also be reviewed in relation to collection costs. If a reasonable collection rate is negotiated, it may be more cost-effective to utilize an agency, particularly if the agency utilizes advanced technology to track and collect bad debt more efficiently. A periodic review of accounts written off to bad debt and accounts referred to a collection agency should confirm the appropriateness of follow-up efforts and adherence to prescribed guidelines. Hospitals should be cautious about the level of effort expended for smaller-dollar balance accounts. It may cost more in employee time and effort to collect an account with a balance of $100 than it would to turn the account over to an agency with more sophisticated means of collecting.

Contractual allowance percentages should be reviewed by payers, particularly for contracted payers who might negotiate to decrease the hospital's percentage of contractual allowances. Many hospitals across the country are experiencing a managed care boom previously experienced only by hospitals in California and Minnesota. With the number of contracts increasing rapidly, it is critical to monitor contractual allowance percentages to ensure that they are beneficial to the hospital in terms of profit or additional service volumes.

Evaluating payer trends in terms of estimated reimbursement requires a meaningful comparison of actual versus expected reimbursement. Because it is difficult to track this information manually, many hospitals may not be aware of underpayments and lost revenue. Managed care and other contracts are particularly difficult to evaluate in terms of late payment penalties, stop-loss clauses, and drug and procedure exclusions. Having the capability to identify underpayments or payments received after the contracted payment time frame allows a hospital to recover revenue it may otherwise have overlooked. The ability to evaluate the profitability of a contract and estimate reimbursement reveals underpayments and contract violations, and allows the hospital to more effectively manage or enhance revenue.

Revenue Enhancement Opportunities

For years, hospitals improved net revenues and reduced related contractual allowances by utilizing reimbursement strategies that effectively used the Medicare cost reimbursement regulations to the hospital's advantage. The concepts today are similar. Contractual relationships and reimbursement formulas continue to provide opportunities to improve payments. The difference in today's environment is that responsibility for revenue enhancement rests not only with the individuals in the finance department, but also involves many operational departments—both revenue-producing and non-revenue-producing.[15]

Although revenue enhancement strategies are available to all hospitals, certain benchmarks can aid in identifying significant opportunities for improvement. These include coding for medical record processes, outpatient CPT-4 review and CDM maintenance, and pricing strategies.

Medical Record Processes—DRG Optimization

The level of Medicare payments is integrally tied to the accuracy and specificity of the codes established for each inpatient confinement. The addition or deletion of a complication or comorbidity can result in significant differences in reimbursement. Additionally, the coding process is dependent on the quality of the documentation provided by the physician and clinical staff. Inaccurate documentation or coding may cause considerable reimbursement loss for the hospital.

The following factors or combinations of factors indicate potential opportunities for maximizing reimbursement:

- Reduction in hospital case-mix index
- Increase in length of stay
- Increase in cost per case
- Increase in contractual allowances
- High volume of DRG changes by the peer review organization (PRO)
- High staff turnover or medical records staff with limited specific training
- Limited technology (for example, lack of an encoder)

Outpatient CPT-4 Review and CDM Maintenance

The importance of accurate coding extends beyond inpatient services. Medicare reimbursement for outpatient surgery, diagnostic imaging, and other diagnostic services is directly tied to the coding and billing function. Payments for these outpatient services are based on the accuracy of CPT-4 and HCPCS codes. Individuals experienced in medical records coding should work closely with clinical personnel in the affected hospital departments to ensure that codes contained within the hospital's charge description master are consistent with Medicare's requirements.[16]

The following factors or combinations of factors indicate potential opportunities for maximizing reimbursement:

- Splintered responsibilities for maintenance of the charge description master
- Increasing level of denied claims due to CPT-4 or HCPCS coding errors
- Increasing level of denied claims due to lack of documentation
- Turnover of coding staff within medical records or responsibilities for coding lying outside the medical records department
- Increase in ambulatory surgery or diagnostic imaging volume

Pricing Strategies

Hospitals traditionally have not been very sophisticated in their charging practices. A review of charging practices to ensure that the hospital has established separate charges for all services payable by third parties, and an attempt to reconcile service delivery to patient bills to minimize lost charges, can provide significant increases in net revenues. Additionally, hospitals should understand the level of resources expended for services and reflect these resources within their pricing structure. Effectively modeling procedure-level payment information to determine the net revenue impact of increases to procedural prices is also essential when considering annual or semiannual price changes.[17]

The following factors or combinations of factors indicate potential opportunities for maximizing reimbursement:

- High cost-to-charge ratios
- High nonfixed payer percentage
- Infrequent charge description master updating practices
- Recent additions of technology
- Frequent third-party claim audits or increasing insurance denials

Short-Term Strategies for Improving Cash Flow and Revenue

Hospitals having immediate cash flow problems may need to focus on short-term strategies to temporarily alleviate their financial shortages. Two strategies to be considered are initiating a cash acceleration project and factoring or selling accounts receivable.

Accelerating Cash Flow

In situations of deteriorating cash flow and a high volume of accounts aged in excess of 90 days, a hospital should seriously consider cash acceleration or account reduction – the single greatest source of cash available to a hospital, other than factoring or selling accounts receivable. Because it can take 16 to 20 weeks to begin realizing the cash flow associated with the acceleration project, this alternative is best suited to hospitals in the position to fund operations without an immediate cash infusion. Hospitals that do not have the luxury of time should seriously consider factoring or selling accounts receivable.

Cash acceleration projects are designed to significantly improve cash flow by reducing the hospital's investment in accounts receivable. In addition to these benefits, the process should aid in identifying system or operational issues that have contributed to the growth of accounts receivable and, specifically, to the growth in aged accounts receivable. Accounts receivable grow because of operational and system inefficiencies. Without an accompanying effort to identify and eliminate these inefficiencies, the hospital will suffer a chronic backlog. A primary objective of a cash acceleration project should be not only to reduce the hospital's investment in accounts receivable and achieve a one-time improvement in cash flow, but also to maintain the new cash flow levels by improving operations.

If time permits, the hospital should perform an intensive evaluation of the noncurrent accounts receivable file prior to initiating the cash acceleration project. One objective of this evaluation is to determine the expected liquidity of the aged accounts receivable file. This requires a thorough review of a statistically valid sample of aged accounts within each payer category to determine whether all measures were taken to ensure payment, for example, insurance verification, precertification, adequate follow-up. Each account is assigned a liquidity factor (likely to collect, unlikely to collect, and so on) summarized by payer class and applied to the total noncurrent accounts receivable file. Once the liquidity of the file is established, the hospital is in a position to quantify the expected cash flow and analyze the adequacy of the reserve for contractuals and bad debt.

Once the evaluation of the file is complete, an important next step is to quantify the projected benefits and cost associated with the project and then determine the most appropriate method for cash recovery: in-house, outsource, or a combination of both. To predict benefits associated with the project, three considerations should be quantified:

- *The impact of the project on bad debt expense.* Some reasonable estimate should be calculated of the aged accounts receivable dollars that would not otherwise be collected without the cash acceleration process, due to such factors as exceeding statutory limits. Because accounts continue to lose liquidity as they age, certain accounts collected under a cash acceleration project would not be collectible if the project were postponed.
- *The impact of the project on interest income.* Some reasonable estimate should be calculated of the timing of the cash acceleration

process relative to the time it would take to collect the aged accounts receivable without the project. Industry experience suggests that approximately 50 percent of cash is collected within 20 weeks of initiating a cash acceleration project.[18] Interest income earned as a result of the project (current interest rates multiplied by the expected cash) should be calculated for the period between the expected receipt of payment for aged accounts with and without the project.

- *The impact of the project on the increased efficiency of staff.* This factor is not easily quantified; however, it should be recognized that certain savings as well as increased cash flow will be achieved by reducing the work load currently assigned to business office staff and increasing efficiencies within the patient accounting department by identifying and improving system and operational inefficiencies.

To predict costs associated with the cash acceleration project, the following factors should be quantified:

- *Project managed and conducted by in-house staff.* It is unlikely that a cash acceleration project can be performed using in-house staff exclusively. External temporary support likely will be needed to augment existing staff. Nevertheless, a considerable portion of the total accounts receivable files will be carved out from the day-to-day responsibilities of billing and collection personnel. Certain in-house staff must therefore be available to staff the project. The hospital should utilize internal staff in some capacity to familiarize them with effective billing and follow-up procedures and techniques.

  The number and level of experience of temporary personnel required will depend on the number of accounts in the aged file and the expected daily benchmark productivity. Once this is determined, the hourly expense associated with temporary personnel over the projected life of the project should be calculated. Qualified temporary personnel for this type of project are usually available only at premium prices; a lower-priced agency likely will provide lower-quality services and, ultimately, recover less cash.

  Also, the availability and quality of resources to effectively manage and control the project in-house should be considered. A cash acceleration project, whether conducted in-house or by an outsourcing firm, requires strong control and management; however, the level of involvement of a project manager will be much greater when the project is conducted in-house. Because managers within the department will be busy running operations as well as developing and implementing procedures and processes to minimize the risk of future backlogs, they may not be able to accommodate the day-to-day demands of the project.

- *Performing the project using an outsourcing firm.* The potential fees charged by the outsourcing firm should be estimated using standard contingency fees charged by firms within the hospital's local market area. These fees may vary from 15 to 30 percent. When anticipating potential costs associated with outsourcing, it must be considered that a minimum fee may be charged per account for the project.
- *Combination of in-house staff and an outsourcing firm.* The hospital may want to carve certain higher-risk accounts out of the file and place them with an outsourcing firm, while retaining those with greater expected liquidity to be worked internally. Self-pay accounts and low-dollar outpatient accounts are often outsourced, whereas third-party inpatient and high-dollar third-party outpatient accounts are usually retained. If this is the preferred course, it must be remembered that the contingency fee charged by the outsourcing firm will likely be higher than a rate negotiated for the whole aged file.

If an external agency is chosen to perform some or all of the cash acceleration project, certain factors for contracting with outsourcing firms should be considered:

- Multiple bids should be evaluated.
- Agency experience should be identified and references carefully checked.
- The experience of the supervisory and billing staff who will be used on the project should be identified, and the hospital should negotiate the ability to refuse unacceptable staff.
- Accounts that cannot be worked cost-effectively should be excluded (for example, past statutory limits, low-dollar accounts).
- Performance-based fee arrangements should be utilized.
- A minimum level of effort for each account should be defined.
- The duration of the project and the period over which subsequent payment will be attributed to the agency should be limited.
- Management reporting should be reviewed and approved prior to project initiation.
- Acceptable procedures for the process should be established—financial class prioritization, denials/appeals, financial class transfer, small balance write-off, and so on.
- Agency performance and fee calculations should be carefully tracked.

Cash acceleration projects can be quite effective if expectations are kept in perspective and if the information obtained during the project is used to enhance operations within the department. The project should not be viewed as a solution to accounts receivable problems but, rather, as a mechanism to provide a needed cash infusion and, more important, to identify and resolve operational issues. Regardless of the method chosen to perform the project, strong management and oversight of project progress is critical to overall success.

Factoring/Selling Accounts Receivable

For hospitals in need of immediate cash to fund operations, selling accounts receivable may be the only option. Receivables funding programs offer a wide range of options for hospitals, and most are available to hospitals with less than investment-grade ratings. The programs value the collectibility of the accounts receivable as opposed to the creditworthiness of the hospital.[19] Unfortunately, funding programs may cost more than some hospitals expect and may still fall short on results.

There has been a significant growth in the number of firms offering funding programs. Prominent firms include Towers Financial, Shearson Lehman Hutton, Premier Hospital Alliance, United Medicorp, CIS Technologies-Sharp Program, and Hospital Billing Collection Services. The products these firms offer generally allow hospitals to finance most of their third-party receivables through off-balance-sheet sale of assets. The hospital pays a fee—it varies widely—to gain immediate access to cash. The deals generally have no recourse to the hospital; if a bill is not collected, the hospital is not held financially responsible. The hospital usually continues to collect the receivables on behalf of the financier, but may receive assistance with collections.[20]

Many of these firms have received approval from the Health Care Financing Administration (HCFA) for funding of Medicare and Medicaid receivables. The Department of Housing and Urban Development (HUD), though, has expressed concern when hospitals have outstanding mortgage-backed loans from the federal government. HUD has therefore established some guidelines and criteria for hospitals seeking to sell their accounts receivable.[21]

There are other potential roadblocks a hospital must overcome to pursue these funding programs, depending on the current status of the hospital's receivables. Previous bond issues, notes, or lines of credit issued to the hospital may preclude any such funding of receivables activity, as they were secured by the hospital's receivables.[22]

Although a funding program may provide short-term relief for a financially distressed hospital, without sound business planning the program may further erode the hospital's creditworthiness. These programs should also not be viewed as a solution for high days of revenue outstanding. Accounts receivable funding is an alternative source of financing that, with proper structure, can provide a fast source of capital for troubled hospitals. Some available research suggests that hospitals could increase their current business office expenses by more than 20 percent before finding a cost justification for the present accounts receivable funding programs.[23] Hospitals in severe financial distress, of course, may not have the luxury of time and available cash to fund these increases or wait for the results.

Long-Term Strategies for Improving Cash Flow and Revenue

Hospitals that are not in imminent danger of closure can concentrate on long-term strategies for improving their cash flow. Proven strategies include accounts receivable operational reviews, coding optimization, and strategic and operational pricing programs.

Accounts Receivable Operational Review

Hospitals need to review their patient accounting cycles regularly. The review process should generate recommendations to ensure the effective use of resources; develop guidelines and tools to monitor accuracy, completeness, and timeliness; and keep patients, physicians, hospital departments, and external customers satisfied. The following sections illustrate the need for review in the various areas of the patient accounting cycle.

Admission/Registration

An operational review of admitting and registration may be more or less complex depending on hospital size and points of entry. The larger and more decentralized a hospital, the more difficult will be the review and implementation of changes. If admission and registration procedures and operations have not changed much in the past decade, tasks and responsibilities should be challenged and investigated in detail. Specific criteria should be reviewed:

- The accuracy, completeness, and timeliness of patient demographic, financial, and insurance information
- The timing or initiation of processes
- The clarity, usefulness, and documentation of policies and procedures
- The effectiveness of insurance verification and financial counseling activities
- Monitoring tools and goals established for each area

The review should focus on:

- Bed reservations and assignment
- Preregistration and preadmitting procedures
- Admission and registration procedures
- Emergency department admissions and registrations
- Insurance verification and certification

Bed reservations should be reviewed to ensure that information regarding inpatient admissions and planned outpatient services is received. Outpatient information may be maintained by individual ancillary areas or departments when scheduling patient services and may not be shared for preregistration uses. It may take considerable effort to determine the level and location of information available. For bed assignments, the proper accounting of the daily census should also be reviewed. With the changes in regulations for observation patients, the thoroughness of this review is playing a greater role in ensuring the accurate capture and recording of revenue.

Preadmission/preregistration procedures should be reviewed for comprehensiveness to minimize financial risk. A comprehensive preadmission/preregistration program should include:

- Timely collection of demographic, financial, and insurance information
- Confirmation of insurance benefits and actual existence of coverage
- Precertification and authorization for services obtained
- Review of open outstanding balances and bad debt accounts
- Communication with patient/guarantor regarding deductibles and estimated liability

Effective preadmission/preregistration procedures minimize financial risk, provide high-quality customer service, educate patients regarding hospital financial and clinical processes and expectations, and collect copayments and deductibles that are difficult and costly to collect afterward. The timing of information processing should be investigated to ensure effective utilization of information. Some hospitals obtain patient demographic, financial, and insurance information in advance of a patient visit, but do not begin the preadmission/preregistration, insurance verification, and financial counseling processes until the day before, the day of, or the day after the patient's admission or visit.

Admission and registration processes and procedures likewise should be reviewed to ensure their consistent application at different registration and admission points. Special attention is required for areas that provide high-cost and high-volume services and that are less likely to be covered by insurance. New procedures or technology should also be investigated with an insurance company to determine any coverage limitations. The accuracy and completeness of information obtained at various registration points should be uniform to ensure the consistent application of and adherence to procedures. To ensure complete and accurate information, an admission/registration checklist of all information to be obtained, reviewed, verified, and signed must be maintained.

Such checklists commonly include:

- Advance directives
- Medicare secondary payer questionnaire
- Release of information form signed
- Primary insurance information obtained
- Secondary insurance information obtained
- Insurance verified
- Patient notified of deductibles/deposits
- Admission/registration form reviewed for completeness

A review of the emergency department (ED) should focus attention on major aspects critical to routine admissions and registrations as well as:

- *The level of effort employed to obtain patient information.* For patients with serious medical conditions, it may not be possible to obtain complete patient demographic, financial, and insurance information. Every effort should be made, however, to gather as much patient information as possible, always with due respect for the patient's condition. Insurance cards, identification cards, driver's licenses, and so on, should be copied and highlighted. If this opportunity to obtain information is not seized, the hospital may reduce or limit its prospects of obtaining payment for services.
- *Opportunities to request and collect payment for services.* Particularly for nonurgent cases, and in accordance with hospital guidelines and policies, a floor layout should be considered in which patients must pass the registrar or cashier in order to exit. Information regarding charges and financial responsibility should also be posted and provided to waiting patients.
- *Patterns and trends in the percentage of admissions from the ED.* Changes in patterns should be reviewed, to the physician level, if information is available. Insurance companies may deny emergency charges if a patient's condition was not documented as urgent. Rising numbers of denials or reductions in reimbursement for ED care are strong indicators of poor documentation or coding.

Emergency departments usually account for more than their fair share of bad debt and small balance write-offs. Collecting payment for services provided in the ED could reduce bad debt as well as the cost involved in collection efforts later in the patient accounting process. Dedicating a financial counselor to the ED is one way to reduce bad debt and identify alternative payment resources for patients in need. If the size and staffing resources of a hospital do not easily permit this, other alternatives should be pursued—for example, cross-training of ED registrars, directing patients to financial counselors, and establishing a rotating position that can be "on call" as patients needing services are identified.

Additionally, high levels of ED admissions that appear to be out of line with a particular type of hospital (community, tertiary, academic) may be an indicator that some physicians are circumventing the preadmission/admission process altogether. In some situations, this circumvention may be in response to complaints from their patients.

Insurance verification has become a problem area in many hospitals. During a review of the area, the following items should be evaluated:

- *The timing of processes.* It is critical to act on and process information at the point it is received to minimize financial risk and provide information to patients. If processing of patient information is delayed until admission or registration, opportunities to enhance revenue or minimize risk could be squandered.
- *The documentation of information.* A patient account should be reviewed for the comprehensiveness of documentation and its accessibility. Is information commonly documented in the system or by hard copy? Are standard phrases or words used to expedite documentation and encourage uniform understanding? Is information documented only by one area or unit, or do all parties handling the account document information?
- *Information review processes.* Due to the volume and complexity of patient information, review processes should be in place to ensure reasonableness and completeness. If a patient is no longer covered under his or her insurance, is an inquiry made to determine the reason? If insurance coverage has been terminated due to unpaid premiums, in some instances it could be to the benefit of the hospital to cover the payment of premiums. The cost of premiums is usually much less than the cost of care for serious medical/surgical conditions and a small percentage of the bad debt that would have been incurred due to the lack of insurance payments.
- *Monitoring tools and methods.* Monitoring tools and methods ensure consistent productivity and effort. Methods to track incoming and outgoing calls, the percentage of accuracy, and the percentage of insurances verified before the time of service are some common examples.

Insurance verification is critical to the effectiveness of the billing process and the reimbursement ultimately received. With employers changing insurance companies so frequently and offering more and more insurance options to employees, maintaining up-to-date information on benefits, contracts, and changes is imperative. Lacking any standardization in the industry, it may be impossible even to determine the insurance company from an employee's insurance card.

Medical Records

The timing of medical records operations and the cooperation of physicians and ancillary departments control the timing of billing. The skill, scrutiny, and experience of the coding staff determines the amount of reimbursement for each patient's account. If procedures or diagnoses exclude complications or comorbidities, the hospital may be underbilling.

A review of the medical records department's interdependent and complex processes and operations should include the following:

- *Investigation and analysis of "discharged, not final billed" or "unbilled" or "suspense" accounts.* If the total in this category is greater than 10 days of revenue, reviewing and revising operations may enhance revenue. The reasons for delays and backlogs should be evaluated and resolved.
- *The volume of uncoded records.* Eliminating uncoded records could dramatically increase revenue. Eliminating the backlog could result in a one-time increase in revenue equal to the number of days of revenue backlogged.
- *The number and dollar impact of records holding for physician attestation.* Minimizing the number and dollars of records holding for attestation may present a straightforward opportunity for revenue enhancement. The number and dollar amount of records holding for attestation should be summarized by physicians.
- *The number of records holding for release of information signatures.* Without a release of information the most accurate and complete information will not enhance a hospital's revenue, and without proper signature a bill will probably be denied. Ensuring the effectiveness of admission and registration checks and reviews and implementing enhancements should minimize the revenue impact of this issue.
- *Diagnosis and procedure coding.* A periodic review of diagnosis and procedure coding could identify lost revenue due to undercoding and serve as a means of focusing education. Accounts that have been undercoded should be rebilled to capture additional revenue.

Billing

Billing is the key to revenue enhancement. The financial impact of delayed, lost, or otherwise incorrect bills could be substantial. Particular areas of focus in reviewing billing operations include the following:

- *The status of bill production.* Billing backlogs, by bill type and financial class, should be investigated and quantified in terms of number and dollars of accounts receivable. Backlogged bills represent potential revenue enhancement.

- *The distribution of billing responsibilities.* Are staff organized effectively in terms of work load and expertise? Regulatory and other informational complexities make it difficult for an employee to master all financial classes and payer types. Narrowing billers' focus to specific financial classes or payer types will increase billing effectiveness and efficiency.
- *Review or audit functions.* Errors and missing information create havoc in reimbursement. With the complexity of patient accounting processes, monitoring tools and functions are essential. In many operations, it may be advantageous to utilize a manual or automated review mechanism that identifies errors, missing elements, and irregularities.
- *Utilization of technology.* Some manual effort is to be expected in a process as complex as billing, but it should be kept to a minimum. Automated processes and technology should be maintained and reviewed for effectiveness:
  - Automated edit reports for billing errors and missing elements
  - Electronic claims submission
  - Fax machines
  - Information system features that minimize keystrokes and level of effort and that enhance accuracy and timeliness of bill submission, such as preestablished codes for account notes and automatic updates of patient information, reducing duplicate entries of patient information
  - Automated monitoring tools and reports: productivity reports by payer and by biller; percentage of claims filed electronically; billing errors by payer and by biller

Collection and Follow-up

Sound follow-up and collection can make quick work of a hospital's accounts receivable. Specific areas to investigate include:

- *Guidelines for documentation.* Information is the key to receivables management and revenue enhancement. Guidelines for documentation, particularly in the information system, are essential for providing all parties with current information.
- *The hospital's statement and letter cycle.* Patients respond to persistent follow-up efforts. Statements, letters, or postcards sent in 10- to 15-day increments increase the likelihood of prompt collection. Hospitals that defer sending statements, bills, and follow-up notices for 30, 45, or 60 days minimize their chances of collection.

- *The number of employees dedicated to follow-up and collection efforts.* If employees are responsible for both billing and follow-up, the effectiveness of follow-up may be minimized. Account follow-up should be the responsibility of a dedicated staff.
- *The use of collection agencies and collection technology.* Technology (autodialers, collection software packages, and so on) and agency assistance could provide a cost-effective means of enhancing follow-up efforts. Many types of assistance, including precollection services, statement and letter assistance, collection letters, or a combination of calls and letters, are available for various fees.

Education and Job Competency

In years past, before the establishment of diagnosis-related groups, the resource-based relative value scale (RBRVS), preferred provider organizations, health maintenance organizations, and leveraged buyouts (LBOs), a hospital could fairly easily hire employees for its patient accounting operation, train them in a relatively short period of time, and keep the process running smoothly. It is becoming more difficult now to hire qualified accounting personnel with backgrounds in medical terminology, broad knowledge of the insurance industry, the mathematical aptitude to calculate expected reimbursement and contractual allowances, and the assertiveness of a tax collector to encourage patient payments. Hospitals are being forced to incur a high cost in training employees. Many hospitals also lose money and suffer additional costs when employees leave the hospital for higher salaries at other area institutions. Many hospitals are not aware of, or are unable to, measure the costs and losses associated with training and employee turnover, even though employees are one of the hospital's greatest assets.

With the pace of change in the health care industry, it is difficult to train employees, but more difficult to ensure that they are always current regarding regulatory changes and developments. Some hospitals have adopted programs of instruction, review, and testing to ensure adequate levels of training and education. Testing employees increases their motivation to learn and identifies weaknesses in the training program and problem areas for employees. Training and testing also can be used to recognize employee achievement and encourage career advancement. Without properly educated employees, it is unrealistic to expect an efficient, effective operation.

Proven education and training techniques include the following:

- Admitting:
  - Insurance card matching with plan type
  - Screen depictions (Employee identifies information to be completed and where to obtain the information.)

  - Description of a situation (Employee identifies the information to be documented in account notes.)
  - Deductible, estimated liability, and copayment calculations (Employee calculates each based on a set of facts regarding insurance information and previous account history.)
- Billing:
  - Itemization of patient bill and insurance facts (Employee calculates expected reimbursement and contractual allowance.)
  - Copy of UB-82 (Employee identifies missing and incorrect elements that would cause rejection.)
- Collection:
  - Description of situation (Employee documents appropriate procedures and amounts for payment arrangement.)
  - Listing of accounts outstanding (Employee identifies priority and approach used in follow-up.)

Coding Optimization

The objectives of coding optimization are to seize every available opportunity to enhance reimbursement through optimal clinical coding and to establish hospital management systems to ensure optimum inpatient and outpatient Medicare reimbursement. Coding optimization opportunities most frequently lie in:

- Medicare inpatient ICD-9-CM coding and DRG classification
- Medicare ambulatory surgery CPT-4 coding and ambulatory surgery center (ASC) classifications
- Medicare HCPCS coding for ancillary departments subject to fee schedules and payment limitations

DRG Optimization

Underoptimization for inpatient DRGs is typically related to three areas: the sequencing, specificity, and existence of secondary diagnoses. Hospital coders and physicians must understand the impact of sequencing on DRG assignment. Improper sequencing of diagnoses and/or procedures can result in the assignment of a lower-priced DRG and lower reimbursement.

Similarly, a lack of documentation or specificity in the record can result in the failure to identify a complication or comorbidity that could significantly affect DRG reimbursement. The lack of a secondary diagnosis in the documentation can also adversely affect DRG assignment and reimbursement.

The financial impact of underoptimization of DRG assignment can reach $1,000 to $2,000 per bed. Conversely, DRG optimization can yield enhanced payments immediately, reveal opportunities for ongoing payment enhancement, and provide baseline data to establish and monitor the quality of the coding process.

Many factors can lead to an incorrect DRG assignment. One issue is a lack of documentation or poor documentation in the medical record, specifically unidentified comorbidities or complications or the absence of operative procedures. Procedures or conditions that may lead to complications or comorbidities may not always appear significant when viewed independently, but they can change reimbursement significantly.

Another source of incorrect DRG assignment is the improper sequencing of the principal diagnosis or the absence of a clear-cut principal diagnosis. The principal diagnosis is defined as "the condition established after study to be chiefly responsible for the admission of the patient to the hospital."[24] Correctly identifying the principal diagnosis requires clear and complete documentation by the physician in the medical record and correct sequencing of the principal diagnosis with secondary diagnoses. In addition, missing ancillary reports make it impossible for coders to identify conditions that might influence the designation of the principal diagnosis or conditions that might constitute complications or comorbidities.

Coding from the face sheet, sometimes practiced as a more expedient method of coding, often overlooks information to optimize reimbursement. Similarly, phone reports often provide insufficient information for the coder to properly assign diagnoses and their corresponding codes.

To properly identify opportunities for DRG optimization, the hospital should perform an intensive review of approximately 100 to 200 medical records, focusing on certain high-opportunity DRGs. The objective of this review is to identify ICD-9-CM coding and sequencing errors, missed diagnoses or procedures, the incorrect selection of a principal diagnosis, or any missing documentation.

For the highest potential change in reimbursement, the sample set should target medical records:

- Without comorbidities/complications
- Without cardiovascular complications
- Without complex circulatory disorders
- Without complicated diagnoses
- For minor operating procedures
- With principal diagnoses that are really symptoms

Implementing DRG optimization begins with experienced, trained coders. Therefore, recruiting qualified people and building a staff large enough to perform thorough chart reviews should be the first order of business. Any procedural problems that extend coding time should be resolved, and physicians should be persuaded to cooperate in providing clear, complete, and accurate documentation.

CPT-4 and HCPCS Coding Optimization

Medicare outpatient reimbursement for outpatient surgery, diagnostic imaging, and other diagnostic services is also based, in part, on fixed-payment formulas directly tied to the coding and billing function. Regulations effective October 16, 1991, require that every hospital outpatient service be assigned an HCPCS code.

As regulations change regarding outpatient reimbursement and UB-82 completion, complete and accurate CPT-4 coding and clinical documentation in the medical record become even more critical. Coding accuracy is essential for appropriate third-party reimbursement, timely payment, and compliance with Medicare and Medicaid regulations.

Working closely with clinical personnel, coders should review the hospital's charge description master to identify procedure descriptions that are inconsistent with those included in the Medicare CPT-4/HCPCS coding description; CPT-4/HCPCS codes included in the charge master that have been deleted, replaced, or that are invalid; and CPT-4/HCPCS codes currently not included in the charge master that should be considered.

A review of outpatient coding should focus on services most frequently utilized by Medicare and Medicaid patients and on other certain high-volume procedures. An important component of the CPT-4/HCPCS coding review is an evaluation of the UB-82 revenue codes for departments where the codes affect HCPCS assignment.

Experience has shown that CPT-4/HCPCS coding reviews reveal the most significant results in:

- Laboratory
- Radiology
- Pulmonary function
- Cardiology
- Gastroenterology
- Vascular laboratory
- Neurodiagnostics

Pricing Strategies

The application of new pricing strategies is equally important in helping the hospital to obtain its long-term goal of improving cash flow through increasing net revenues. Two approaches to consider in this long-term strategy are strategic pricing and operational pricing.

Strategic Pricing

Strategic pricing applies payment information to enhance net revenues. Instead of initiating annual across-the-board rate increases to achieve budget requirements for increases in gross revenue, strategic pricing targets price increases for specific procedures that have high charge-based and/or high cost-based participation. Additionally, strategic pricing should consider all payment attributes of each high-volume procedure to ensure that the hospital's rate structure is truly optimized.

The strategic pricing initiative should have one singular objective: to achieve the highest net revenue at the lowest overall price level, while considering market and political price sensitivities. This approach can significantly improve operating margins compared with across-the-board price increases or even selective departmental methods.

Effectively modeling procedure-level payment information to determine the net revenue impact of increases to procedural prices is essential when considering annual or semiannual price changes. A procedure-level analysis is superior to department-level analyses due to the fluctuations in payer mix among procedures in any given department. Similarly, careful consideration of all payment attributes (cost reimbursement, bad debt percentages, and so on) for each procedure can further enhance the net revenue impact of proposed price increases.[25]

Simply stated, strategic pricing is designed to:

- Rank procedures based on each individual procedure's marginal contribution factor (the increase in net revenue per one dollar increase in charges)
- Reduce all prices for the related procedures to their lowest defined limits
- Raise procedure prices individually to their highest defined upper limit based on a rank ordering of marginal contribution factors

This methodology maximizes the net revenue per procedure for every dollar of rate increase. As a result, prices for procedures with a high utilization by collectible charge payers and/or a high utilization by cost-based payers will be increased, whereas procedures with a high utilization by fixed-price payers and/or a high utilization by uncollectible payers will be decreased. The outcome is the highest net revenues attainable for the given level of gross revenues.

For a strategic pricing process to be successful, it must:

- Develop a price structure that provides rational, consistent, and competitive pricing of all procedures. Global departmental price changes may spark physician and patient concerns.
- Ensure that at least 80 percent of the hospital's revenue is represented by the procedures isolated for pricing consideration.
- Provide a price structure that remains competitive in the hospital's local marketplace.
- Consider organizational sensitivity to certain rate increases (for example, room rates, delivery charges, and supply items).

- Allow targeting of overall gross revenue and net revenue limits as well as targets and limits by individual payer or department.
- Incorporate varying payment methodologies (Medicare, Medicaid, HMO/PPOs, commercial insurance, self-pay, and so on) into the analysis in order to accurately model and project procedural profitability.
- Adjust historical procedural data by payer to budget-year volumes to incorporate budgeted procedure mix changes and/or payer shifts.
- Consider the impacts of any physician sharing in hospital charges.
- Allow for the determination of pricing constraints on an individual procedure level.

The purpose of strategic pricing should be to identify a procedure-specific net revenue contribution margin for each significant procedure based on its utilization patterns by payer, bad debt percentage, fixed-payment utilization, and impact on departmental cost reimbursement. This information will provide benefits not only in maximizing net revenue through logically placed price increases or decreases, but also in evaluating the profitability of specific product lines. Payment information, combined with the market and cost information identified through the charge capture process, will assist the hospital in making decisions regarding the future investment of its resources and in identifying inappropriate pricing methodologies. Furthermore, this process will provide the hospital with precise information for use in evaluating proposed new services or joint ventures. Meanwhile, the hospital will be maximizing net revenues for the services it currently provides.[26] However, the hospital must realize that the benefits available through a strategic pricing initiative depend on the specific circumstances of the hospital (for example, payer mix, current price structure, and the flexibility in pricing that management feels is acceptable in the marketplace).

Several additional considerations should be weighed when embarking on strategic pricing initiatives:

- *Pharmacy/central supply room (CSR) formula analysis.* Hospitals have typically elected to price pharmacy and CSR items using a cost-based markup formula. Tremendous benefits can be realized if formula pricing is abandoned for procedure-based strategic pricing.
- *Routine revenue maximization.* Many large hospitals have separate nursing units, obstetrical units, neurological units, pediatric units, and so on for varying types of patients. The room rates usually do not vary significantly by patient type and result in a potentially inefficient price structure. Hospitals may wish to consider separately pricing the various nursing units according to their contribution margins to build a pricing structure that maximizes net revenue in routine areas.
- *Two-tier pricing.* Most hospitals today have specialized outpatient centers that must share their service area with other outpatient

providers. Strategic pricing can be used to analyze the effects of reducing certain outpatient rates, while maintaining current inpatient rates for procedures that have high outpatient utilization (and consumer visibility), such as laboratory and radiology. Procedures can be separated into inpatient and outpatient components and priced independently.

Operational Pricing

Operational pricing involves a thorough review of operating activities within revenue-producing departments. The intent is to increase net revenue by identifying services rendered for which no charge has been made or by creatively revising and/or expanding the existing charge structure.

Hospitals should give thoughtful consideration to performing an operational pricing review. Historical approaches to pricing for services have focused on market constraints, budgetary goals and objectives, and rate increases unrelated to procedure-specific costing. As a result, the evolution of charge structures at most hospitals has not accurately reflected resource consumption or the cost of doing business.

Similarly, the maintenance of the charge description master (CDM) at most hospitals is fragmented. Many assign the function to finance department personnel with little or no input from the operating departments. Additionally, many hospitals only update the CDM during the budget process to account for annual price increases. The lack of a comprehensive CDM management process, involving key personnel from all revenue-producing departments, causes loss of revenue for services performed but not reflected in the charge structure. Most often, revenue losses occur due to ineffective charge capture processes and inadequate training of clinical personnel as to the critical need for accurate recording of all services, procedures, and resources consumed.

An operational pricing review can produce favorable and immediate results as well as valuable information to improve the operational effectiveness of a hospital. Although all revenue-generating departments should be considered initially, the greatest opportunities typically lie in:

- Pharmacy
- Central services
- Surgery
- Nursing
- Laboratory
- Emergency department

An operational pricing initiative can generate additional net and gross revenue, build a more comprehensive base of charges, improve the charge capture process, and establish firmer control over charge capture and maintenance. The study can also provide an enhanced understanding of cost structure, a better match of resource consumption to charges, and a foundation for operational improvements to ensure the ongoing optimization of net and gross revenues.

Conclusion

In recent years, several internal and external factors have combined to have a significant impact on hospitals' ability to manage both cash flow and days of net revenue in accounts receivable—two vitally important measures of a hospital's financial position. An effective and lasting turnaround will depend in large part on the hospital's application of strategies that will enhance net revenue and thus improve cash flow. A variety of methodologies and strategies may be used to identify opportunities for revenue enhancement for both the short and long term, including accounts receivable operational reviews, coding optimization, and strategic and operational pricing programs.

References

1. Anderson, H. J. Business office innovations improve hospital cash flow. *Hospitals* 65(7):50, Apr. 5, 1991.
2. Bradford, C., and Simoni, A. Strong medicine: rethinking the PFS director's role. *Healthcare Financial Management* 45(8):25 Aug. 1991.
3. Nemes, J. Hospitals put teeth into efforts to collect bad debt. *Modern Healthcare* 21(24):42, June 17, 1991.
4. Nemes.
5. Committee on Ways and Means, U.S. House of Representatives. *1991 Green Book.* Washington, DC: CWM, USH, 1991, p. 318.
6. Ashby, J. L., Jr. The burden of uncompensated care grows. *Healthcare Financial Management* 46(4):66, Apr. 1992.
7. American Hospital Association. *AHA Hospital Panel Survey, ProPac, Hospital Outpatient Background Report, C-90-2.* Chicago: AHA.
8. Interstudy. *Managed Care: A Decade in Review.* Excelsior, MN: Interstudy, 1990.
9. Cleverly, W. O., senior editor. Accounts receivable management. *Topics in Health Care Financing* 8(3), Spring 1992, foreword.
10. Cleverly.
11. Cleverly.
12. Anderson, p. 50.

13. Anderson, p. 50.
14. American Hospital Association. *HAS/Monitrend II.* Chicago: AHA, 1992.
15. Deatsch, D. G. Revenue enhancement strategies. *Topics in Health Care Financing* 17(3):22, Spring 1991.
16. Deatsch, p. 27.
17. Deatsch, p. 28.
18. The statistics reflect the experience of Ernst & Young and the author conducting more than 250 similar projects.
19. *The Zimmerman Letter* (monthly newsletter published by Zimmerman & Associates, Hales Corner, WI). Nov. 1990, p. 1.
20. Anderson, p. 51.
21. *The Zimmerman Letter,* p. 2.
22. *The Zimmerman Letter,* p. 1.
23. *The Zimmerman Letter,* p. 3.
24. Healthcare Financing Administration quoted by: Dingess, R., Brickell, B., and Tarplee, S. Improving the hospital's bottom line through effective accounts receivable management. Presentation to the Healthcare Financial Management Association, Chicago, Oct. 1990.
25. Deatsch, p. 28.
26. Deatsch, p. 28.

Chapter 6

Cost Reduction and Quality Improvement

Mark Van Sumeren

Cost reduction is a fundamental and necessary element of any financial turnaround strategy. Reducing costs can enhance cash flow to fund continued operations and buy time while the turnaround strategy is implemented. In addition, organizations in financial trouble often find that many expenses can be delayed or avoided, at least temporarily, while management struggles to achieve more permanent structural changes.

Achievement of Cost Reductions in a Turnaround Situation

Cost behavior is discretionary within narrow bounds. Management may dictate that spending patterns be sharply curtailed, but the effects of such pronouncements are rarely long-lasting. Classic examples of this phenomenon involve such mandates as eliminating travel and education expenses, reducing professional dues and related expenses, restricting overtime, and, in the extreme, implementing across-the-board layoffs. These activities can certainly be successful in generating immediate changes in cash position, but they are rarely sustained because they do not modify the underlying factors (professional requirements to maintain certification, requiring nursing staff to work overtime to complete paperwork, and so on) that influence such costs in the first place. The organization enjoys the immediate gratification of influencing the effect but without changing its root cause—and so, like the drug addict, the organization soon requires another, probably stronger dose.

As this chapter demonstrates, achieving short-term savings in a turnaround situation does not necessarily ensure long-term viability. In lieu of tempting quick fixes, a successful turnaround strategy employs a rigorous and systematic cost restructuring. In this approach, management pays particular attention to understanding the underlying factors driving existing cost behavior and then adjusts those factors so as to cause permanent, structural change in the cost behavior of the organization.

A successful approach also requires that management take a nontraditional view of the organization and its operations. A traditional view focuses on the organization as a long list of various functionally distinct departments or cost centers. Some organizations that apply this traditional construct pursue across-the-board layoffs in an effort to spread the pain equally. Others focus staff reductions in "noncritical" areas (for example, housekeeping and cafeteria), assuming that cuts in these areas will have the least impact on patient care.

A better way to view the organization is from a horizontal or process-oriented perspective, as opposed to the vertical, functional orientation. This nontraditional concept envisions major operating systems (surgical services, patient flow, critical care, material management) and critical processes (admitting, drug distribution). Operating systems and critical processes, which typically cross traditional functional boundaries, offer the greatest opportunity for effecting structural changes in cost behavior. A horizontal perspective also more closely resembles the key customers' view of the organization. A patient only knows that there was a glitch in his or her admission; he or she does not care whether it could be the fault of seven separate departments. Making operational changes from a process perspective rather than a functional perspective improves the chances that quality—the *customer's* idea of quality—will be improved and not degraded.

Traditional Approaches to Cost Reduction

Often, the organization in distress is hungry for cash and seizes every opportunity to realize quick improvements in cash flow. The more common responses to this challenge are often tactical.

Methods

An organization in distress may employ a few or more of the following tactical methods to achieve immediate cost reductions:

- Freezes on "discretionary" expenditures, such as travel and education, training, professional dues, and consulting fees
- Extending payments
- Hiring restrictions, except in "critical" areas
- Overtime restrictions

- Wage and salary freezes or reductions
- Inventory spend-downs
- Delays in capital expenditures
- Elimination of staff or noncritical functions (for example, planning and marketing, public relations)
- Selective staff reductions
- Across-the-board layoffs

This might be viewed as a checklist of progressively severe tactics the organization can use, depending on the severity of its financial distress. With the exception of the final two, any single action from this checklist will have only a limited impact on the organization's cash position. Therefore, this discussion concentrates on the specific methods and implications of selective and across-the-board staff reductions as tactics within the financial turnaround strategy.

Staff Reductions

When expediency is a primary consideration in a turnaround, management generally acts within the organizational, operational, cultural, and political realities of the moment at the hospital. For example:

- Decision making is swiftest along existing organizational lines. Because the hospital is likely organized along traditional, functional lines (for example, nursing, laboratory, radiology, admitting), it is best equipped to make decisions within these boundaries. In a turnaround situation, managers are ordered to make adjustments within their spheres of control—their respective departments. Activities or linkages that span departmental boundaries are usually ignored.
- Typically, management information that could benefit the organization in making intelligent choices regarding expense reductions is inadequate. Data systems in most health care organizations have been developed to serve reimbursement requirements, rather than decision support needs. When pressed for information to help in assessing relative efficiencies within the organization, management is burdened with data that are organized to maximize cost-based reimbursement (in spite of its outdated relevancy) and that response does not effectively match costs to reasonable measures of work load.
- Lacking effective decision-making structures and adequate management information, an organization's decisions about staff reductions mirror the relative political power of the affected constituencies. For example, nursing can either escape a turnaround untouched or bear the brunt of layoffs, all depending on the political standing of the nursing executive among fellow executives and on the support for the nursing department among influential physician leaders.

Limitations

The traditional approach to cost reduction offers the value of expediency and will likely provide immediate cash benefits to the organization. Nonetheless, this approach is excessively limiting to the long-term success of the turnaround strategy. In particular, the traditional approach suboptimizes the performance of the organization; service levels to key customer groups usually decline and, ultimately, cost savings cannot be sustained.

Suboptimization

By following functional organization lines, staffing adjustments and the operational changes necessary to support these adjustments occur almost exclusively within departmental boundaries. But the most significant opportunities for performance improvement lie at the point of interaction between departments. Breakdowns in communication and turf battles between departments arise from organizational constructs and informational architecture that promote control within, but not between, functional units.

Examples of this phenomenon are abundant in health care. Administrative mandates to department managers sometimes do not serve the overall good of the hospital. For example, a dietary director under mandate to reduce staffing expenses unilaterally discontinues passing meal trays to patient rooms. Although the director is successful in meeting the mandate, the inpatient nursing areas experience greater overtime costs in order to absorb the additional work load. It is similar to squeezing an inflated balloon: When the sides are pushed in, the top and bottom of the balloon expand to compensate.

Lack of Sustainability

Faced with the need to achieve quick cost reductions, managers often will achieve them without changing the underlying factors that drive the costs. In a traditional cost reduction approach, managers often implement staff or other expense reductions without modifying the work processes or systems that supported the preexisting expense levels. For example, the medical records director might eliminate filing clerks without changing the filing system or its related work processes. Sooner or later, the department experiences intolerable backlogs and delays, and is forced to rehire the laid-off staff in order to return to acceptable performance levels. Once the pressure is removed, the balloon retains its original shape.

Deterioration of Service Levels

By focusing cost reduction efforts on departments or functions rather than on systems or processes, an organization sacrifices the needs of its external customers. Putting the needs of internal customers (departments) before the needs of patients, physicians, and the community cannot help but diminish service quality in the eyes of these external customers. When a manager scales back registration staff and/or hours of coverage in response to a mandate to reduce departmental expenses, the net savings may achieve the manager's target cost reduction at the expense of lower accessibility and longer wait times during the admitting process. The patient is handed a bouquet of limp balloons and told to please wait.

A Systems View of Cost Reduction and Quality Improvement

The alternative to traditional approaches to cost reduction is to view it from the standpoint of improving performance within the hospital's major systems. This approach involves assessing the productivity of the internal processes that enable the hospital to deliver service to its customers and restructuring them to perform that function more effectively and cost-effectively.

Process Orientation

The functional (departmental) view of the hospital organization makes sense internally, but has little relevance to its external customers. External customers view themselves as the recipients of the organization's products or services. The processes used to transform resources (inputs) into these products or services (outputs) concern only the hospital and its internal customers. This relationship is depicted, somewhat simplistically, in figure 6-1.

A patient visiting the hospital for an outpatient radiology procedure, for example, might experience the visit as a series of processes: registration, ancillary testing, results reporting, and billing. To the hospital organization, these processes involve a number of distinct organizational units: admitting, financial counseling, radiology, outpatient registration, medical records, business office, general accounting, and so on. But the patient is not concerned whether the registration clerk captured his or her insurance information correctly at the time of registration, only that the bill is executed properly. Thus, cost reduction or productivity improvement efforts that

Figure 6-1. A Customer's View of the Organization

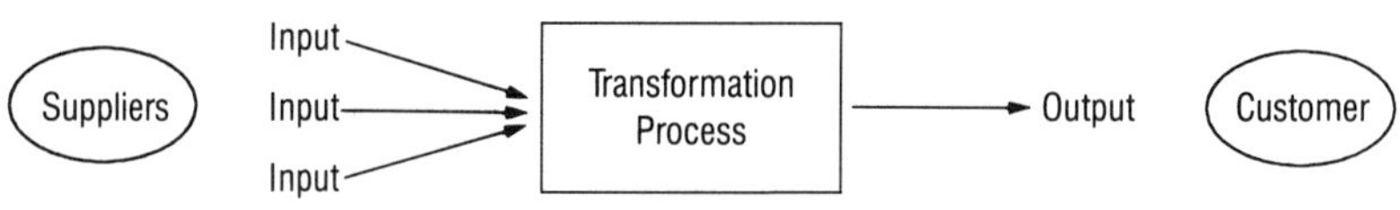

emphasize functional needs over process needs are missing the whole point, which is to keep the external customer satisfied. Figure 6-2 identifies some of the significant systems and major processes within the hospital environment, and depicts how these systems and processes cut across the organization's functional boundaries.

Performance Improvement Techniques

In this systems view, cost reduction is a by-product of serious efforts to improve performance, a challenge to the traditional notion that higher quality must cost more. A more accurate cause-and-effect model might be as follows:

Cause	*Effect*
Emphasis on cost reduction	Reduced quality
Emphasis on improved quality through process improvement	Reduced costs

Or, put simply, if the primary objective is to reduce costs without modifying underlying systems, quality will likely suffer. Alternatively, when the focus is on improving service through a process improvement orientation, it will result in the added benefit of lower costs by eliminating non-value-added activities.

Performance improvement can be realized in a variety of modes, depending on the specific needs of the organization. One means of categorizing these alternative modes is in regard to the timing or pace of change required—fast versus measured—and the degree of change—tactical versus strategic. Figure 6-3 depicts five alternative performance improvement modes: focused improvement, continuous improvement, strategic definition, business process innovation, and focused restructuring.

In the previous section, it was argued that the traditional cost reduction approach is tactical. By contrast, the systems view of performance improvement calls for a fast-paced, strategic mode in a turnaround situation—focused restructuring. As the name and description imply, *focused restructuring* concentrates the organization's turnaround efforts on those parts of the business enterprise that are one of the following:

- Not central to the core business strategies of the organization
- Supportive of, but not central to, the core business strategies and not related to the organization's core competencies
- Central to the core business strategies, but not satisfying the fundamental needs and expectations of key customer groups
- Fundamental to the core business strategies, but not performing at competitive levels, as evidenced by external benchmarking

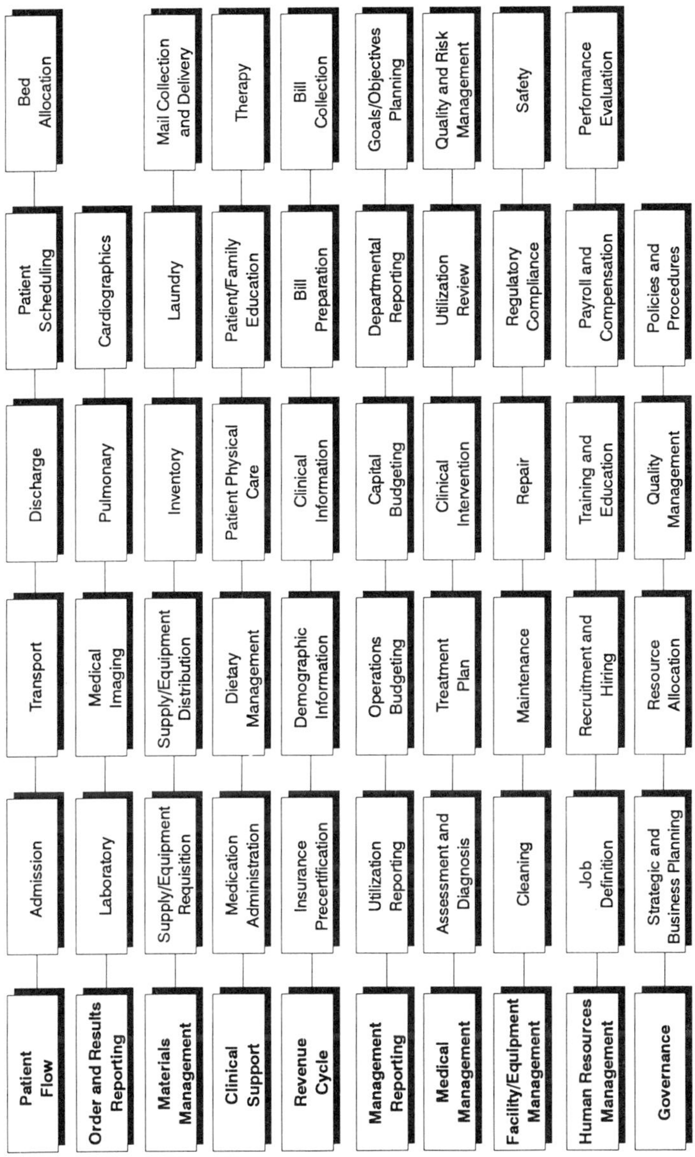

Figure 6-2. Cross-Functional Organizational Chart

Figure 6-3. Performance Improvement Modes

<table>
<tr><td colspan="2"></td><td colspan="2">Pace of Change</td></tr>
<tr><td colspan="2"></td><td>Fast</td><td>Measured</td></tr>
<tr><td rowspan="3">Degree of Change</td><td>Tactical</td><td>Focused Improvement</td><td>Continuous Improvement</td></tr>
<tr><td rowspan="2">Strategic</td><td rowspan="2">Focused Restructuring</td><td>Strategic Definition</td></tr>
<tr><td>Business Process Innovation</td></tr>
</table>

Areas that are not central to the core business strategies are primary candidates for divestiture or elimination. It is not uncommon to find hospital organizations burdened with significant costs in outreach and other services tangential to the core business and mission of the organization. Common examples are extensive catering functions provided by many hospitals' dietary departments, geographically dispersed home health and community health programs, social service functions unrelated to the discharge planning activities of the hospital, and so on.

At many hospitals, nonessential services have long been incubated by well-intentioned managers who looked for opportunities to keep their people busy as inpatient activity began to erode. Lacking sufficient financial controls and information regarding profitability and impact on market share, the value of the services to the organization's mission can go unchallenged for years. One mid-size hospital, with no other providers in the immediate community, ran a $4 million home health program with no identifiable influence on market share and that was losing an estimated $700,000 annually. The same hospital operated a community health program, again with no discernible impact on market share, that was losing $100,000 annually. In many cases, eliminating such programs reduces revenues as well as expenses, so the hospital needs to be vigilant about eliminating all the costs associated with the terminated program.

Areas that are supportive of the organization's core strategies but are unrelated to its core competencies are prime candidates for make-versus-buy decisions. In one turnaround situation, the chief operating officer (COO) expressed his view on this matter: "The patient will continue to receive [this service], it just won't necessarily be provided by a . . . hospital employee."

In a perhaps extreme case, an executive of a large tertiary hospital promoted the idea that his product line managers had the freedom to shop for laboratory services; if they could obtain better service at a better price outside the hospital, they were not obligated to use the hospital-based laboratory.

Services central to the core business strategies that are not meeting customer needs and expectations or not achieving performance levels achieved by other organizations represent the greatest challenges during the turnaround process. In this case, the challenge is to restructure or reorganize these services to become more responsive to customer needs and expectations and to demonstrate substantially greater operating performance.

An example of a service area that many hospitals would consider to be central to their core business strategies is the outpatient service area. Yet, as important as this area is to organizational success (frequently accounting for 35 percent or more of total revenues), most hospitals do a poor job of meeting customer needs and expectations for outpatient service delivery. Outpatient services are often highly fragmented and uncoordinated. In one hospital, a group charged with improving outpatient service delivery discovered that patients had to select from more than 60 different telephone numbers to schedule an outpatient procedure, depending on what type of procedure was to be performed and in what office. Patients requiring multiple outpatient procedures had to schedule each one individually, because the hospital had no capability to coordinate schedules among departments. One manager cited the difficulty for her patients: "Since we can't get our act together, we expect the patient, in an anxiety-driven state and with no knowledge of our internal operations, to coordinate our services for us."

Focused restructuring of outpatient service delivery will likely entail a significant realignment of roles and responsibilities in order to provide a seamless system to patients and physicians. In the case just cited, traditional organizational constructs were challenged by viewing outpatient services as an interdepartmental process instead of the distinct products of the myriad functional departments that provide outpatient services. Outpatient services began to be viewed internally as a life cycle of activities:

- Scheduling
- Registration
- Treatment
- Discharge

Although the life cycle concept was given a warm reception, each department soon organized its part of the life cycle differently, thus meeting the needs of each department but creating mass confusion among the hospital's customers. This prompted exploration of ways to restructure operations to improve service and reduce costs, including centralized patient registration, centralized scheduling, and clustering of services around patient characteristics (for example, organizing common outpatient procedures in a treatment area, as opposed to retaining them within the respective ancillary departments).

Example of Focused Restructuring

A community hospital, part of a regional health system, was experiencing considerable problems with its surgical instrument processing system. Costs were rising dramatically. Instrumentation was deemed woefully inadequate, equipment was at the end of its useful life, and staff were routinely working overtime to hold a patchwork system together and keep the surgery schedule from crashing. Two chief quality problems were evident:

- Flash sterilization rates exceeded 25 percent of all trays supplied to the operating suites. *Flashing* is the quick, but inferior method of sterilization that hospitals use whenever sterile instrumentation is not available through central sterile supply in time for a case to begin. Implications include delays in case starts, higher OR staff costs, reduced instrument life, and greater risk of infection.
- Approximately 25 percent of all surgical cases did not have the correct number of instruments or sufficient instrumentation available in the suite at case start.

Recognizing that other hospitals in the system were experiencing similar difficulties, representatives from each hospital met to pursue alternative structures and systems to provide sterile surgical instrumentation to their operating suites. Breaking down the traditional barriers between the three hospitals and the various operating departments within each hospital, the instrument processing system will be restructured into a centralized processing function with local case cart assembly and distribution. The following benefits are anticipated:

- A 30 percent return on invested dollars in new instruments, space, and equipment through productivity gains, reduced instrument wear, and longer instrument life
- A decrease in the flash sterilization rate to less than 1 percent of all cases
- An increase greater than 99 percent probability that correct and sufficient instrumentation will be available in the suite prior to case start

Role of Comparative Data

As a starting point in the performance improvement effort, the hospital's cost structure should be compared to similar data from other representative hospitals. This analysis provides useful insight into:

- Cost areas/departments where the number of full-time equivalents (FTEs) appear unfavorable
- Cost categories, such as wage rates, supply usage, or costs, that appear to be out of line
- Resource utilization issues, including lengths of stay and ancillary utilization, that warrant further attention
- Cost areas/departments where operating differences warrant further analysis to determine the potential for change

There are a number of reliable sources for this type of data, including:

- State hospital associations
- American Hospital Association
- Regional and national associations (for example, VHA)
- Proprietary consulting firms' data bases

The important considerations for a comparative analysis include the cost data base used for the comparison and the characteristics of the hospitals to be included in the data base. The hospitals included in the data base should be very cost-effective. The best performers in the data base—those who represent a "best-demonstrated practice"—should be singled out. There is no value in comparing the organization to average performers.

The integrity of the data is crucial to the success of the comparative analysis. It is important to seek out a comparative data base that is:

- *Comprehensive.* The data set includes all operating expenses, for example, labor, nonlabor, patient care departments, nonpatient care departments, insurance costs, interest expense, and both inpatient and outpatient costs.
- *Selective.* The comparison should be with peer institutions that are better than average, or "best performing."
- *Highly structured.* For "apples-to-apples" comparisons, the data set needs to be highly structured for consistency. The application should require all users to adhere to a common chart of accounts, common procedure definitions, and common relative value unit measures.
- *Normalized.* Differences in operations should be normalized to the extent practical and required for valid comparisons. The data base should be normalized for procedure mix within departments, case mix, volume, and regional price differences.

Using a data base that meets these criteria, the hospital can evaluate its cost structure in several ways: cost per case, departmental cost per unit of service, and, where feasible, number of units of service per adjusted case. The output from these comparative analyses should include summary variances that show differences within both the hospital's cost structures and those of the peer set of hospitals.

Comparative data are typically viewed suspiciously by managers. This must be recognized up front, and efforts should be made to properly communicate the objectives for using comparative information. This effort should be structured to use the data base to identify where the hospital's cost structure appears to be out of line, indicating where operating policies and strategies may need to be challenged. Information developed from the comparative analysis should be used to focus further inquiry, not to identify problems or determine their appropriate solutions.

Translation of Cost Differences into Opportunities

The comparative analysis identifies differences between the hospital and a peer group of hospitals. Of course, not every difference pinpoints an opportunity. For example, there may be differences due to plant configuration that may never be eliminated. To complement the comparative analysis, opportunities should be further validated in terms of the operational features, policies, and strategies that are germane to the hospital. Particular attention should be paid to systems issues that cross department lines (for example, the revenue cycle, which includes admitting, medical records, and patient accounting). Significant differences from benchmark hospitals in resources allocated to these systems, coupled with low service quality (for example, high error rates, long cycle times), are evidence of cost-reduction/quality-improvement opportunities. The objectives for provider validation are to support and verify findings from the comparative analysis and to develop management consensus on cost improvement opportunities through interviews and discussions of general findings from the comparative analysis, hospital-specific data, and other pertinent information.

Each administrator and key executive should be interviewed during this process in order to develop a fuller understanding of operations, strengths, opportunities, and quality service issues. These meetings should include discussions of alternative approaches successfully in operation at other facilities that have application to the hospital. Such discussions often identify valuable, cost-effective ideas. In addition, department managers responsible for the primary and secondary activities of each department should be interviewed.

Any other internal data should also be reviewed to enhance understanding and analysis. These data may include management engineering and productivity reports, Blue Cross and other agency comparative analyses, any multiyear baseline of FTEs, other department statistics and productivity measures, and financial information on program profitability.

The findings from both the comparative analysis and the provider validation will be used to identify opportunities for operational improvement and to specify subsequent actions to improve productivity, efficiency, and quality of service. In other words, these findings will be used to improve hospital financial performance through focused restructuring.

Typical Results from the Use of Comparative Data

In comparing themselves to a best-demonstrated practice data set, hospitals in distress or embarking on a performance improvement process typically identify operating cost differences, relative to the best-performing hospitals, of up to 40 percent of total operating costs. Depending on the severity of their turnaround situations, these hospitals can eliminate up to one-half of the identified cost differences within a three-year period. In other words, hospitals that use comparative data wisely can reasonably expect to reduce their total operating costs by up to 20 percent over the course of three years.

Conclusion

An essential step in helping the hospital in financial distress to effect a turnaround is to concentrate on reducing costs in an effort to enhance cash flow. Traditional approaches to cost reduction have been tactical, such as freezing expenditures, limiting hiring, effecting across-the-board layoffs, and so on. However, focusing on these functional changes can have the effect of diminishing the hospital's service quality. A more effective approach is to improve the performance of the systems or processes that enable the hospital to deliver service to its customers. A comparative cost analysis, by department and by major system/process, with other representative institutions will enable the hospital to assess departmental and system operation and restructure service areas, as needed, in order to reduce costs and at the same time improve the quality of care delivery.

Bibliography

Davenport, T. H. *Process Innovation.* Cambridge, MA: Harvard Business School Press, 1993.

Davenport, T. H., and Short, J. E. The new industrial engineering: information technology and business process redesign. *Sloan Management Review* 31(4), Summer 1990.

Hirschhorn, L., and Gilmore, T. The new boundaries of the "boundaryless" company. *Harvard Business Review,* May–June 1992, pp. 104–15.

Ostroff, F., and Smith, D. Redesigning the corporation: the horizontal organization. *The McKinsey Quarterly* (1), 1992.

Prahalad, C. K., and Hamel, G. The core competence of the corporation. *Harvard Business Review,* May–June 1990.

Senge, P. M. *The Fifth Discipline: The Art & Practice of The Learning Organization.* New York City: Doubleday/Currency, 1990.

Shapiro, B. P., Kasturi Rangan, V., and Sviokla, J. J. Staple yourself to an order. *Harvard Business Review,* July–Aug. 1992.

Stewart, T. A. The search for the organization of tomorrow. *Fortune,* May 18, 1992, pp. 92–98.

Chapter 7

Medical Staff Issues in a Turnaround

Charles Musfeldt, M.D., and Thomas Collier, M.D.

The medical staff of a financially troubled hospital must be educated on the costs of care and permitted to implement changes that will raise the level of cost consciousness, decrease the medical legal risks, and improve the quality of care and service. With appropriate and correct data, and the support and cooperation of administrators, physicians can identify the causes of problems in these areas, recommend and implement practical solutions, and become a vital resource in the turnaround of a financially distressed hospital.

Raising Fiscal Awareness among the Medical Staff

Appropriate education can help correlate the clinical with the financial. The traditional premedical school curriculum for physicians emphasizes scientific studies, affording little time for economics, business, and finance. Medical school and postgraduate training likewise stress the science and techniques of diagnostic workups, with little regard for their cost-effectiveness. Residents must acquire an impressive command of obscure clinical information, but may never be asked a single question about the cost of care. Often, in fact, the more tests a resident has performed, the more highly regarded is his or her work.

With the change in reimbursement from open-ended fee-for-service arrangements to fixed reimbursement, such as Medicare diagnosis-related groups (DRGs), teaching hospitals can begin by promoting cost-effective practice patterns among their residents. Medical school faculty need to ask residents why a study is necessary if it is unlikely to change the diagnosis.

Individual discussions, displayed costs of ancillary items, and economic grand rounds all serve as useful educational tools in this effort.

Sharing Financial Data

When presented with pertinent financial data, most physicians are capable of making beneficial suggestions. However, administrators are quick to give reasons for not revealing hospital financial data to the medical staff. Some administrators use information as an instrument of power, to be withheld or released only as they see fit. Some withhold data for fear that physicians might take them to competing hospitals.

All that must change in a turnaround situation. Armed with coherent financial information presented in a manner that implies urgency, the medical staff can act quickly to change a troubled hospital's financial picture by admitting more patients, performing more on-site outpatient procedures, and managing patients in a cost-effective manner. For this process to begin, small group sessions as well as individual discussions are generally necessary to adequately answer physicians' questions and clarify administrators' expectations of physicians.

In preparing to show financial data to the medical staff, three steps are essential to ensuring credibility:

1. Hospital financial data should be verified to ensure that they correspond to patient bills.
2. Patient bills should be examined to ensure that they correspond to care as recorded on the medical record.
3. A pilot group of three or four medical staff leaders should be appointed to run through the financial data before they are issued to the entire medical staff.

Hospital administrators should perform several tests with the assistance of hospital auditors to ensure that patient bills correspond to hospital financial data. Have all the patients been appropriately classified into payer groups? A graph showing the percentage increase in patients in fixed-reimbursement payer groups can help to persuade physicians that hospital revenues are lagging and that there is a need for cost-effective care.

In addition, patient charts and bills need to be matched. This issue may bring to light several problems, including the need for more appropriate coding of DRGs, missed charges, or opportunities for price reductions from vendors for high-cost items.

Finally, presenting to a small group of physicians in advance allows administrators to anticipate questions, simplify difficult audiovisuals (too many numbers or too many slides can have a positively sleep-inducing effect on a physician audience), and garner support. Physicians frequently ask what the "real" costs are to the hospital if they are being shown only patient charges. A particularly helpful technique is to encourage physicians themselves to make the presentation. A medical staff is less likely to react negatively to any message if one of its own members is the messenger.

Providing Individual Profit and Loss Statements

A financially troubled hospital must be effective in relaying financial information to individual clinical practices. Each physician should receive a profit and loss statement, a profile of inpatient service comparing the cost of care to actual reimbursement and thus the practice's profitability contribution to the hospital. The statement can be general (for example, listing all patients seen in a fiscal year) or specific (for example, listing patients classified by DRG). The hospital's net revenue should be reported rather than charges; charges include the hospital's markup on patient bills, which is not paid by certain fixed-rate payers. The medical staff should understand the method of cost determination, whether through a cost accounting system or a cost-to-charge ratio.

It is essential that financial reports be presented to physicians individually. This is the least intimidating method and does not subject physicians to the stigma of being held up as a bad example among peers. In a typical community hospital, department heads should present the information, always in a positive tone, emphasizing an exchange of helpful ideas and asking the physicians what the information means to them. Although names should not be disclosed, it is often helpful to display profit and loss data in context with examples presented for unnamed physicians in order to give physicians an understanding of their comparative performance.

Minimizing the Physician's Medical Legal Risk

Physicians are more likely to participate in turnaround activities if they perceive that they will not be placed at increased risk of professional liability. Luckily, most quality improvements reduce medical legal risk as well as cost, so such efforts can easily be sold to physicians concerned about liability. Reducing medication errors is one good place to start.

Cefazolin™, for example, need only be given every eight hours according to its manufacturer, but it is frequently ordered every six hours. A concerted effort by the Pharmacy and Therapeutics Committee to promote the ordering of Cefazolin™ every eight hours rather than every six is likely to yield quality improvements as well as cost reductions. Administering the drug less frequently should also reduce medication errors, with substantial cost savings.

Another example relates to intravenous H_2 blockers, such as cimetidine or ranitidine. Patients in the intensive care units are customarily placed on intravenous H_2 blockers to prevent gastric ulcers. Once the patient has regained consciousness, is clinically improved, and begins taking liquids or solids, it is appropriate to switch from intravenous to oral H_2 blockers. But physicians may not always make the switch soon enough. Getting physicians to act promptly will reduce the number of complications associated with intravenous medication, a quality improvement that will potentially reduce the physicians' legal liability and at the same time yield significant cost savings.

Improving Quality and Cost-Effectiveness

Improved quality saves physicians time, and anything an administrator can do to save the physicians time will go a long way toward winning their loyalty and cooperation. The shortest route to a physician's heart is through the swift and accurate communication of lab results and speedy operating room (OR) turnovers. Delays in getting radiology results, for example, create both a quality problem and a nuisance. If an ultrasound of a patient's gallbladder reveals gallstones, treatment in many cases will not begin until the patient's physician has the radiology report in hand. Any delay in communication causes an unnecessary delay in treatment and increases the chance for clinical complications. Sluggish OR turnover can further delay treatment. Left unattended, gallstones may cause obstructions and further complications, such as acute cholecystitis or pancreatitis. It is clear that improved communication and coordination among hospital departments can positively affect quality and outcomes.

Saving the Hospital Money

Delays can result in significant financial losses for the hospital. Because Medicare, for example, reimburses a fixed amount to take care of a patient with congestive heart failure, delays must be kept to a minimum if patient care is to be delivered efficiently at a cost that is appropriate given the fixed reimbursement. Reworks must be avoided so that the patient can be discharged in a timely manner.

If laboratory reports are not back to the physician in time or the nurses have not documented the patient's daily weight, the physician may not be able to ascertain response to therapy. Several days' delay can compromise the effectiveness of patient care as well as overutilize the hospital's resources beyond the fixed payment it is destined to receive.

Private insurance companies are also converting to prospective payment systems (PPSs), and employers are contracting directly with hospitals. As fixed reimbursement becomes the prevalent method of third-party payment, attention to quality and cost may well separate the hospitals that survive from those that do not. Hospitals already on the verge of failure have no choice but to scrutinize their operations and seize every opportunity to lower costs and improve quality.

Reducing Readmissions

Peer review organizations (PROs) contract with the federal government to review Medicare patient charts for possible compromise of clinical quality. Among other indicators, the readmission of a patient within 30 days of discharge raises a red flag and may earn a PRO citation. Readmissions can be prevented by planning for discharges in consultation with social service or home health agencies. Allowing nurses to take more time with cardiac patients to explain their medications and giving physical therapists enough time to explain the use of a walker will also serve to reduce readmissions and PRO citations.

Keeping track of patients readmitted within one week or one month is also a good way to monitor quality. Physicians would just as soon not see their names on a list of chronic readmitters. External audits of hospital admissions performed by insurance companies or utilization review firms are likely to detect and report readmissions as well.

Developing the Medical Staff–Administration Relationship

In financially distressed hospitals, administration and medical staff must communicate effectively. Without considerable effort, a we–they mentality can pervade health care institutions and paralyze decision making. Even worse, physicians and administrators at some hospitals will not sit down at the same table but, rather, resort to blaming one another for all sorts of problems. Success comes when administrators and physicians find a common cause—a mutual challenge, such as improving quality of care, seeking contracts from desirable managed care entities, or ensuring compliance with the changing demands of government agencies.

It is important that hospital administrators and physicians work together for the common good of the hospital. For example, great mutual benefit can be realized simply by stationing a nurse in the admissions office to ensure that patients are directed to the appropriate floor in a timely manner; that admissions screening calls are made to insurance carriers, relieving the physicians' office staffs of this task; and that all necessary history and physical, lab, X-ray, and EKG reports are on the chart, preventing unnecessary delays in diagnostic or surgical procedures.

Physicians and administrators can also find mutual benefit in cooperating in the purchase of surgical supplies and pharmaceuticals. Hip and knee prostheses are a strong case in point. It used to be that orthopedic surgeons, relying on their training, experience, and perhaps a relationship with a particular surgical supplies sales representative, enjoyed their choice of vendor and prosthesis for hip replacements. An OR nurse simply ordered the prosthesis, the vendor set the price and sent an invoice, and the hospital was reimbursed via patient charges to the insurer.

Today, under the PPS, Medicare reimbursement for total hip and knee replacement is fixed at approximately $8,000 for the entire hospitalization and all supplies. Administrators would do well to persuade orthopedic surgeons to join them in negotiating with a single surgical supply vendor to lower costs. Offered an exclusive deal, the supplier can be persuaded to waive rental fees, take back unused equipment for credit, or discount prices based on early payment. The negotiation process itself will create an awareness of the administration's and physicians' common interests and will potentially create a fresh atmosphere in which to approach the hospital's problems together.

Dealing with Inefficient Systems

In a financially distressed situation, administrators need to find out from physicians what it is that slows their care of patients. Their answers to this question quickly reveal the bottlenecks in the process of admitting patients, performing diagnostic workups, implementing therapeutic plans, and discharging patients. In the quest for financial success under a fixed-reimbursement system, such wasteful hindrances must be discovered and removed.

Behind surgeons' frequent complaints about slow turnover in the OR, for example, lie several possible contributing factors: slow personnel in the nursing, anesthesiology, or housekeeping functions; excessive paperwork; lack of planning for the next case; lost paperwork; patients not properly evaluated for their capability to undergo anesthesia; or surgeons arriving late to the OR. The Operating Room Committee bears responsibility for recognizing such problems and remedying them. If the committee is not functioning effectively, a task force should be assembled to review objective data, establish possible reasons for delays, and act to eliminate them.

Without thoughtful procedures, the simplest processes have a way of becoming complex and cumbersome. At one hospital, every urine sample had to be evaluated microscopically, at great cost to the hospital, because the time was not routinely marked on specimen labels. Dipstick tests occasionally show false negative readings if a urine sample is more than two hours old, so the lab had to examine each specimen under the microscope. The importance of completeness in labeling had not been explained to the nursing assistants. As the urine container passed from nursing assistant to ward clerk to transporter to lab clerk to lab tech, no one was aware that an additional test would be required if delivery time were greater than two hours, and no one was encouraged to keep the specimen moving along. To them, quality amounted to not dropping the specimen. Physician complaints found an ear among the hospital's administrators, and soon every specimen arrived at the lab with a complete label.

Breaking Down Barriers with the Hospital's Internal Customers

If a hospital—operating in the red or in the black—is to survive and prosper, its administration must accurately identify both internal and external customers and discern their expectations. Some administrators fail to recognize the physicians as their internal customers and thus make the mistake of sometimes treating the medical staff with disdain. A small number of administrators even ignore their medical staffs, making little attempt to understand their needs or motivations.

Recognizing the physician as an internal customer, the administrator should make every effort to break down barriers that impede the care of patients. Without acceding to their every request or demand, the administrator should work to understand and help fulfill physicians' expectations. Open communication is, of course, a prerequisite to a good working relationship between administrators and medical staff.

Spending More Time in the Field

The late Sam Walton found enough time to visit almost every Wal-Mart store from coast to coast. The least a successful hospital administrator can do is spend a few moments every week walking about the hallways, clinics, and patient rooms of his or her facility. An administrator's presence in the hallways of the hospital instills a sense of accountability among employees and conveys the message that their leadership cares. Nothing a chief executive officer (CEO) can say will speak as loudly or as clearly as his or her personal involvement. Attending a meeting of the Medical Executive Committee supports the development of capable physician leadership. Attending a meeting of the Pharmacy and Therapeutics Committee promotes cost-effectiveness in formulary management and drug use.

High on the list of priority visits should be physicians' offices. Physician office staffs are important external customers of the CEO. A commitment to spending time with them will improve the financial situation of the hospital by preventing the miscommunication that so often hampers the admitting and outpatient scheduling processes.

The successful administrator learns about physicians' and employees' individual needs and concerns. CEOs of financially distressed hospitals commonly grasp for solutions before they have gathered enough information and fully analyzed it. Resolving the turmoil of a turnaround begins with a leader who is a good listener.

Physicians who assist the administration in times of financial distress should, of course, be duly rewarded. Those who care for patients with skill and compassion and with an eye toward cost, quality, and effective communication contribute to the future success of the hospital. The administrator of a troubled hospital would wisely involve the medical staff early in the turnaround effort, moving quickly and assuredly to tap the resources of the hospital's most valuable allies.

Conclusion

It is vitally important that the administration of a financially distressed hospital recognize the potential of its medical staff as a resource in achieving a long-term turnaround. Including physicians in the financial picture, alleviating their concerns over medical legal risks, and working to improve the quality of service will go a long way toward achieving physician participation in the turnaround process. Opening the channels of communication and cooperation will enable administrators and physicians to work together as partners in the common cause of securing the hospital's financial future.

Suggested Readings

Burda, D. Changing physician practice patterns. *Modern Healthcare* 19(7):18–24, Feb. 17, 1989.

Burda, D. Tennessee hospital finds it can reduce its costs by improving quality. *Modern Healthcare* 20(16):36, Apr. 23, 1990.

Collier, T. The medical staff in the financially distressed hospital. *Topics in Health Care Financing* 17(2):26–38, Winter 1990.

Collier, T., Doyne, M., and Hoover, J. Physician leadership in clinical resource management. *Healthcare Productivity Report* 4(1), Jan. 1991.

Musfeldt, C. 10 attributes of a hassle-free hospital. *Hospitals* 66(16):76, Aug. 20, 1992.

Musfeldt, C. 25 warning signs of quality problems. *Hospitals* 65(1):42–43, Jan. 5, 1991.

Musfeldt, C., and Hart, R. MD-directed critical pathways: it's time. *Hospitals* 66(23):56, Dec. 5, 1992.

Musfeldt, C., Engler, D., and Collier, T. Outlines for improvement of clinical care quality. *Journal of the Society for Health Systems* 2(3):25–43, 1991.

Nackel, J., and Collier, T. Implementing a quality improvement program. *Journal of the Society for Health Systems* 1(1):85–100, May 1989.

Chapter 8

Phaseout Options

Catherine Mazanec

Not every hospital is capable of a turnaround. Employing the strategies addressed in this book may only postpone the inevitable. Hospitals that cannot evolve to meet current market needs and effectively sustain their share of the market will eventually have to merge with other institutions, close their doors, or convert to alternative uses for which there is sufficient demand.

The implementation of prospective payment and the shift to outpatient care promoted by managed care and other third-party payers accelerated the process of change in the health care field. The effect has been reduced utilization of inpatient beds and financial distress for a number of hospitals, as reflected in the high rate of hospital closure. The major determinant of eventual closure appears to be low utilization.[1] The Office of the Inspector General reports that, in 1990, rural hospitals that closed had an average occupancy of 23.5 percent, and urban hospitals that closed were operating at 30.5 percent.[2] Although bed capacity has declined in all parts of the country, the decline has not kept pace with declines in utilization, creating more overcapacity and increased division of market share.

In 1990, average occupancy nationwide was 64.5 percent; in some markets it was much lower. For example, in Northeast Ohio average hospital occupancy was 57.4 percent.[3] There were, on average, 4,530 empty beds per day, representing a substantial amount of excess capacity.[4]

Historical Perspective

Hospital closure and conversion is not a new phenomenon, although the rate of closure has accelerated in recent years. Historically, declines in utilization resulted from a reduced need for certain types of specialized hospitals or from neighborhood demographic changes. When specialty hospitals were closed, they were often converted to another health care use. Acute care facilities in declining neighborhoods were often replaced by new facilities in a better location. Again, Northeast Ohio provides a number of examples (see figure 8-1).

Several inner-city hospitals established by physicians in Northeast Ohio also closed. The need for these hospitals, established to provide a place for osteopathic, black, and female physicians to practice, diminished as these groups were accepted on general hospital medical staffs.

With one exception, all these hospitals closed before 1980, well before the implementation of the Medicare prospective payment system (PPS) and the shift in focus to ambulatory care.

Alternatives to Closure

The choice to close a hospital is difficult, and hospital managers and board members are justifiably reluctant to proceed without first exhausting all their options. Fixing their attention and energy on strategies that will enhance market share and use excess capacity, they most frequently concentrate their efforts on changing the mix of services to attract additional volume. The number of skilled nursing and other long-term care units, for example, nearly doubled between 1980 and 1990.[5] In certain states, however, certificate-of-need (CON) laws make it difficult to convert units to specialty care, limiting the appeal of this option.

Hospital management may determine that merger with another, stronger hospital is required to forestall a closure. In many instances, though, a merger extends the life of the hospital only to have the merged system convert it for other uses. A recent study of 17 hospital mergers shows that 7 converted

Figure 8-1. Examples of Types of Hospitals and Dispositions

Type of Hospital	Disposition
Tuberculosis hospital	Converted to skilled nursing care
Convalescent and crippled children's hospital	Physically relocated to a university teaching hospital and eventually merged with its pediatric hospital
Obstetrics, focusing on unwed mothers	Sold to an HMO and converted to a full-service acute care hospital
Psychiatric hospital	Closed and transferred to an existing acute care hospital
Primarily obstetrics, operated by the Salvation Army	Sold and operated as a women's and children's hospital

a facility to an alternative use—4 to long-term care, 2 to psychiatric care, and 1 to outpatient care.[6] In other cases, troubled hospitals were acquired and later closed by their purchasing hospitals. Although this may seem to have been a poor investment of funds for the purchasing hospitals, sometimes acquiring and then closing excess capacity has provided healthy economic returns by consolidating the patient population at one facility and eliminating a second set of overhead costs.

The decline in inpatient care in short-stay acute care hospitals may, in fact, be due in part to increases in the number of patients admitted to specialty hospitals, which continue to be reimbursed on the basis of reasonable costs. Figure 8-2 illustrates the growth in hospitals and hospital units that are excluded from the Medicare PPS.

Phaseout Options

Essentially, a hospital that can no longer survive at its current location with its current mix of services has three options. It can:

- Close the hospital as an acute care facility and convert it to another use
- Sell the hospital to a third party who may convert it for an alternative use or raze the facility, developing the land for another use
- Close and abandon the facility

Figure 8-2. PPS-Excluded Hospitals/Units

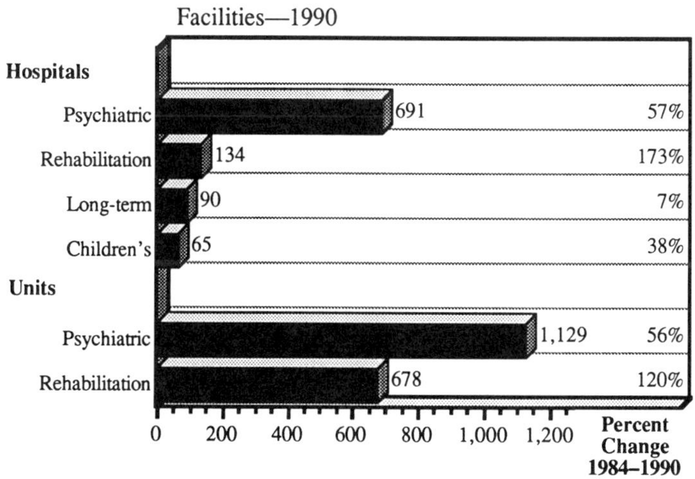

Source: HCFA, Health Standards and Quality Bureau, 1991.

Each of these options has implications that must be considered and evaluated by the hospital. In truth, a hospital's flexibility to choose among these options may be greatly restricted by its location, the condition of its facility, local and state regulations, and available financial resources.

Issues Associated with Closure

Regardless of its final disposition, a facility contemplating closure as an acute care hospital must first address a number of issues. These include regulatory requirements, public relations, community resistance, cost of closure, and Medicare reimbursement.

Regulatory Requirements

In 1988, Congress passed the Worker Adjustment, Retraining Notification Act (WARN), which requires businesses with 100 or more employees to give 60 days notice of a mass layoff or plant closing. For hospitals, it is very difficult to continue operating once public announcement of closure is made. Physicians begin to admit patients elsewhere, and volume drops dramatically. Employees begin to focus attention on finding a job, creating an atmosphere that is not conducive to the best patient care. In addition to employee notification requirements, numerous other state, city, and other agency notification requirements are imposed on a closing hospital.

Public Relations

A great deal of emotion surrounds the closing of a hospital as an acute care facility. A carefully crafted public relations campaign should be developed to explain the circumstances. Such a campaign is important in any closure, but it is particularly critical if the hospital to be closed is part of a system with other hospitals serving the community. In this situation, it is essential to ensure that physicians retain their allegiance to the system and, if geography permits, to keep patients in the system. The communication strategy must consider each of the hospital's key constituencies, including medical staff, employees, patients, and the general community.

Community Resistance

However much attention a hospital pays to the public relations aspects of its closure, there will still be community resistance. As one chief executive officer (CEO) who closed a hospital notes, "No matter how well you communicate the objective data on how and why the decision was made, some elements of the local community will make a major issue of this."[7]

In some instances, community pressure can be strong enough to cause a hospital to reopen. Since 1986, 16 closed acute care facilities have reopened, most of them reestablished after their communities raised the required funds. Most of these facilities have fewer than 50 beds and, even with community support, many continue to have low census (one is operating with an average daily census of 1.3) and operating losses.[8]

Cost of Closure

The costs associated with closing a hospital are extremely high. An organization that decides to close a hospital and convert it to another use or that is part of a larger system that retains the financial liability for the institution must estimate and then manage these costs to the extent possible.

Unemployment expenses can be significant. One recently closed hospital that was self-insured for unemployment estimated its unemployment expenses at $2.5 million; through outplacement, organizing job fairs, and working with employees, the hospital was able to reduce its actual cost to approximately $500,000.

Other expenses include those associated with the liability for long-term leases and contracts, losses on sale of equipment and other assets, staff time required to handle the close-down, costs associated with appraisal and sale, and legal, consulting, and other fees. The costs associated with the restructuring of debt and assumption of the liability by another provider within a system can also be high. A hospital that closes with insufficient cash to pay off outstanding debt creates a major event of default. In this situation, bondholders become creditors and may seek a judicial remedy. Trustees, management, auditors, and other advisors may actually be sued.

Medicare Reimbursement

Medicare payment policy requires that a gain or loss resulting from a bona fide sale or scrapping of an asset be recognized in the year that the asset disposal takes place. Theoretically, the gain or loss represents an adjustment to the depreciation expense recognized during the years the provider participated in the Medicare program and the asset was in service. A gain resulting from the disposal of an asset indicates that too much depreciation was taken during the years the asset was in service, and recognition of the gain is made to "recapture" the excess depreciation taken. Conversely, a loss resulting from the disposal of an asset indicates that too little depreciation was taken during the years the asset was in service, and recognition of the loss is to correct for the depreciation shortfall.

In the 1970s and early 1980s, it was not unusual for a hospital to be sold at a profit. Today, many hospitals are being sold at a loss, resulting in millions of dollars in reimbursement claims. A number of these claims have been rejected by the government, and it is expected that the affected hospitals will appeal the decisions to the Provider Reimbursement Review Board.[9]

The issues surrounding Medicare reimbursement are complex. A hospital contemplating closure and eventual sale must understand Medicare reimbursement regulations and should obtain expert advice in allocating the purchase price among the assets.

Conversion to an Alternative Use

According to a *Modern Healthcare* survey conducted in 1989, approximately one-third of hospitals that closed in the prior five years have converted to another type of health care use or continue to provide nonacute care.[10] For the remaining two-thirds, conversion is either undesirable or infeasible. In some instances, the value to the purchaser rests solely in the real estate, and the sale is followed by demolition of the facility; in others, a hospital cannot find a buyer and the facility is abandoned. Given the amount of excess capacity in today's health care system and the predicted acceleration of hospital closings, more abandonments may be seen as hospitals confront a scarcity of buyers while lacking the resources to convert to alternative uses.

Conversions to other health care uses occur, whether through merger with another provider or within existing systems, when there is a commitment to maintaining a health care presence in a community and when the financial resources are available to convert the facility to another use. Among the most common alternative uses are:

- Long-term care
- Specialty care (for example, substance abuse, rehab, psych)
- Assisted living
- Ambulatory and emergency care
- Office space

Conversions require careful planning, significant resources, and, often, compliance with numerous regulatory requirements. The following case examples describe three successful conversions:

- *Merger of two hospitals followed by conversion of one facility.* In this situation, three hospitals were providing care in the same small community. Two of them determined, as a result of independently conducted planning processes, that the market could not support three hospitals and decided to merge their facilities. As a result of that merger, all acute care services were moved to one facility. Although studies indicated that $5 million could be saved by closing the other

facility, a number of factors, including public sentiment, dictated keeping it open. The second hospital was therefore converted to a mixed-use facility providing a number of non-acute care services, including:
– Adult and adolescent chemical dependency
– Physical rehabilitation, both inpatient and ambulatory
– Inpatient psych and outpatient mental health
– A condominium complex housing a number of physician offices
Although there were some volume drops in the first year following the merger and conversion, both facilities and their operations have seen an increase in market share and profitability.

A tremendous investment of time went into community and medical staff education to explain the rationale for the conversion and the benefits that would result. From a regulatory perspective, the hospital had to apply for certificates of need (CONs) for several of the services to be provided in the converted facility. Contracts for mental health were actively pursued and obtained from several of the surrounding counties to enhance utilization.

- *Hospital closure followed by conversion to another use.* This system closed one of its hospitals in 1989 and transferred its operations to another recently constructed hospital within the system that was in a better location and had sufficient capacity to handle the volume. Plans are now under way to convert the closed hospital to a skilled nursing and elderly residence facility. The residence component will focus on assisted living and congregate care. The costs to effect the conversion have been substantial. Actual facility renovations are estimated at close to $5 million. The organization also had to purchase three nursing homes so that it could transfer the licenses for the 78 skilled beds, because it operates in a state with a moratorium on new long-term-care beds. Even with the purchase, the hospital still had to apply for a CON to renovate the hospital and to operate the skilled beds.
- *Sale of facility followed by conversion.* This 200-bed inner-city hospital was closed and sold to an area nursing home by its parent system. The nursing home's decision to purchase the facility was made after a detailed analysis of the costs to convert the facility. The very high conversion costs, estimated at $4 million, dictated a low purchase price in order to make the operation financially viable. The Catholic sponsorship of both organizations created a strong desire to execute the agreement. Given the very low purchase price that could be supported from reimbursement sources after conversion, however, the hospital had to actively seek a buyer willing to pay a higher price and had to conduct an arm's-length negotiation in order to recapture Medicare capital reimbursement. The hospital also had long-term debt, which was assumed by the system.

After conversion, the facility will house long-term and skilled beds, a unit for patients with traumatic brain injury, an AIDS unit, a dialysis unit, and an emergency department (ED).

The system agreed to lease some of the space in the hospital for a heavily used dialysis unit needed by the community and for the ED, which it continued to operate. Closure of the hospital was preceded by an extensive period of planning and a public relations campaign to educate the public on the need to close and the intention to support a continued health care presence through the ED and the dialysis unit.

Rural Hospital Conversions

The preceding examples demonstrate conversions that were facilitated and, in part, financed by systems. But a large number of the nation's troubled hospitals are small, rural facilities that lack the resources to convert. Closures of rural facilities create access problems in the sparsely populated communities they serve. In response to this problem, Congress, through OBRA 1989, authorized grants to assist conversions of hospitals that are members of rural health networks. In essence, rural primary care hospitals (RPCHs) can convert to outpatient facilities with 24-hour EDs and will receive cost-based reimbursement for their services. These hospitals must be networked with essential access community hospitals (EACHs) that provide inpatient care. By law, the grant program is limited to seven states, including California, Colorado, Kansas, New York, North Carolina, South Dakota, and West Virginia. Current grant funding is focused on establishing transportation and communication linkages between the EACHs and the RPCHs.

Currently, 750 rural hospitals are operating with fewer than 10 patients a day, most of them outside the 7 designated states for the RPCH program. In addition to the EACH/RPCH program, a number of other initiatives are being considered to assist in closing or converting some of these facilities, while ensuring that access is retained.

The Conversion Planning Process

Although conversion may be a viable option for a number of hospitals, it can require a fairly lengthy planning process that is fraught with legal, financial, and regulatory woes. Many hospitals unfortunately neglect to seriously consider conversion until their financial condition has deteriorated to the point that they lack the manpower or funds to successfully convert. The sooner a troubled hospital begins the planning process, the easier is its conversion.

Sound conversion planning involves:

- Evaluating the demand for the new service(s) needs
- Understanding third-party payment rules and assessing the financial viability of the new service
- Determining whether the existing corporation will provide the service or whether a new corporation will be created
- Identifying regulatory and legal requirements, such as state closure notifications, provider licensure, and CON
- Organizing a public relations campaign
- Developing a staff plan to support all the tasks associated with closure as an acute care hospital
- Estimating the costs of conversion (for example, in many hospitals the cost of asbestos removal is extremely high)

Shortchanging the planning process can condemn the conversion to failure. A focus on community needs and a true assessment of the associated costs are the key ingredients of success.

Conclusion

A financially distressed hospital that is unable to effect a turnaround is faced with three options: It can close its doors and cease operation; it can close and reopen as a new facility offering different services (for example, an acute care hospital converting to a specialty care facility); or it can merge with or sell out to another institution that will either close or convert it. The hospital that opts to close its doors must first address a number of complex issues, including, for example, the cost of closure, compliance with regulatory requirements, and Medicare reimbursement. The hospital that opts for conversion must address a likewise serious set of issues within the course of a long planning process. Both options are expensive and time-consuming for hospitals whose time and finances have run out.

Notes and References

1. Cleverley, W. O. Hospital closings: fact and fiction. *Healthcare Executive* 47(2):26, Sept.–Oct. 1990.

2. Hospital Closures: 1990, Report OEI-04-91-00560, January 1992, Department of Health and Human Services, Office of the Inspector General.

3. Northeast Ohio is defined as a five-county region including Cuyahoga, Geauga, Lake, Lorain, and Medina counties.

4. American Hospital Association. *National Hospital Panel Survey.* Chicago: AHA, 1991.
5. Perry, L. AHA traces hospital shakeout in '80s. *Healthweek News* 5(23):2, Dec. 2, 1991.
6. Greene, J. The costs of hospital mergers. *Modern Healthcare* 22(5):36, Feb. 3, 1992.
7. Levine, P. CEOs as risk takers: from vision to reality. *Hospitals* 64(22):25, Nov. 20, 1990.
8. Greene, J. Towns breathe new life into closed hospitals. *Modern Healthcare* 21(12):24, Mar. 25, 1991.
9. Greene, J. Feds slow to part with paybacks for losses. *Modern Healthcare* 21(42):42, Oct. 21, 1991.
10. *Modern Healthcare* survey conducted in Jan. 1993.

Chapter 9

Capital Restructuring

Darrell J. Tamosuinas

A cash crisis may be resolved in a variety of ways, depending on the severity and immediacy of the crisis and the prospects of reversing its causal factors. A performance deficiency may be recognized early and addressed adequately, or it may fester until the crisis becomes severe. Unfortunately, management, boards of directors, and other parties-in-interest (or stakeholders) sometimes ignore early warning indicators or lack sufficient information to detect a pending crisis.

When the magnitude of the crisis dictates a formal debt restructuring process, whether in or out of court, the hospital and its management, board, and staff face some profound changes. Control over the fate of the organization (as opposed to operating control) must be effectively shared and, in extreme cases, virtually abdicated to outside parties-in-interest, such as banks and bondholders. Creditors will assert their rights, contracts will be renegotiated, and pressure for change will come from a variety of often contradictory sources.

Interpreting financial information in actual or anticipated distress situations and developing an appropriate restructuring or reorganization strategy that considers the rights and priorities of parties-in-interest both inside and outside the hospital requires a full understanding of the rationale, the players, and the processes typically involved in a restructuring situation.

The Process of Capital Restructuring

Formal restructuring may be regarded as part of a hospital's "action continuum," presented in figure 9-1. Each stage of the continuum encompasses elements of its preceding stage.

Figure 9-1. Action Continuum

Troubleshooting

Remedial actions that address specific aspects of financial and operational management; accomplished *within* the organization.

↓

Turnaround

Remedial actions that encompass the full scope of the organization's operations; accomplished *within* the organization.

↓

Restructuring

Reaction to a current or pending financial and operational crisis, requiring participation and negotiation with parties *outside* the organization; accomplished out of court.

↓

Reorganization

Restructuring in which the magnitude of changes required and/or the difficulty of the negotiating process requires court supervision.

Restructurings involving acute care hospitals and other health care facilities, as with all organizations, require a combination of specific industry knowledge and familiarity with common restructuring practices. Each situation is unique, and thus the courses of action undertaken by restructuring teams will vary. The individual hospital's market and other business imperatives, debt characteristics, number and type of creditors, management capabilities, and governing tax law will all play a role. But whatever the hospital's circumstance, the process of restructuring generally involves three phases, each incorporating a number of process steps as presented in figure 9-2. The phases are not strictly sequential.

Assessment

The need for accurate assessment of financial and operational information is a constant in the management of any hospital. Ongoing analysis coupled with an ability to recognize the development of fundamental problems and the need for strategic changes is the best method for preventing a crisis.

When a crisis situation does develop, it often becomes apparent that this ongoing process of operational assessment has broken down. In all hospitals, both administrators (including chief executive officers, chief financial officers, and board members) and certain creditors (such as banks or bond trustees) are provided with some type of periodic financial and statistical information. Ideally, this information should provide insight into the operational performance and strategic direction of the hospital, with well-interpreted income and expense presentations along with indicators of the quality and efficiency of services provided at department and total entity levels. In practice, however, the information provided is all too often inaccurate, not timely, and/or vague. If the information is sound, the parties receiving it may lack the necessary skills to interpret it. Even when good information is presented to parties with requisite expertise, there are often attitudinal hurdles to overcome in admitting that a problem exists and that something must be done about it.

Consequently, it is common to find that the first step in a restructuring process must be an assessment of the assessments, that is, a reevaluation of available information on the past operations of the hospital. Such a reevaluation must be conducted in light of the knowledge that a problem has occurred; it should be an active search for contributing trends. In many cases, additional analyses (beyond what has been provided on a routine basis) must be conducted on specific aspects of operations. Figure 9-3 poses some key questions that must be addressed and considerations for interpreting such information. Historic analysis will provide the basis for the next steps in the restructuring process: the preliminary development of plans going forward.

Figure 9-2. The Restructuring Process

Phase	Process Steps
Assessment	• Historical analysis • Development of plans and projections or forecasts under a going-concern scenario • Development of a hypothetical liquidation analysis
Negotiation	• Arrangement for a short-term working capital line • Negotiation of deferrals on payments, amendments to payment terms, or refinancing • Negotiation of new contracts, trade credit agreements, and, possibly, new management • Development of short- and long-term business plans
Implementation	• Crisis management to curtail cash hemorrhage • Stabilization of operations and implementation of turnaround measures • Execution of long-range plans, including strategic changes in financial and functional operations

Figure 9-3. A Reevaluation of Available Information

Questions regarding: Erratic earnings/losses	Information and use of information regarding: Erratic earnings/losses
• Are erratic earnings and/or losses due to the sale of assets or refinancings?	• Normalize operating results excluding erratic factors in order to measure trends.
• Are periodic losses due to substantial year-end adjustments regarding reserves for contractual allowances?	• Accounting or finance department may not be responsive to regulatory requirements or other contractual or pricing strategies.
• Are earnings or losses due to fluctuations in payer mix?	• Potential issues regarding physician practices; requires review.
• Are earnings or losses due to increases in malpractice reserves or losses?	• Medical staff relations may be poor.
	• High medical staff turnover or poor quality control.

Questions regarding: Periodic or sustained cash flow crises	Information and use of information regarding: Periodic or sustained cash flow crises
• What are collection periods for accounts receivable?	• Potential problems with billing sequence including completion of medical record and/or coding.
• Does the organization over time cash out a percentage of its net revenue?	• Collection follow-up procedures may be inadequate or nonexistent.
• Are capital expenditures consistent with budget?	
• Are settlements with Medicare and/or Medicaid anticipated?	• Potential miscoding.
• Is there a short-term and long-term cash plan and reconciliation process?	• Purchasing department or other management decisions may not be consistent with timing of cash flow availability.

Questions regarding: Declining census and occupancy levels	Information and use of information regarding: Declining census and occupancy levels
• Is there new competition?	• Potential market saturation (overcapacity).
• Is there a shift in inpatient or outpatient service?	• Potential technological or regulatory change.
• Is there a major demographic shift in the service area?	
• Is there a decline in the length of stay?	
• Is the hospital losing primary care physicians and/or admitting specialists?	• Recruitment programs in effect.
• Is there a decline in admissions?	• Quality of care of hospital may be declining and will need to be upgraded.

Figure 9-3. (Continued)

Questions regarding: Aging receivables and increased bad debt reserves	Information and use of information regarding: Aging receivables and increased bad debt reserves
• Are charitable and indigent care levels increasing?	• Improve admissions screening regarding Medicaid eligibility.
• Is there an increase in private-pay patients?	• Poor follow-up on private-pay collections segment.
• Is there a socioeconomic change in the service area?	• Other business office management issues may need to be addressed.

Questions regarding: Increasing FTE per AOB* levels	Information and use of information regarding: Increasing FTE per AOB* levels
• Is there increased use of agency personnel?	• FTEs should be measured against industry standards as appropriately applied.
• Is there a decline in admissions?	• Physician practice patterns may need attention.
• Is the reduction in staff consistent with declines in utilization?	• Seasonal staffing may be appropriate, if possible.

* Full-time equivalent (FTE) per adjusted occupied bed (AOB)

Questions regarding: Increasing Medicare/Medicaid census as compared to market service area	Information and use of information regarding: Increasing Medicare/Medicaid census as compared to market service area
• Why is the commercial or managed care base declining?	• Physician relations may need to be improved.
• Have expense levels been adjusted correspondingly?	• Expenses may need further control.
• Is there a significant change in the patient population in the service area?	• Service offerings may need adjustment.
• Are commercial-pay admitters moving to other hospitals or to other areas (for example, to more modern facilities, from city to suburbs)?	• Service offerings may be inferior requiring technological and/or medical staff adjustments.

(Continued on next page)

Figure 9-3. (Continued)

Questions regarding: Aging plant	Information and use of information regarding: Aging plant
• Is there a master plan, and is it being followed?	
• Is there significant deferred maintenance?	• Estimated cost to bring hospital up to code.
• Are life safety code issues being followed?	• Establish master plan in order to minimize disruption to operations.
• What is the capital expense in relation to depreciation, and what are the anticipated equipment and plant expenditures?	• Estimated cost to meet expenditures necessary to upgrade to master plan requirements.
• Has the technological status of the hospital changed, and is the technology obsolete?	
• Is the hospital in jeopardy of losing its JCAHO accreditation?	
• Are capital projects considered based on economic feasibility?	• Economic feasibility and expenditures should be consistent with master plan.

Questions regarding: High departmental management turnover	Information and use of information regarding: High departmental management turnover
• What is reason for turnover?	• Compensation analysis should be performed and incorporated in restructuring.
• Are hiring policies appropriate?	• A change in leadership may be appropriate.
• Are compensation levels appropriate?	• Institutions in the same market may be responsible and associated activities need analysis.
• Is there a medical staff relations problem?	
• Is there a leadership issue?	

Questions regarding: Budget, strategic plan, and process	Information and use of information regarding: Budget, strategic plan, and process
• Is there a short- and long-term cash plan and reconciliation process?	• Management may not recognize effects of operating and investment decisions.
• How frequently is a cash budget prepared?	
• Is a strategic plan or budget prepared?	• Outlook and assumptions may be unsubstantiated and/or unrealistic.
• Is there a reconciliation of actual to budget or plan?	• The management of disbursements may not be coordinated with receipts.

Depending on the severity of the crisis, two types of plans may be required:

1. *A short-term plan.* This plan focuses on cash inflows and outflows in the upcoming 6 to 12 months. It may be necessary to develop a weekly or, in some cases, even a daily plan. This plan should identify critical "cash crunch" points and will help determine the degree of urgency for the restructuring.
2. *A long-term plan.* This plan begins to anticipate strategic changes over a five-year period. It should help further quantify the magnitude of the crisis and whether restructuring is the appropriate option. Analysis of the plan may indicate that either an internal turnaround process could be sufficient or immediate progress toward court-assisted reorganization is advisable.

If results anticipated in the long-term plan are very poor, it may also be advisable to prepare a liquidation analysis. A variety of hypothetical liquidation scenarios may be tested, depending on the level of projected financial distress. A hospital suffering from a poor strategic or geographic position, overpowering competition, and severe cash hemorrhaging may have to consider a so-called bricks-and-mortar liquidation, in which the anticipated proceeds will be limited to a quick sale of hard assets. In such cases, the condition of, and the market for, all inventory and removable assets must be evaluated. The value of the land and building will be determined with reference to the conditions of the market, the desirability of the location, and the adaptability of the building, if any, to other uses. Data on recent sales of comparable properties are useful in such an analysis, but are not always readily available.

In calculating liquidation value, it must be remembered that a portion of the loss on a hospital's sale of assets may be reimbursable by Medicare. An estimate of this amount, if applicable, should be included in the anticipated liquidation proceeds. A full discussion of Medicare's guidelines for such reimbursement may be found in the Health Care Financing Administration's (HCFA's) *Provider Reimbursement Manual,* section 132.[1]

If the strategic position of the hospital has weakened due to operational problems and there is substantial risk that management will be unable to implement a long-term turnaround, a "going-concern" sale or merger with a competitive facility may be examined. Estimations of going-concern value usually involve a more or less formal valuation process. Although there are no strict guidelines for such valuations, they usually involve some type of discounted cash flow analysis. The hospital's operations are projected for a period, generally five years. Often, projections are adjusted for certain operating burdens (such as specific labor contracts or charity care mandates) that would not necessarily attach to a new owner. The hospital's ability to generate free cash flow is estimated based on these projections and then discounted using a weighted average cost of capital (WACC) factor. This WACC factor is determined by examining the actual costs of both debt and equity funding for hospitals similar to the subject hospital in terms of corporate structure, size, and location. As with a liquidation analysis, the ability to construct a valid group of comparable properties greatly enhances the reliability of the valuation analysis.

All these plans are likely to be revised many times as the restructuring progresses. However, a thorough analysis and the development of well-thought-out plans at the beginning of the process will greatly enhance the hospital's initial position as it begins to negotiate with the various parties-in-interest. As discussed later in this chapter, hospital management may find it necessary or desirable to engage assistance from outside the organization in accomplishing these tasks. If utilized correctly, such assistance may bring both a fresh perspective and a degree of credibility to the assessment process.

Negotiation

The process of negotiating a restructuring begins when creditors are alerted to the crisis, either through deliberate contact from the hospital or because events such as late payments or defaults have come to their attention. At this point, the assessment process will be expanded to include the various parties-in-interest. These parties will focus on:

- The potential future profitability and cash generation capacity of the operation
- The hospital's management needs and the ability of current management staff to fill these needs
- The hospital's market and regulatory environment
- The current and proposed capital structures

Each party will evaluate these issues in light of its own level of involvement and relative economic position in the hospital. The general guideline for utilizing certain information gathered in the assessment process will likely be the U.S. Bankruptcy Code. Even if a restructuring is not carried out in a courtroom setting, creditors and other interested parties will gauge their interests against the positions they would occupy if the situation were to progress to that extreme. The respective rights of parties-in-interest, for example, would be formed based on contracts such as indentures and loan agreements in conjunction with Absolute Priority established under Section 507 of the Bankruptcy Code. The rights and assertions of parties-in-interest are further delineated when considering potential avoidance actions with regard to preferential transfers under Section 547 of the Code, and equitable treatment considering what is known as the Best Interests Test under Section

1129. A thorough understanding of reorganization proceedings under the Bankruptcy Code (see chapter 10) will facilitate the negotiation process.

When the cash crisis is immediate, the hospital's first goal will probably be to arrange or extend a short-term working capital line with one or more of its major lenders. If successful, securing this line can provide short-term relief and allow breathing space in negotiations on long-term debt; if unsuccessful, negotiations must proceed under high pressure, often characterized by rapid deterioration of operating conditions.

In approaching long-term debt, the hospital will seek to obtain short-term deferrals and long-term rescheduling of interest and principal payments; it will also probably seek amendments to certain terms, such as required debt service coverage ratios. Various avenues of debt consolidation and refinancing may be pursued. The hospital will also find it necessary to renegotiate contracts, including trade credit agreements and possibly management and staff contracts. Not-for-profit hospitals may also consider negotiations with key donors, for example, in an attempt to free funds granted for endowment or capital additions and allow them to be used for operating expenses. In such cases, attention must be paid to state and federal statutes so that the hospital's tax-exempt status is not impaired. In all instances, the willingness of parties-in-interest to deal and cooperate is critical to successful restructuring.

In addition to normal operating requirements, there is generally a need for cash to fund the restructuring. The need may be sufficiently accommodated through deferrals or working capital loans, as noted previously. In the case of restructurings under Chapter 11 Bankruptcy, a debtor-in-possession line of credit is often required to fund the high level of administrative expenses and operating deficits associated with the process.

In an out-of-court restructuring, the hospital will most likely begin formal negotiations with its major secured debt holders—its banks and bondholders. If results at this level are sufficiently favorable, the hospital may receive the cash relief it needs to satisfy other parties, such as trade creditors; otherwise, at some point negotiations will be extended to this group, dealt with either on an individual vendor basis or, as is common in reorganizations under bankruptcy, through a committee. Depending on the structure of the organization and the extent of the restructuring, shareholders in for-profit hospitals may enter the negotiation process at many points.

All parties-in-interest will evaluate the potential success of a restructuring by assessing the ability of the hospital, as presented in long-range plans, to generate cash and by estimating the level of risk associated with assumptions regarding that ability. Sophisticated creditors will consider key performance drivers for the health care industry in general and for the specific hospital in question, including pricing, medical records and billing systems, levels of full-time equivalents (FTEs), trends in hospital usage, and technological enhancements. They will evaluate the hospital's business plan in light of these factors and will assess management's ability to carry out such plans. Ultimately, creditors will ask certain key questions and consider two primary avenues of approach:

Option	*Key Questions*
Liquidation	• Is the liquidation value (expected proceeds) of greater value than what could be realized under a going-concern scenario?
Workout/Going Concern	• What are the prospects and assumptions in a workout? • What is the present value of the cash stream in a workout/going-concern scenario after adjusting for risk factors? • Should the operation be stabilized in the mid-term and sold at a later time for higher value?

The present value of risk-adjusted discounted cash flows presented in the plan as compared to the proceeds expected under liquidation is the essential consideration in restructuring. Should the perceived risks be too high to execute a successful turnaround, senior lenders may pursue liquidation or going concern sale.

Implementation

Upon first consideration, it might appear that the implementation of a restructuring begins at the conclusion of the negotiation phase. But in a sense the implementation phase begins as soon as the crisis is recognized. The first steps taken to stop the cash hemorrhage, however temporary, are the real start of an implementation process, which carries through and beyond the formal restructuring period.

Once a plan is in place to deal with the immediate cash crisis, the implementation phase focuses on the stabilization of operations and on the hospital's progress in turnaround measures. This forward motion should begin even as negotiations are still proceeding, based on the results of the assessment phase. Key areas involving large potential dollar results must be addressed as soon as practically possible; staff adjustments may be made, unproductive units or services curtailed, trade credit terms renegotiated, and pressure brought to bear on outstanding receivables. If weak upper management is identified as an issue, turnaround consultants or more qualified long-term replacement executives may be brought in.

If negotiations conclude successfully, the final phase of implementation will involve the execution of long-range plans, including all identified strategic changes in the operations and financing of the hospital. In some senses, this phase will represent a return to normalcy in the hospital's operations, though it will be obvious in the wake of a restructuring that the stakes for success have been heightened and scrutiny is more intense.

At this point in the discussion, it is worthwhile to mention one outgrowth of the negotiation phase that will in part shape expectations during implementation: negative and affirmative covenants in restructured debt instruments. A variety of debt instruments may be issued by a hospital, distinguished by characteristics such as taxable or tax-exempt and secured or unsecured properties. Depending on the purpose of the loan, the nature of the holder's debt, and the anticipated source or sources of repayment, certain requirements will be imposed on the hospital.

Various covenants will be created based on the interest of the debt holders. Two common objectives of such covenants are: (1) to preserve conditions that will enable the hospital to repay its debt, and (2) to alert debt holders of potential developing financial problems. Lending covenants designed to restrict further changes in the hospital's capital structure or other business characteristics may place limits on additional debt, liens on assets, and restrictions on merger and acquisition activities. Covenants designed to alert debt holders to potential problems may be structured around measures of earnings, liquidity, and leverage.

The development of appropriate covenants requires that consideration be given to adequate flexibility, reporting, and corrective or "cure" periods, so that the hospital can continue to properly manage its business and adjust its strategy based on market and regulatory changes. An event of default on a covenant should be regarded as an alert to debt holders to foster corrective action, not a license to shut down operations. Some negative deviation from plan and intermediate defaults (sometimes referred to as "technical defaults") may be expected in the course of implementing a restructuring. Covenants such as those defining excessive collection or trade payable periods, or violations of debt service coverage ratios and net worth requirements, should be regarded as early warning signals designed to urge prompt corrective action.

The Parties Involved

The process of debt restructuring is above all else a process of negotiation. Regardless of the size of the organization, this negotiation is likely to involve a diversity of parties. Inevitably, many will have contradictory interests—not just on the financial level, where each party will predictably seek its own maximum gain, but also on functional and emotional levels, where motivations may be less apparent. Relational histories (for example, between board and lenders or between management and staff) will affect the willingness of various parties to bargain in good faith and accept necessary concessions. Parties will also differ in the degree of distress they bring to negotiations, depending on the relative magnitude of their perceived stake. Thus a thorough understanding of all facets of the hospital's operating history is vital.

In addition to these considerations, it should also be reiterated that possible outcomes for the hospital under liquidation or bankruptcy scenarios will provide a backdrop to out-of-court restructurings. If the restructuring leads to liquidation or bankruptcy, each party's anticipated position will or should inform its evaluation of any proposals offered in negotiation.

For-Profit and Not-for-Profit Hospitals

The parties involved in restructuring for-profit and not-for-profit entities will differ. Clearly, some parties will be common to either form of organization: trade creditors, possibly commercial lenders or bondholders, and physicians, management, and staff employees. Others, such as shareholders or donors, will be peculiar to one type of entity. But even parties common to both forms of organization may differ widely with respect to their attitudes toward the bottom line and the mission of the organization.

For-profit hospitals will be distinguished primarily by the presence of shareholders, who regard the operation as an investment first and foremost. With respect to projected plans for operating under restructuring, shareholders will be concerned that the organization profit, not merely survive. In many instances, shareholders may therefore be inclined to make more stringent demands on financial performance; however, they may also be more amenable to allowing whatever changes are deemed necessary in order to maximize such performance. The boards of such entities are often more business-oriented, emphasizing financial and functional oversight and realization of fiduciary responsibility to shareholders and lenders.

In place of shareholders, the not-for-profit hospital has donors or funders. This group may include a broad range of public-sector funders, private foundations, and individuals; there may also be an endowment fund(s) that generates significant income. Profit in such operations is usually regarded as desirable but may not be considered necessary; funders will generally perceive break-even, or even modest deficits, as acceptable. Both funders and board members will be more focused on ensuring that the mission of the hospital is carried out. On the negative side, the mission may constrain a not-for-profit hospital from negotiating changes or concessions that would maximize financial viability. On the positive side, many parties involved in the negotiation process may have a special dedication to or "soft spot" for the altruistic nature of the operation, or a connection based on other than strictly financial considerations (such as religious affiliation), and thus may be more willing to consider sacrificing some of their own interest in restructuring.

Internal Parties

Various key groups within the distressed hospital have a stake in the restructuring process, and some of them will want to become involved in it in order to influence the outcome. These parties include the board of directors, physicians, management, staff, and hired advisors.

Board of Directors or Trustees

In some sense, the board of directors bears a fiduciary responsibility to all the other parties-in-interest in a restructuring; that is, the board's duty is to attempt to ensure that the hospital survives, discharges its debts, and carries out its mission with respect to either shareholders or donors as well to patients and the community at large. Boards will often become concerned during restructuring with the issue of retaining control of the organization, and will frequently resist what they perceive to be attempts at interference by creditors or certain shareholders. In addition, in recent years board members have become increasingly concerned over issues of personal liability, particularly the threat of shareholder lawsuits. Thus, boards may be highly conservative in their reactions to innovative or unusual proposals during restructuring, and uncooperative with solutions that involve sharing the power for operational decision making.

Physicians

Whether their primary concern is to maximize their individual practices, serve a particular public, or a combination of the two, physicians will generally have a high interest in preserving the public image of the hospital and ensuring that it provides an amenable environment for their practices and their patients. Physicians tend to resist changes that might decrease or limit investment in the physical plant, such as equipment and renovations. Although they may not participate directly in the restructuring process (except to the extent that they may also fill positions on the board or in management), physicians may wield considerable influence through their ability to decrease or cease admissions to the hospital and simply take their business elsewhere.

Management

In general, hospital management will share many of the board's concerns: survival, discharge of debt, and so on. However, management is closer to the front lines and, like the physicians, will be concerned with securing the resources it perceives necessary to carry on operations without undue stress; management may be highly resistant to cuts in administrative resources and will tend to seek a comfortable operating cash position. Individual managers will, of course, be concerned with preserving their own jobs and will wish to avoid being blamed and possibly punished for events leading to the restructuring. Thus, management may tend to present negative past performance as resulting from uncontrollable forces (and consequently resist operational changes going forward) and may be overly optimistic in projecting future improvements. On the other hand, management is likely to have suffered the greatest stress in dealing with disgruntled creditors, and is often eager to facilitate a speedy resolution to the restructuring crisis. Management must be willing and able to cooperate with the demands of all parties-in-interest for financial and operational information on both past and projected future operations.

Staff

Staff in a distressed hospital will be concerned, perhaps above all else, with the preservation of jobs. Depending on the nature of the market, trained staff, like the physicians, may be able to wield the threat of departure if faced with longer or less flexible hours and reduced or stagnant pay scales. Staff or its representatives may also be direct players in the negotiation process if the hospital bears responsibility for funding pension and other employee benefits plans. Unions will fight to protect their contracts and their members' jobs.

Advisors

Before and during restructuring, most hospitals are likely to require the assistance of outside advisors. In distressed situations, though, it is not uncommon to find that hospitals have acquired a welter of inappropriate, ineffectual, and duplicative consultants, all of whom have a vested interest in prolonging their engagement as long as they are paid. The scrutiny of operations required in restructuring should dictate a close evaluation of the need for, and integration of, advisors in all areas.

External or Constituent Parties

There are also a number of concerned parties outside the distressed hospital that have a stake in the outcome of the restructuring process and whose cooperation can help determine its success or failure. These parties include secured lenders, unsecured lenders, shareholders, donors, and the community at large.

Secured Lenders

Secured lenders may include commercial institutions providing working capital or capital construction loans, bondholders of either public or private debt, and certain trade creditors, such as those offering lease/purchase agreements on capital equipment. Secured lenders can anticipate a priority position under bankruptcy and will typically demand full or nearly full satisfaction of the hospital's obligations. However, they may be willing to consider either extended payment schedules or reduced interest rates on outstanding loans, particularly if they perceive that the survival of the hospital is at stake, because liquidation proceeds are rarely adequate to fully discharge existing debt.

Unsecured Creditors

Unsecured creditors may also include commercial lenders and bondholders and will typically include the vast bulk of trade creditors. Unsecured creditors are aware that they often fare poorly in bankruptcy and may therefore be willing to take deep discounts on existing receivables. Vendors forced to accept punitive discounts, though, may refuse to supply the hospital in the future, a particular concern with single-source vendors of highly specialized goods or services.

Shareholders

To the extent that the value of their investments rests on earnings retained by the hospital, shareholders' interests in restructuring will often be opposed to the interest of secured and unsecured creditors. In addition, like the board of directors, shareholders will often become concerned with retaining control of the organization and will be reluctant to share such control with creditors. Shareholders will also often bring pressure to bear for drastic cost-cutting, putting them at odds with medical and management staff. In addition, if shareholders perceive that they are holding virtually worthless stock with little prospect of a short- to mid-term increase in value, they may care far less than other parties-in-interest about the survival of the corporate entity. The nature of the shareholders as a party in restructuring may vary widely, depending on whether shares are held by only a few investors or are distributed over a wide base with no individual investor holding a dominant share.

Donors

Unlike shareholders, donors typically have little technical ongoing control over the entities they fund. But donors who feel their funds have been misused are highly likely to direct their future support elsewhere. In addition, under certain circumstances donors may have the right to "reclaim" donations that have not been spent according to the terms of their granting. Funding organizations and major individual donors also form a distinct "community within the community," with its own potential for spreading negative perceptions. Donors dissatisfied with the direction and terms of a restructuring may not only withhold their own future contributions, but may sour potential new donors who may be vital to the hospital's continued viability.

Community

With regard to the community at large, as with donors, the hospital's primary concern is image and perception. Depending on a variety of factors in the marketplace, such as overall affluence levels and the level of participation in managed care programs, individual community members may have a high degree of control over which hospital facilities they use. If a restructuring becomes highly publicized (whether acrimonious or not), physicians and staff begin to defect and hospital services begin to suffer visibly; the hospital may lose the public's confidence, which will be difficult to recover. The community can also have a significant impact on the willingness of state and local governments and private funders to continue to support the facility.

The Hospital Strategy

In essence, the hospital strategy is the game plan undertaken by the distressed hospital during the implementation phase of the restructuring process. This final section discusses two factors that have a tremendous impact on the success of the implementation phase: the use of outside assistance, and the adoption of a realistic financial and operational plan.

The Need for Outside Assistance

This discussion has alluded to the many factors that lead hospitals in restructuring situations to seek assistance from outside the system. Because most, if not all the parties involved will be tainted by conflicting interest in the eyes of certain other parties, it is extremely difficult for any group inside the process to successfully negotiate a restructuring settlement; outside parties with some measure of perceived objectivity are usually required. In addition, during the intense process of negotiation, the demands for financial and operational analysis and reporting often exceed the capabilities of hospital management. The sheer quantity of information demanded may be beyond the capacity of a staff already pressed by cutbacks and the stress of juggling inadequate resources day to day. In addition, there is often a need for specialized expertise in the legal, accounting, and technical considerations presented by various restructuring strategies.

Many outside firms provide operating and management analysis, assistance with the assessment of financial strategies, and participation in restructuring negotiations. Such firms typically work intensely with hospital management in the early phases of restructuring to assess past operations and develop future projections. If the restructuring process expands to include all or most constituent groups (as opposed to a single lender or a limited group of creditors), and particularly if it appears that the process is moving toward liquidation or bankruptcy, such constituents often engage their own advisors. Typically, the hospital will come under pressure to reimburse the cost of such advisors. These advisors do not become directly involved in the day-to-day management of the hospital, and generally, though not always, the scope of their services is limited to the period of the restructuring with only occasional monitoring and follow-up after its conclusion.

Other, so-called turnaround firms provide more extensive, day-to-day involvement with the operations of the hospital. Such firms generally provide a key management team of executives who may either work with existing management or actually replace them, whether for a defined transition period or on an open-ended basis. These firms often have a wide latitude in proposing and implementing organizational changes. Typically, they are called in when confidence in management has been so seriously eroded as to impede or prevent successful restructuring negotiations.

In addition to these options, constituent groups in a restructuring often negotiate for participation, or greater participation, on the board of directors. Board members may be added either to provide an expertise currently perceived as lacking, or simply to represent the interests of the constituent group.

Proposed Operating and Financing Plans

As noted above, demands for information and document preparation tend to increase dramatically in a restructuring situation. Hospital management and its advisors in this situation may expect to face some or all of the following demands with respect to operating and financing plan preparation and reporting.

A thorough financial and operational plan going forward under restructured terms will be perhaps the single most important document prepared by hospital management in conjunction with its advisors. Such a plan must be focused on the permanent rather than the temporary fix; that is, it must incorporate long-term strategic assessments rather than being geared solely toward short-term survival. The plan must include a realistic assessment of the hospital's strategic viability and its component services in the marketplace and of the adequacy of current management and staff to implement the plan.

In practical terms, it will usually be necessary to run several iterations of the plan during restructuring negotiations, as various terms and operating scenarios are proposed and evaluated.

As negotiations proceed, the parties involved must decide at some point whether the restructuring can be accomplished within the framework of existing loan, bond, and other documents, or whether some or all of these documents must be rewritten. Obviously, the production of new documents can be anticipated to require significant additional time of management and its legal and financial advisors.

Finally, hospitals emerging from a restructuring will generally face more stringent requirements for ongoing reporting. At a minimum, existing covenants on reporting are likely to be strictly enforced. Periodic reporting requirements may be increased; for example, reports originally required to be produced quarterly may be required monthly. New reporting focused on specific areas of concern may also be required. Time lines for production of reports may also be tightened, especially if there is a perception that tardy reporting contributed to the problems that led to the restructuring.

Conclusion

When a hospital fails to recognize the warning signals of financial distress, a debt restructuring process may be warranted. Regardless of the hospital's circumstance, the process typically involves three phases: assessment of the hospital's past operational and financial performance in order to project the type of corrective strategy to undertake (for example, liquidation, merger, or workout); negotiation with the hospital's creditors and other interested parties, either under the guideline of the U.S. Bankruptcy Code or through an out-of-court agreement; and implementation of both short- and long-term action plans. Because a number of internal and external parties with diverse interests will be affected by the restructuring process, it may be in the hospital's best interest to seek outside expertise to negotiate an option that will be acceptable to all parties, and to structure the operational and financial planning that will make that option work.

Reference

1. HCFA. Gains and losses on disposal of depreciable assets (excluding involuntary conversions). In: *Medicare and Medicaid Guide: Provider Reimbursement Manual.* Chicago: Commerce Clearing House Inc., 1990, section 132, pp. 1679-4 through 1679-11.

Chapter 10

Bankruptcies and Workouts

Robert M. Fishman, James B. Riley, Jr., and Kimberly A. Warnke

A hospital in financial distress can manage a turnaround by seeking protection from its creditors under the bankruptcy laws or by securing their cooperation in an out-of-court workout. Filing a petition for bankruptcy, though often a long and trying process, may be the most effective turnaround strategy for a hospital that wishes to maintain control of its operations during restructuring. A workout is an attractive option for a hospital that does not require the protection and structure of formal bankruptcy if its creditors are willing to take part in its financial transformation.

Bankruptcy or Workout: Making a Choice

The first step in choosing between bankruptcy and workout is to decide on a course of action. Selecting the best course of action begins with a careful assessment of the hospital's goals, resources, liabilities, operations, and particular problems.

Goals

Formulating a bankruptcy or workout strategy involves the identification and prioritization of goals for the hospital. These goals will be dictated by the particular hospital's situation and will greatly influence, if not determine, the selected strategy. The goal formulation process requires consideration of not only economic and legal elements, but health care and public interest issues as well.

The goals of a failing health care institution must be determined through an assessment of its assets and liabilities, as well as the specific factors contributing to the facility's decline. The administrators of the institution must identify the cause of the distress and offer a proposal(s) designed to cure the ills or make the inevitable termination as painless as possible. If the problems are caused by a change in the industry, such as a modification in reimbursement policy, or by a competitive change in the surrounding environment, a discontinuation of some of the services currently provided may be part of the strategy.

If the revenues and ultimate profitability of a facility are overmatched by the level of its debt service, the resulting cash flow problem may require a financial restructuring. Such a restructuring might include an infusion of capital, the sale of certain assets, or the sale of the entire facility as a going concern. If the distress is the result of operational or management deficiencies, including accounts receivable mismanagement, outside sources may have to be tapped to provide appropriate expertise. Finally, where the economic and operational realities leave no hope for revival, a liquidation designed to maximize the return to creditors may be the best resolution strategy. The formulation of an appropriate strategy follows the enumeration of the institution's goals and requires a careful analysis of the present state of the hospital's affairs and the various factors that led to the distress.

Creditors and Debt

One of the crucial elements to consider in designing a workout or bankruptcy strategy is an analysis of the institution's debt including the creditors to whom it is owed. The type and amount of a troubled hospital's debt may greatly affect the choice of a financial resolution. It is self-evident that those creditors with the most at stake will likely become the most active participants in any workout or bankruptcy process. Creditors holding indebtedness for which the hospital has pledged collateral (the "secured creditors"), such as holders of tax-exempt secured bonds, will certainly play a prominent role in either an out-of-court workout or a formal bankruptcy scenario. Issues that will affect the secured creditor are the magnitude of debt, ratio of debt to collateral, and the creditor's assessment of the likelihood that the collateral securing that debt will diminish in value over time. The secured creditor can impose its leverage into the situation by initiating a foreclosure action, seeking to sell tangible personal property pursuant to the Uniform Commercial Code or the applicable bond documents, or by collecting directly from the institution's debtors under the terms of the security agreement. Any of these actions might force a hospital to seek the protection of the bankruptcy court.

The unsecured creditors (creditors who do not have a security interest in assets of the debtor) of a distressed hospital can also impose leverage on the institution by refusing to continue to do business with it. The impact of this action by an unsecured creditor will depend on whether the goods or services provided by the creditor are readily available in the marketplace or are unique and essential. The unsecured creditor, however, is likely to have less money at stake and consequently may have less incentive and ability to become a roadblock to a hospital's reorganization attempts. Additionally, the large number of competing suppliers in the health care industry should reduce the leverage available to unsecured creditors, although these suppliers may be willing to continue relationships with a reorganizing hospital on a cash basis only.

A bad relationship with even a few creditors could result in the filing of an involuntary bankruptcy petition under Section 303, Title 11, United States Code (hereinafter, Title 11 will be referred to as the "Bankruptcy Code"). This section of the Bankruptcy Code allows an involuntary petition to be filed against for-profit entities (nonprofit ventures are specifically excepted) by only three eligible creditors (assuming the hospital has at least 12 such creditors) with aggregate unsecured claims in excess of $5,000. Thus, fostering cooperation among creditors can be a crucial part of any attempted workout or bankruptcy.

Regardless of the type and amount of debt owed, a good relationship with creditors can afford the hospital enough time to explore all its financial options; a poor relationship with creditors may limit the hospital's choices or eliminate them altogether. In either a workout or a bankruptcy situation, strong creditor support, especially from larger and more influential creditors, may help to persuade other creditors and the bankruptcy court to give the hospital debtor some breathing room.

Creditor attitude toward a debtor hospital may be influenced not only by direct interaction with the hospital, but also by the type of creditor involved. A more sophisticated institutional lender or bank may be more experienced with the bankruptcy or workout process and may, through its understanding of the issues and the process, be more inclined to cooperate as long as its interests are perceived to be protected.

An experienced lender may also be more aggressively hostile toward a debtor if it perceives its interests are threatened by continued operations. A less sophisticated creditor may be more passive, due to a lack of familiarity with the process and the opportunities it presents. If the less sophisticated creditor becomes angered by the nonpayment of the hospital's debt, though, it will more likely personalize the situation and respond with animosity, and may be less easily persuaded to cooperate. But this emotional component can also work to a debtor's advantage. A creditor with a long-standing and satisfying relationship with a debtor and its administrators may be inclined to lend support, especially if the debtor is an institution that is seen as providing an important community service. A particular creditor's situation may also make the creditor more difficult to deal with in a reorganization attempt; for example, a creditor that is a trustee for a group of individual interest holders (such as holders of public debt instruments) may have additional concerns and constraints based on its fiduciary role, which may cause its decision-making process to be much more complex. If a hospital has obtained financing through the issuance of a bond or a similar vehicle, it may be more difficult, as a practical matter, to obtain the cooperation of a bond trustee that may have problems obtaining the consensus of numerous public bondholders.

Assets

An evaluation of the hospital's assets is another important element in determining whether to attempt a workout or file a bankruptcy petition, as well as in defining whether to undertake a reorganization or a liquidation. Clearly, the most crucial component in any attempted workout or bankruptcy is the availability of cash. The more cash available to a financially distressed hospital, the greater its chance for a successful reorganization. Further, the more unencumbered property or equity realizable from encumbered property, the more options there are available to design a reorganization strategy. Either unencumbered assets or assets in which the hospital has equity may provide comfort to creditors, which may buy the debtor some cooperation or provide additional tools for financing or sale, enabling a distressed hospital to obtain the cash necessary to continue operations both during and after its reorganization. Salable assets might include real property; personal property, such as machinery and equipment; and contracts, licenses, and permits that may be valuable to an entity interested in taking over the hospital's operations.

In evaluating a hospital's assets, the value of those assets may be subjective, rather than objective, and may depend on whether the hospital continues operating, on the purpose for which a potential buyer intends to use an asset, or on the financial strength of a potential buyer. Continuous operations may be crucial to the potential purchaser of the institution, as closure may result in the loss of valuable licenses and permits (such as certificates of need) necessary to a buyer that wishes to continue operating the health care facility. A cessation or sale or change of operations may also jeopardize a hospital's tax-exempt restricted funds, including grants, loans, and donations that are restricted to a particular use or dependent on an institution retaining its not-for-profit, tax-exempt status. The value of real property may vary depending on the specific use a potential buyer contemplates for such property.

The value of the real property portion of a hospital's assets may be extremely variable. For example, real property that a purchaser intends to convert from a health care institution into a shopping mall may have a value to the developer that is quite different from a potential purchaser intending to use the property as a not-for-profit rehabilitation center. The value of real property may be vastly enhanced if the potential purchasers include a rapidly expanding private university whose campus abuts the hospital property or a wealthy religious organization that is not profit-motivated and does not require the use or sale of the property to pay for its purchase.

In deciding whether a reorganization is possible, the hospital's assets must be valued and compared with the amount and type of debt. A determination must then be made as to whether a package of cash, property, and liens may be provided by continued operations, accounts receivable collections, and the sale or refinancing of property, which will satisfy creditors and prevent the need for a complete liquidation.

Business Operations

An additional consideration in choosing a financial strategy is the current status of the hospital's business operations. The more problematic the hospital's financial situation, the more difficult it will be to conduct a reorganization effort—inside or outside bankruptcy court. A workout strategy is more appropriate for a health care institution that is currently maintaining stable business operations and that projects the ability to continue stable operations for the foreseeable future. The more unstable the operations, the riskier the attempt to effectuate a workout. If an institution has reached the crisis stage, its only alternative may be to seek the protection of the Bankruptcy Code to prevent the immediate cessation of operations. The further an institution is along the crisis continuum, the more inevitable will be a bankruptcy petition and the more difficult the reorganization effort.

A facility may also experience additional trauma upon the filing of a bankruptcy petition. This trauma may take the form of an immediate cash crisis occasioned by a lender with a revolving credit facility that will not agree to the use of cash which constitutes the lender's collateral or a depository institution with an interest in the debtor's assets, freezing the hospital's bank accounts and preventing access to the cash necessary to continue daily operations. The more control an institution has at the time it begins its reorganization efforts, the more likely those efforts will proceed smoothly. The more chaotic the situation, the more difficult survival will be.

Advantages and Disadvantages of Bankruptcy Filing

A hospital considering filing a bankruptcy petition or attempting an out-of-court workout must be fully aware of the advantages and disadvantages of the formal bankruptcy process. Filing a petition may be the only option if creditor pressure becomes too great and begins to debilitate the hospital's operations. Absent such acute pressure, various considerations will enter into the distressed hospital's decision regarding how to proceed.

Advantages

Filing a bankruptcy petition can be advantageous to the distressed hospital in a number of ways. Benefits include evoking automatic stay and enabling the hospital to reject certain leases or contracts.

Automatic Stay

Upon the filing of a bankruptcy petition, an automatic stay arises by operation of law under Section 362 of the Bankruptcy Code, preventing all entities from commencing or continuing the enforcement of any action against the debtor and its property. Evoking the automatic stay by filing a bankruptcy petition can provide a debtor with the breathing room it needs in the short term to attempt a reorganization or other orderly financial resolution. The automatic stay can be a great help to a troubled hospital, but may be lifted with regard to a particular creditor under certain circumstances.

Right to Reject Certain Leases and Contracts

Another bankruptcy tool offering protection to a troubled hospital seeking to reorganize is found in Section 365 of the Bankruptcy Code. This section of the Code provides a debtor the opportunity to pick and choose among its executory contracts and unexpired leases, by either assuming or rejecting them. The time allowed a debtor to decide whether to assume or reject such a contract or lease differs, depending on the type of bankruptcy petition filed and the type of contract or lease involved. The net result of these provisions, however, is that the filing of a bankruptcy petition can provide the debtor with additional time to make decisions regarding which contracts and leases are necessary to support the business operation contemplated through the reorganization process and which contracts or leases are unnecessary and should be discarded. Upon a proper rejection of a contract or lease under Section 365, any damages due pursuant to such rejection are treated as a prepetition claim along with other unsecured claims in the bankruptcy proceeding.

Disadvantages

Although filing a bankruptcy petition can create certain advantages for the distressed hospital, the action can also result in some serious disadvantages. Creditors already alienated by the hospital's inability to pay its debts will be further alienated by the protections provided by a bankruptcy petition. Furthermore, the bankruptcy procedure itself will place additional stress on the hospital in terms of both tasks to be performed and the money required to perform them.

Creditor Alienation

The general inability to pay debts as they become due, which precedes many bankruptcy filings, can certainly create alienation or animosity among creditors. The additional blow of filing a bankruptcy petition and thereby obtaining the protections discussed in this chapter can cause additional creditor alienation. Although the cooperation of creditors is essential to any out-of-court workout, the lack of such cooperation can also make formal reorganization efforts much more difficult. Where filing a petition is a choice rather than a necessity, it is important to assess creditor attitudes and potential responses to the filing. It may be helpful to initiate contact with certain key creditors, such as secured lenders, if it is believed that this might assist in creating alliances that will promote a cooperative effort and in avoiding hostility that may hamper the reorganization attempt subsequent to the filing.

Bankruptcy Burdens

Reorganizations inside or outside bankruptcy court create additional work and stress for the hospital attempting the reorganization. Therefore, the duration of the reorganization effort can affect its success. The filing of a bankruptcy petition brings with it an additional set of requirements and obligations with which the hospital must contend. The Bankruptcy Code requires a debtor to complete a number of tasks according to specific procedures and within specific time periods.

A debtor that files a bankruptcy petition, referred to in the Bankruptcy Code as the *debtor-in-possession,* must promptly prepare and file a Statement of Financial Affairs and Schedules of Assets and Liabilities in the format required by the court.[1] A debtor-in-possession must also prepare and file monthly operating reports in the prescribed forms, by the fifteenth day of each month of operations subsequent to the filing. To maintain maximum control over its future operations, the debtor-in-possession must also file a plan of reorganization within the exclusive period of time specified by the Bankruptcy Code, or run the risk of having a creditor file its own plan, which may produce an outcome that is inconsistent with the goals of the hospital.

Beyond the specific tasks imposed by the Bankruptcy Code, a debtor that has entered the bankruptcy process must confer with and respond to creditors and the court in numerous additional circumstances. A debtor-in-possession is required to give appropriate notice to creditors and obtain the court's approval of transactions for which creditor consent or court approval would not have been necessary prior to the filing. Such notification and approval is required for postpetition financing and certain transactions that are considered to be outside the ordinary course of the hospital's business.

Along with the protection afforded a hospital by filing a bankruptcy petition comes the obligation of responding to all creditor motions and complaints filed with the court and to all court orders. Although the automatic stay precludes the continuation of ongoing litigation against the debtor with regard to prepetition claims, the filing of a petition provides creditors with a new forum—the bankruptcy court—and another set of tools with which to pursue or protect their interests or claims against the debtor. A prime example of an additional avenue of attack provided by the Bankruptcy Code is the ability of a creditor to file a motion to appoint a trustee in a Chapter 11 case or a motion to convert such a case to a Chapter 7 liquidation case. A creditor pursuing such tactics must present sufficient evidence to prevail on the merits of such an attack but, by filing one of these motions, can require the debtor to defend its right to control an orderly reorganization and can, if successful, either remove the debtor's control over its reorganization or force a liquidation.

The additional tasks and pressures of a bankruptcy case will require a significant deployment of human resources, including the hospital's personnel, its legal counsel, and other qualified professionals, such as accountants. These additional resources create additional expense, which must be paid by the hospital. In a case where groups of creditors form committees, such as an unsecured creditors' committee or a bondholders' committee, legal counsel and other professional advice for such committees will also be funded by the debtor institution, if approved and allowed by the Bankruptcy Court. Although the situation, and thus the amount, can vary greatly from case to case, the additional cost of the administration and professional services necessary to support a formal bankruptcy proceeding can be exorbitant.

Bankruptcy

In conjunction with a hospital's determination to file a bankruptcy petition, it must also decide whether to file under Chapter 7 (liquidation only) or Chapter 11 (reorganization or liquidation) of the Bankruptcy Code. If reorganization is the aim, the hospital must file a Chapter 11 petition. If a liquidation is planned, either a Chapter 7 or a Chapter 11 petition could be filed, and the choice would depend on the amount of control desired, the level of resources and time to be committed, and the specific needs and goals of the hospital.

Liquidation

When a hospital decides to liquidate, it typically files a bankruptcy petition under Chapter 7 of the Bankruptcy Code and a Chapter 7 trustee is appointed to oversee the liquidation process. In addition, the hospital must begin the task of addressing a number of other issues associated with closure, such as notification of state and federal agencies and the orderly transfer of patients to other area providers.

Chapter 7 Trustee

Unlike a Chapter 11 petition, a Chapter 7 petition prompts the automatic appointment of a trustee by the Office of the United States Trustee. A Chapter 7 trustee takes control of the debtor and its assets, thus relieving the hospital and its administrators of these tasks. Although the trustee basically steps into the shoes of the prior hospital owners, directors, and managers, he or she owes a fiduciary duty to the creditors of the institution. Although a debtor is entitled to its own legal representation in a Chapter 7 proceeding, the role of the debtor and its legal counsel in a Chapter 7 case is quite minimal, consisting mainly of the fulfillment of certain administrative and reporting tasks. Under certain circumstances a debtor can conduct a liquidation in the context of a Chapter 11 proceeding, but this approach will not be specifically addressed in this chapter.

Hospital Closure Issues

In addition to the general bankruptcy issues common to any liquidation case, there are a number of important considerations that are specific to the liquidation of a health care facility. A hospital or other health care institution cannot simply close its doors when the financial strain leaves no alternative. The life-sustaining services of a medical facility cannot be withdrawn from its patients and the community at large without attending to numerous legal and ethical considerations. The closure and liquidation of a hospital require a heightened degree of planning and coordination not always necessary in the case of other commercial businesses. Extra time and consideration must be given to the closure of a health care facility if it is to be accomplished without risk or injury to the hospital, its patients, and the local community.

The closure of all or a portion of a medical facility requires prompt and adequate notice, which may include obtaining a state permit or, at a minimum, notifying the applicable state licensing and health planning agencies. State health planning agencies may also require the preparation of a closing plan and the opportunity to review and approve the proposed closure. Whether legally mandated or not, preparing a closing plan is advisable because it provides the framework for an orderly closing. A closing plan should address all the necessary legal and practical issues involved in a proper hospital closure.

In addition to notifying state public health agencies, the hospital should notify all federal, state, and local agencies responsible for the reimbursement, licensure, operation, and regulation of all its various services and facilities.

The notification of nongovernmental agencies may also be required in the case of closure, partial closure, or sale of a health care facility. The hospital may need to provide notice of its closure to certain accreditation agencies and other professional associations. The hospital should be aware of notice requirements contained in plant closure laws and should review its various contracts and agreements, including collective bargaining agreements, and attempt to comply with notice requirements these agreements may contain regarding a closure or a change in operations. In addition, the hospital considering closure should take care to ensure continuous professional liability insurance coverage during and after a closure or sale.

In the sale of all or a portion of a hospital to a buyer wishing to continue the facility's operations, the hospital's licenses and certificates of need (CONs) may be its most valuable assets. If financial or other constraints demand the closure of a facility before a proposed sale can be completed, the hospital may seek the suspension of its licenses and CONs. If successful, this approach may preserve the licenses and certificates for sale to the buyers, who, depending on the circumstances of a particular community, might be unable to obtain new ones.

In addition to the applicable licensing and regulatory agencies, early notification of other governmental and public service agencies is necessary for a responsible closure or reduction of operations. Providers of health care, emergency, public, or social services, including police and fire departments, ambulance companies, and other hospitals and health and welfare providers in the area, should be promptly notified of the closure of a hospital or its emergency department (ED). Alternative health care facilities must be contacted and the orderly transfer of patients arranged. The date of the anticipated closure should be determined and widely publicized well in advance of the termination of emergency services. Admissions and ED services should be terminated as far in advance of the closure of a facility as possible, in an effort to reduce the risk that a severely injured patient will enter the hospital and remain in a condition that medically prohibits his or her transfer on the anticipated closure date.

Hospital employees are crucial to the safe and effective performance of the patient care and transfer tasks necessary during the closure period. They should be informed of the anticipated closure as early as possible and kept abreast of developments and information. Providing assistance with job placement and referral services may aid employees in maintaining the commitment necessary for an orderly closure.

In addition to the necessary health care personnel, a reduced team of administrators, record keepers, and other professionals will need to complete tasks such as collecting accounts receivable, administering employee benefit plans, complying with environmental laws and regulations, and completing the remaining accounting and record-keeping functions. The hospital must provide for the careful transfer and storage of medical and financial records to ensure compliance with confidentiality requirements and Medicare and state reimbursement program requirements, and to ensure appropriate access by patients and their physicians.

Reorganization under Chapter 11

Whether its goal is liquidation or reorganization, a Chapter 11 case requires the consideration of a number of issues not involved in a Chapter 7 case. The following sections provide an overview of the nature and complexity of many of the issues the hospital filing for bankruptcy under Chapter 11 must address.

Debtor-in-Possession Status

In a Chapter 11 case, a trustee is not automatically appointed and the debtor-in-possession and its administrators and board members maintain control of the hospital's assets and business operations. The debtor's retention of counsel must be approved by the bankruptcy court at the commencement of the case, and the debtor's counsel will perform an active function in the bankruptcy process. In addition to selecting and having its choice of counsel approved, the hospital, through its board of directors, should designate one or more individuals to be responsible for making the day-to-day decisions necessary to continue hospital operations. The choice of those in control of this administrative function can be crucial to a successful outcome. For example, in the case of diverging agendas, having more than one individual in charge can create disagreement that may weaken or at least retard the progress of the reorganization.

Public Perception

Although filing a bankruptcy petition does not invoke the stigma present in prior decades, a bankruptcy filing can raise concerns in the minds of creditors, patients, and admitting physicians. The concerns raised by a bankruptcy filing can impede the reorganization process and should be minimized. Creditors may have an incentive to continue their dealings with a hospital in bankruptcy if they believe that the potential for collecting on the debt owed them is greater if the hospital continues operation than if it closes its doors. Promoting the reorganization effort through positive public relations can prevent the abandonment of the facility by creditors who may be necessary providers of goods and services, and may prevent those creditors from creating additional obstacles for the reorganizing hospital. Additionally, incoming patients may wish to avoid a health care facility if they perceive it to be beset with financial and related problems that could compromise the health care services they need. More important, physicians who are concerned about the viability of a hospital, and who do not have a financial or personal investment in the facility, may be more reluctant to admit their patients there. Thus, the public relations efforts of a hospital involved in a Chapter 11 case should be aimed at improving its relationships with its creditors, who are the source of its supplies, and with the medical community and the public, who are the source of its income.

Trustee in Chapter 11

Although a trustee is not automatically appointed following the filing of a Chapter 11 petition, Section 1104 of the Bankruptcy Code provides that a trustee may be appointed for cause such as fraud, dishonesty, and incompetence (occurring either pre- or postpetition) or if such appointment is in the interest of creditors, equity security holders, and other interests of the estate. Thus, maintaining the control allowed in Chapter 11 by continuing as a debtor-in-possession may depend on the hospital's ability to avoid the concerns of interested parties who might prompt a request for, and the appointment of, a trustee. Developing public relations that promote creditor cooperation and avoid a request for a trustee is time and effort well spent.

Cash Collateral and Postpetition Financing

Cash flow following the filing of the Chapter 11 petition can be even more constricted than prior to the filing. Pursuant to Section 363 of the Bankruptcy Code, the trustee or debtor-in-possession may not use cash collateral if the entities with an interest in cash collateral perceive that they will suffer a "loss" through such use and therefore object.[2] Cash collateral commonly becomes an issue in a case if the hospital has a revolving credit arrangement with a lending institution that has a blanket lien on virtually all the hospital's assets. In such a situation, counsel for the hospital will move at the commencement of the bankruptcy case for authority to use cash collateral and will likely attempt to obtain the agreement of the lender and other interested parties. If such consent is withheld, the hospital may have to proceed with a hearing and ask the court to order the use of cash collateral over creditor objections.

The debtor hospital may be required to provide a creditor with assurances of "adequate protection" of its interest in cash collateral before being granted the use of cash collateral. Adequate protection as defined in Section 361 of the Bankruptcy Code requires the debtor to provide a creditor with cash payments or a continuing lien on assets and at least a break-even operation that keeps the debtor's level of assets constant and prevents a deterioration in the creditor's position.

It is also possible for the hospital to obtain additional financing after filing a Chapter 11 petition. Section 364 of the Bankruptcy Code provides that the court may allow a debtor-in-possession to obtain unsecured credit or incur unsecured debt out of the ordinary course of its business. Such debt will be allowed as an administrative expense entitled to priority status in the distribution of the estate's assets. The court can also authorize the hospital to obtain credit or incur debt with a priority status superior to all other administrative expenses or a debt that is secured by a lien on unencumbered property or a junior lien on encumbered property. Under certain circumstances the court, under this section of the Bankruptcy Code, can even allow the debtor to obtain credit or incur debt by granting a lien on encumbered property that is equal or senior to the lien already existing on the property. However, this option is available to a debtor-in-possession only if it cannot obtain credit otherwise and if the prior lien holder's interest is adequately protected. The practical consequences of these rights are that, if there is equity (value in excess of existing indebtedness) in the current assets of the debtor or if the debtor can demonstrate that its future operations will generate revenue in excess of future expenses, new credit may be obtainable. The new credit can be collateralized by this perceived future "profit" or equity, thereby providing a resource to the debtor-in-possession to assist in the reorganization effort.

Automatic Stay Benefits

As noted earlier in this chapter, upon the filing of a Chapter 11 petition, all proceedings against the hospital and its property are automatically stayed by the provisions of Section 362 of the Bankruptcy Code. The automatic stay is a helpful buffer against ongoing litigation and against the debt collection efforts of unsecured creditors and secured creditors alike. The stay can assist the hospital in limiting the battlefields and in focusing its attention on the reorganization effort.

Although the stay is very broad and provides a great deal of protection, it is not without its limitations. Upon the request of a party in interest, the stay may be modified or terminated for cause, including the lack of adequate protection of the interest of the party in certain property or the debtor's lack of equity in property that is not necessary to an effective reorganization. Section 362 also contains a list of activities that are not subject to the stay. This list includes, without limitation, a criminal proceeding, the enforcement of a police or regulatory power by a governmental unit, and an action by an accrediting agency or state licensing body regarding the accreditation status or licensure of the debtor as an educational institution.

Utility Service

Maintaining the necessary flow of goods and services to a debtor after it has filed for bankruptcy is crucial to the reorganization effort. If particular vendors and service providers refuse to continue their business with a Chapter 11 debtor, their role in the operations can be replaced in the marketplace in most cases. However, there is usually no substitute for electric, gas, and telephone companies. Section 366 of the Bankruptcy Code protects the debtor from the discontinuance of such utility service, but not without providing extra protection for the utility. Under this section of the Code, a utility is prohibited from altering, refusing, or discontinuing service or from discriminating against the debtor due to the commencement of the case. However, this section further provides that the utility may alter, refuse, or discontinue service if the debtor, within 20 days after the commencement of the case, does not furnish adequate assurance of future payment in the form of a deposit or other security for future services.

Counsel for a debtor that has filed for Chapter 11 protection generally contacts the utility providers immediately after the commencement of the case and procures their written commitment to provide future services, negotiating deposit amounts as required by the utilities. The court, if requested, may order a reasonable modification of the deposit or security provided to the utility. Although the continuance of utility service such as electricity and gas could be crucial to any company, this is a much more serious matter in a hospital setting, where the lives and health of the hospital's patients are directly dependent on uninterrupted utility service.

Employee Issues

As important as it is to guard against the alienation of creditors and the public during a reorganization process, preventing the alienation of the employees of a debtor-in-possession is equally important. In the case of a hospital filing for bankruptcy protection, disruption of employee services could be fatal to the reorganization effort. Thus, in a hospital setting efforts to maintain employee morale must be a priority in the reorganization scheme, especially where employees such as nurses may be difficult to replace due to their skill level or their shortage in the marketplace.

Promoting employee cooperation should begin before filing a petition and must continue after the filing. Although the hospital may not wish to inform its employees of its intent to file for bankruptcy protection prior to the actual filing, financial troubles rarely occur overnight and employees may suspect problems well before the filing. Meetings or other communications should be designed to ensure employees that the hospital's administrators are aware of the financial constraints facing the hospital and are taking appropriate measures to solve those difficulties. Immediately after the filing of a petition, it is advisable to hold a face-to-face meeting, if possible, with hospital employees so that they learn of the bankruptcy filing from the hospital administration and so that their concerns and questions may be addressed at the outset. It is important that the communications to the employees be honest as well as uplifting, and it is inadvisable to make promises that cannot be met.

In an effort to reduce employee alienation during a Chapter 11 proceeding, potential payroll problems can be avoided by prepetition planning or by seeking postpetition relief from the bankruptcy court. Cash flow restrictions following the filing of a Chapter 11 petition may interrupt the regular flow of employee compensation. Difficulty can arise when payroll checks are issued before the petition, but are not honored afterward due to the freezing of depository accounts or the inability to obtain immediate use of cash collateral. This problem may be lessened by filing the petition immediately after a payroll has been made and the payroll checks have been cashed, though there likely will be a few straggling checks that are not cashed promptly.

If the situation is such that a hospital cannot perform the prepetition planning necessary to ensure continuous payment of employees, the debtor's counsel may seek an order from the court after the filing of the bankruptcy petition allowing the immediate payment of employee claims for prepetition wages, salaries, or commissions. This request would be made pursuant to Section 507 of the Bankruptcy Code, which designates such claims earned by an employee within 90 days before the filing as priority claims up to a $2,000 limit per employee. If the amount earned by any employee in any one pay period does not exceed the $2,000 limitation, the court may allow the immediate payment of these claims in order to ensure employee commitment. The payment of amounts that exceed the $2,000 limit may be sought, but will be more difficult to obtain. The ability to obtain this relief in a particular case may be a function of the judge before whom the case is pending, as well as the reactions of key creditors.

Insurance

The maintenance of adequate insurance is important for any debtor-in-possession operating under the protection of the bankruptcy court. The lack of insurance or inadequate insurance can provide the "cause" necessary under several sections of the Bankruptcy Code for the removal or modification of protections or benefits otherwise afforded a debtor-in-possession and its property.

As with any debtor, the types of insurance that must be maintained include the following: casualty insurance covering losses for all types of damage to property caused by such things as fire, water, wind, and theft; general liability insurance to cover injury to persons incurred while on the hospital premises; and workers' compensation insurance. The level of insurance maintained must provide adequate coverage and comply with all requirements imposed by law or by contract with a party holding an interest in the debtor's property.

In addition to the insurance coverage just noted, a hospital or other health care facility also requires the uninterrupted maintenance of professional liability insurance if the hospital is to continue operations. Although professional liability insurance can be costly, its absence may prove to be much more costly. Although self-insuring all or a portion of a hospital's malpractice insurance is not uncommon, there is a limit to the amount of self-insurance that is accepted in the industry or that will be tolerated by creditors in a bankruptcy. Self-insuring a portion of a hospital's malpractice insurance requires setting aside a large sum of money in a trust account specifically designated as a self-insurance fund. The cash necessary to provide adequate self-insurance for even a portion of the hospital's malpractice liability may be prohibitive. If the health care institution is unable to obtain adequate insurance from a commercial insurer or a combination of an insurer and a self-insurance fund, the hospital's administrators should immediately make the only prudent decision available to them and prepare to close the health care facility as quickly as possible. Operating a hospital or other health care institution without adequate insurance creates an enormous degree of risk to both the hospital and its creditors.

Executory Contracts and Unexpired Leases: Assumption or Rejection

Section 365 of the Bankruptcy Code provides certain time periods within which a Chapter 11 debtor may assume or reject executory contracts and unexpired leases. This section of the Bankruptcy Code allows the debtor the time necessary to determine which contracts and leases it will need to assume in order to continue the operations that it contemplates will survive the reorganization and to reject those that will not be necessary to the hospital facility as it emerges from the bankruptcy process.

This Code section applies to unexpired leases and executory contracts. Any true lease whose term is unexpired as of the date the petition is filed qualifies as an unexpired lease under Section 365. In analyzing documents with regard to the application of this section, a debtor and its counsel may find certain transactions that appear to be leases but that are actually financing transactions. An arrangement in which a financing transaction is disguised as a lease will be subject to the automatic stay and the adequate protection requirements imposed pursuant to Section 362, rather than the provisions of Section 365. Factors that may be taken as evidence that a purported lease is not a true lease include: (1) "lease" payments for the entire length of the term totaling approximately the value of the property leased, and (2) the "lease" containing an option or requirement that the lessee purchase the subject property at the end of the lease term for nominal consideration.

The term *executory contract* "generally includes contracts on which performance remains due to some extent on both sides."[3] The Bankruptcy Code further limits Section 365 by prohibiting the assumption or assignment of certain types of executory contracts such as those involving a loan or other debt financing or financial accommodation for the benefit of the debtor or a contract regarding the issuance of a security of the debtor.

In a Chapter 11 proceeding, Section 365 allows the hospital to assume or reject an executory contract or unexpired lease of residential real property or of personal property at any time before the confirmation of a plan of reorganization. Upon the request of a party to a specific contract or lease, the court may set a date by which the debtor hospital must assume or reject such a contract or lease. With respect to an unexpired lease of *nonresidential* real property under which the hospital is a lessee, the Code allows only a 60-day period for the debtor to assume or reject the lease. The period may be extended by the court for cause if the hospital requests such an extension prior to the expiration of the initial 60 days.

By using the provisions of Section 365 of the Bankruptcy Code, the hospital operating as a debtor-in-possession is afforded the time necessary to decide, in the context of preparing its plan of reorganization, whether to assume or reject its executory contracts and unexpired leases. Pursuant to Section 365, the rejection of an executory contract or unexpired lease constitutes a prepetition breach of such contract or lease, and the damages flowing from such a breach will be deemed to be a prepetition claim. However, if a contract or lease is initially assumed and thereafter breached, the claim for damages flowing from such a breach is a postpetition claim entitled to administrative priority. Thus, assumption followed by rejection elevates a claim for damages pursuant to such rejection to a higher priority for payment, and adds additional expense to maintaining the debtor's estate. Therefore, although preconfirmation assumption may be encouraged by a particular creditor, the hospital should avoid assuming contracts or leases prior to confirmation of a plan of reorganization, if possible.

Arguing that the potential harm to creditors from premature assumption is outweighed by any inconvenience to a particular creditor should persuade most courts to grant the necessary extensions of time to assume or reject. However, if a decision on assumption or rejection is forced upon a hospital, business considerations must govern the choice.

If the hospital intends to assume a particular contract or lease in which there has been a default, Section 365 requires that the hospital cure all defaults or provide adequate assurance that all defaults will be promptly cured, and provide adequate assurance of future performance under the contract or lease. In addition to determining relative priorities of claims for damages pursuant to contractual breaches by a debtor, the Bankruptcy Code places limitations on certain damage claims. Included in these limitations are allowable damage claims resulting from the termination of a lease of real property or an employment contract.

Some of the hospital's contracts and leases will be required for the continuing operation and others may be eliminated as they become unnecessary for the hospital to continue in its reorganized form. Executory contracts that are likely to play prominently in the reorganization efforts of any health care facility include third-party payer agreements, such as Blue Cross/Blue Shield, managed care contracts, and Medicare and Medicaid provider agreements. Although it is clear that any hospital will need to continue its participation in the Medicare/Medicaid program, there may be a great deal of money allegedly owed the government. This may present an obstacle to the assumption of these agreements, as the outstanding amounts generally must be cured under Section 365 prior to the assumption of the agreements. However, in the case of Medicare/Medicaid, due to the nature of the ongoing reimbursement system, determining exactly what the hospital owes the government and what the government in turn owes the hospital at any point in time will probably prove to be an elusive task. The government may attempt to pressure the hospital to assume the provider agreements, and the hospital will have to negotiate with the government to verify alleged outstanding amounts and propose a repayment schedule that both parties can live with. This illustrates that the cure of defaults under an executory contract or unexpired lease may not have to be an immediate lump-sum payment, but may be made over time if acceptable to the parties or ordered by the court.

If a hospital is not required to assume its Medicare or Medicaid provider agreement but continues to operate under these agreements postpetition, the government may attempt to obtain repayment of prepetition overpayments in exchange for postpetition reimbursement. In a recent case decided by the United States Court of Appeals for the Third Circuit, the Court held that (1) postpetition provision of Medicare services did not constitute assumption and, therefore, did not compel the cure of outstanding prepetition debt; (2) the government violated the automatic stay by withholding postpetition payments in an effort to recover prepetition overpayments; and (3) the common-law "recoupment" doctrine did not allow the government to offset prepetition overpayments and postpetition payments. This decision may be invoked to allow a hospital to continue its participation in the Medicare/Medicaid program postpetition without being immediately forced to assume its provider agreements and cure its prepetition obligations.

A hospital contemplating a sale of the facility should consider whether it might be eligible for Medicare reimbursement for a portion of the loss it may incur on such a sale. If the reorganization strategy is to sell the facility, the hospital should have the potential Medicare reimbursement for loss on the sale calculated by someone experienced in this area and should obtain the professional advice necessary to ensure that it will qualify for the reimbursement.

Adjusting and Achieving the Goals

Following the filing of a Chapter 11 petition and the stabilization of operations, the focus and energy of the hospital turn toward the reorganization process. The hospital and its administrators must reevaluate the goals formulated in making the initial determination of whether to file a bankruptcy petition and what sort of petition to file. These goals must be refined and in some respects reformulated to suit the evolving circumstances of the health care facility and to guide the facility toward its ultimate restructuring.

Depending on its particular situation, a hospital's reorganization effort may contemplate continuing all operations and services existing prior to the filing of the Chapter 11 petition or discontinuing certain operations, services, or facilities that may be the source of the institution's financial problems. A hospital may also determine that part of its reorganization efforts will focus on the sale of certain assets that, if encumbered, may be used to pay off secured creditors and, if unencumbered, may produce the capital necessary to revitalize the facility's operations. Another method of producing capital may be to enter into a sale-lease-back transaction, whereby the hospital may sell property to another entity that will, in turn, lease the property back to the hospital. This type of transaction can produce capital when the hospital has equity in the property that can be liquidated to provide additional funding, without having to give up the use of the property. Another option that may be appropriate is the refinancing of a loan whose interest and penalty payments may be reduced by procuring a different lender and renegotiating the terms of the loan.

Decisions regarding the sale of a hospital or the change in or discontinuation of particular services must include the consideration of not only economic, but also other factors unique to the health care field. These considerations include the maintenance of the licenses, loans, grants, or donations necessary to continued operations. If a licensed hospital changes or cuts certain services, its remaining services must satisfy its licensing requirements. If the restructuring cuts programs essential to its hospital license, the facility might maintain the license by providing the essential services through an independent contractor. If the hospital license cannot be salvaged, the facility might consider continuing its remaining operations pursuant to alternative health care licenses, such as those required for nursing homes or rehabilitation centers.

A change or cutback in services may constitute a default on a hospital's agreements, such as its loan documents. These agreements should be carefully reviewed, and, if a problem exists, the hospital should discuss the changes with its lenders and attempt to renegotiate the documentation to allow for the reorganization strategy. An alteration in hospital services may also create problems with regard to the facility's ability to maintain governmental and charitable loans, grants, and donations (including the Medicare/Medicaid reimbursement program). The hospital considering a service reduction or change should carefully review these additional sources of capital and revenue to identify and attempt to minimize any problems encountered that might reduce the facility's funding. As the strategies become more specific, the hospital and its counsel will turn to various tools provided by the Bankruptcy Code to implement those strategies in achieving its goals.

Preferences and Fraudulent Conveyances

An additional potential source of income for funding a hospital's plan of reorganization may be found in the sections of the Bankruptcy Code that allow a debtor-in-possession to avoid certain prepetition transfers that constitute preferences or fraudulent conveyances and to recover the property or cash transferred. A prepetition transfer of a debtor's interest in property may be avoided under Section 547 of the Bankruptcy Code if the transfer (1) was for the benefit of a creditor; (2) was on account of a debt owed prior to the transfer; (3) was made while the debtor was insolvent; (4) was made on or within 90 days prior to the filing of the petition (or made between 90 days and 1 year prior to the filing if the transfer was to an insider); or (5) the transfer enabled the creditor to receive more than it would if the case were under Chapter 7, the transfer had not been made, and the creditor received payment according to the Bankruptcy Code. There are also a number of points a creditor may assert in defense of preference allegations. The preference provisions of the Bankruptcy Code are designed to prevent a debtor from preferring certain of its creditors by paying debts owed to them and not paying others just prior to filing its Chapter 11 petition.

Under Section 548 of the Bankruptcy Code, a hospital may also avoid the transfer of an interest in property or may avoid an obligation it incurred within one year before the date of the filing of the petition, provided that the hospital (1) actually intended to hinder, delay, or defraud its creditors; or (2) received less than a reasonably equivalent value in exchange for such transfer or obligation and was insolvent at the time of the transfer, was rendered insolvent thereby, or was left with unreasonably small capital.

Plan of Reorganization

The final major step in the reorganization process in a Chapter 11 case is the negotiation, preparation, and confirmation of a plan of reorganization. The plan of reorganization is the documentation of the various strategies the hospital intends to utilize, woven together to create a new contract between the hospital and its creditors. The plan must contain a classification of the claims of creditors and interests of equity holders (if any), and provide for the treatment thereof, including the means by which the claims and interests will be satisfied, whether in whole or in part. In conjunction with the plan, the hospital must prepare a disclosure statement that provides a history of the hospital, a summary of the plan of reorganization, and information intended to assist creditors in determining what type and percentage of repayment they can expect pursuant to the terms of the plan and in assessing the plan's feasibility. In a nutshell, the plan of reorganization and disclosure statement indicate specifically what the hospital is offering the creditors in exchange for their acceptance of the plan and an explanation of the means by which the hospital will obtain the cash or other assets or benefits that it proposes to provide to creditors.

The preparation, filing, and confirmation of a plan of reorganization is usually the culmination of a formal bankruptcy process, including many of the elements discussed in this chapter. Thus, although a bankruptcy filing can provide protection to a debtor, it also adds a layer of complexity that generally requires additional time, effort, and expense. One alternative may be to shortcut the bankruptcy process by preparing a prepackaged plan, drafted and filed simultaneously with the petition. The advantage of this approach is that the length of the process may be greatly reduced, thus minimizing the strain on the debtor's financial and other resources. This may be an option if the financial situation of the hospital allows the time for such prefiling preparation. However, due to the creditor and financial pressures that precipitate most filings, this is not always a feasible alternative. After the plan has been filed and the disclosure statement has been approved by the court, the creditors will be given ballots with which they may vote to accept or reject the plan, and a hearing will be held regarding objections to the plan and whether it will be confirmed. For confirmation, a plan of reorganization must be accepted by a vote of two-thirds in dollar amount and a majority in number of the voting members of each class of impaired creditors.[4] A plan that does not obtain the accepting votes necessary to satisfy these requirements may still be confirmed if it fulfills the complex "cram-down" provisions of Section 1129 of the Bankruptcy Code. Upon the confirmation of its plan, the hospital receives a discharge of all claims listed in its schedules of assets and liabilities and all claims of those creditors who received proper notice of the bankruptcy proceedings. Following the confirmation, the hospital continues to operate and perform pursuant to the plan's provisions, and remains subject to such rights and remedies of creditors as the plan and applicable law provide.

Workouts

A workout, which is attempted without the formal structure and protection afforded by the Bankruptcy Code, offers both advantages and disadvantages. However, an attempted workout is doomed to fail unless the debtor and its creditors can work together to arrive at a solution that is acceptable to all parties.

Control over the Reorganization

Although the constraints of court approval, reporting, and official creditor involvement imposed by the Bankruptcy Code do not exist in a workout situation, the absence of the protective mechanisms provided by the Bankruptcy Code can make it much more difficult to maintain control over the reorganization effort. With no automatic stay of creditor actions, a hospital attempting a workout will have to either persuade creditors to delay enforcement actions or continue to defend (raising both cost and success issues) against such actions while attempting the workout. Without the right (provided by the Bankruptcy Code) to reject unnecessary executory contracts or unexpired leases, there will be no statutory limitation on damages or formulaic treatment of claims. Because of the absence of the cram-down provisions found in the Bankruptcy Code, a hospital pursuing a workout strategy cannot force recalcitrant or unreasonable creditors to accept treatment over their objection. Further, there is no legal mechanism for resolving even reasonable disagreements over proposed restructuring terms.

Thus, an effective workout requires the cooperation of all creditors. A workout is likely to take less time than a formal bankruptcy case, because numerous trips to court to obtain "approval" and the additional administrative tasks required by the Bankruptcy Code are avoided. However, the debtor's limited ability to maintain creditor cooperation, absent court protection, will generally require a quicker resolution. Although there are costs associated with a workout effort, including professional fees for lawyers and accountants, these costs will almost certainly be less than those likely to be incurred in a Chapter 11 case.

Flexibility to Be Creative

One of the primary benefits of choosing a workout over a formal bankruptcy is the lack of constraints, such as the statutory requirements for confirmation of a plan, imposed on the type of financial solution that will be acceptable. The corresponding detriment is that without the assistance of the bankruptcy court, a restructuring plan cannot be thrust on a creditor body that opposes it (the cram-down rights provided under the Bankruptcy Code have no counterpart in a workout). Thus, although a workout may provide more room for creativity, the parameters of the proposed solution are defined by what will be acceptable to the creditors. Conversely, a transaction structure that might not be "legally" acceptable to a bankruptcy court might prove to be acceptable to creditors and become a workable solution in a workout setting.

Discharge from Obligations

A workout does not culminate in a legal discharge, as in a bankruptcy proceeding. At the end of a workout process, the debtor is left with the commitments and obligations of the creditors with whom agreements have been reached, but it has no global emancipation (discharge) from their claims. Accordingly, any creditor with whom agreement is not reached is free to continue to pursue all of its rights and remedies. Such a situation can disrupt, or even destroy, the benefit of a workout and may ultimately force the hospital to resort to the formality of the Bankruptcy Code in order to make the results stick.

Conclusion

A formal bankruptcy filing provides numerous protections and tools for achieving a distressed hospital's contemplated financial liquidation or restructuring. Such a filing can temporarily stay enforcement of creditor claims and provide a method of limiting and treating claims, such as malpractice claims, pursuant to a plan of reorganization. But filing a petition for bankruptcy also poses additional risks, burdens, and expenses that should be weighed carefully. The transfer or liquidation and closure of a health care facility requires close attention to a host of considerations in order to ensure an orderly and responsible shutdown and transfer of patients.

A reorganization under Chapter 11, though often a lengthy and difficult endeavor, may provide the best means available to an institution that desires to maintain control of its operations and achieve a restructuring that will allow those operations to continue. An out-of-court workout may be an appropriate vehicle for effecting a financial transformation in a setting where creditor cooperation is available and where the protections and structure of a formal bankruptcy process are not required. The successful formulation and execution of any of the strategies discussed in this chapter will depend on obtaining the administrative, legal, and professional expertise necessary to implement the strategy, while maintaining an acceptable level of control over the process through creditor cooperation—whether forced or voluntary—and through employee and community support.

Notes and References

1. The term *debtor-in-possession* refers to a debtor which has filed a bankruptcy petition under Chapter 11 of the Bankruptcy Code and which remains in possession and control of its assets and its operations. A debtor is a debtor-in-possession in a Chapter 11 case in which no trustee has been appointed and the debtor-in-possession possess all of the rights and duties of a trustee under Sections 1106, 1107, and 1108 of the Bankruptcy Code.
2. Cash collateral under this section of the Bankruptcy Code includes cash, negotiable instruments, documents of title, securities, deposit accounts, or other cash equivalents in which the debtor's estate and any other entity have an interest.
3. King, L. P. *Collier on Bankruptcy.* Vol. 2, 15th ed. New York City: Matthew Bender & Co., Inc., 1991, pp. 365–415.
4. A creditor is "impaired" if the legal, equitable, or contractual rights attaching to its claims or interests are modified, other than by curing defaults and reinstating maturities or by cash payment in full.

Chapter 11

Case Study: Turning Around a Multihospital System

Roger Green and Tim Hanson

HealthEast is a multihospital system based in St. Paul, Minnesota. Its story is a textbook example of how to achieve a successful organizational turnaround by working hard to identify problems and then answering the call to action.

Merging to Secure the Financial Future

HealthEast was created out of a desire to turn around the fates of a diverse collection of East Metropolitan area hospitals. The hospital environment in the Twin Cities was becoming increasingly hostile in the mid-1980s. Although St. Paul and Minneapolis share a Mississippi River border spanned by many bridges, residents seldom crossed the river for health care services. In the greater St. Paul area alone, 11 different hospitals—some within walking distance of each other—were competing for payers, patients, and the allegiances of the same 1,000-plus physicians. Technology wars were waged as each hospital tried to duplicate the comprehensive, state-of-the-art services demanded by physicians and furnished by other hospitals. Competition for health maintenance organization (HMO) contracts was fierce, with payers leveraging one hospital against the other with threats of "taking their patients down the street." Hospital occupancy levels were low—under 40 percent for the eight St. Paul hospitals that would join together in 1986 to form HealthEast, a provider network aimed at reducing expenses and negotiating more favorable contracts with HMOs.

The merger involved eight hospitals from five hospital systems with three different religious backgrounds: Baptist, Catholic, and Lutheran. Shared values were identified, and preservation of these values became a goal of the merger. Each of the founding organizations had its own varied menu of diversified services—nursing homes, home health, transportation, medical equipment, pharmacies, medical office buildings, and so on. The new creation was a large, complicated, somewhat unwieldy organization offering a duplication of services to the same markets. The potential for cost and labor efficiencies from the merger was great, and the outlook was optimistic.[1]

The newly combined hospital system formulated a mission that consolidated the objectives of its once-separate entities. HealthEast defined its mission ". . . to extend the religious heritage of its sponsors in providing a ministry of caring for and promoting the total health of East Metropolitan area residents. Through functional integration of physicians, staff, and volunteers, and the sponsors' Christian heritage, HealthEast will establish the standard for a quality health care services network."[2]

Consolidation of the System

The new organization set out with a vengeance to take advantage of the merger, combining services and eliminating inefficiencies and duplication of services.[3] Management staffs were consolidated and organized along service lines in an effort to focus on decision making in the system's interests, rather than along historical, parochial lines.[4] Corporate support services were consolidated into systemwide finance, accounting, human resources, marketing, planning, public relations, pastoral, and legal services. The medical staffs were blended into a single staff for all HealthEast hospitals; physician privileges at any one HealthEast hospital entitled the physician to privileges at all the others. A single JCAHO accreditation was achieved for the entire system. Planning began for a unified management information system (MIS).

Several facilities were closed, phased out of service, or merged with others. Mounds Park Hospital's short-term acute services were discontinued, its chemical dependency and mental health services were moved to HealthEast St. Joseph's Hospital, and the Mounds Park campus was eventually sold to Catholic Services for the Elderly for development as a long-term care and senior housing site. St. John's Eastside Hospital was closed and the building was sold to the St. Paul Port Authority for eventual development as a Metro State University campus. Samaritan Hospital was sold to a local developer and torn down to make room for subsidized housing. HealthEast Bethesda Hospital's short-term acute services were transferred to HealthEast St. Joseph's, and a Medicare waiver was obtained to develop the campus as a long-term rehabilitation center. Remodeling occurred at HealthEast Midway, HealthEast St. John's Northeast, and HealthEast Divine Redeemer hospitals to accommodate physicians and patients shifting from the closed facilities.

The financial markets were satisfied that the organization was making many of the right moves. Thus, in 1987, $139 million of bonds for refinancing and new debt were sold, consolidating all debt for the hospitals in the HealthEast system.

Signs of Distress

Even with these sweeping changes, HealthEast's losses grew to more than $2 million per month, and the system was facing a third consecutive year of major losses.[5] The extent of the losses caused debt service coverage to be too low to meet bond covenants.[6] By year-end 1989, HealthEast had accumulated losses of $73.6 million and total liability had increased to $230 million.[7] In fiscal year 1988, HealthEast's debt service ratio dropped to 0.66 from the 1.1 required by lenders, and HealthEast went into technical default on the nearly $139 million bond issue.[8]

In an article written in 1990, HealthEast trustee board chairman Roger Foussard listed the major early warning signs of impending financial crisis: deteriorating cash position, significant adjustments being recommended by auditors, swings in cash flow resulting in reduced liquidity, increasing amounts being owed to vendors, growth in discounts (deductions from revenue) that did not lead to increased business, and significant monthly and annual variances from expected results.[9]

Outside Assessment

In April 1989, with the bond issue in jeopardy, HealthEast hired consultants to fulfill bond requirements[10] and make turnaround recommendations.[11] Although the bond indenture required a consultant study only of the HealthEast "obligated group" (essentially the hospitals and selected other HealthEast services and facilities), the HealthEast board and management elected to ask the consultants to review the entire organization and make recommendations for all of HealthEast.[12]

A comprehensive review of HealthEast was conducted by Arthur Andersen & Co. and The Hunter Group from March 6, 1989, to April 17, 1989.[13] The objectives of the Andersen–Hunter review were:

- To identify the underlying causes of HealthEast's deteriorating financial position
- To make recommendations with respect to rates, fees, and charges; the obligated group's methods of operations; and other factors affecting the financial condition of the obligated group in order to increase debt service coverage to the highest practicable level (at least 110 percent)[14]

The project team comprised consultants experienced in hospital management, finance, physician practices, managed care, information systems, productivity, nursing, and marketing.[15] To ensure that the assessment would be thorough and objective and that the implementation of recommendations would lead to desired results, a member of The Hunter Group's CEO Advisory Board and a senior executive of Arthur Andersen & Co.'s health care practice reviewed the project's approach and recommendations.[16]

The review was completed in two phases:

- Phase I, an overall assessment identifying and prioritizing various financial, strategic, and operational issues for in-depth review in Phase II, was conducted primarily through interviews and high-level data analysis. At its conclusion, an oral presentation was made to management, representatives of the Board of Directors, and the bond trustee.
- Phase II, a focused examination of issues identified in Phase I, involved an in-depth analysis, including interviews, data accumulation, and financial modeling. Alternative strategies were identified and evaluated, recommendations were selected, and HealthEast management was involved throughout the process.[17]

Commitment to Change

HealthEast worked to find solutions instead of scapegoats.[18] "Early in our troubled situation," wrote Foussard in his November 1990 *Trustee* article, "the board wanted to identify fault. That mentality actually led to some important information being withheld from the board. The board quickly learned that the environment must be conducive to reporting bad news, and that honesty and candor should be rewarded."[19]

Each of HealthEast's constituencies needed to be involved in the consultants' review process and "sold" on adopting the eventual implementation measures. These constituencies included management, middle management, employees, physicians, third-party payers, vendors, community members, and trustees. Working together was acknowledged as the key to success. "There was an absolute commitment of board, medical staff, and management to implement the turnaround plan," said HealthEast President and Chief Executive Officer (CEO) Timothy Hanson in a December 1990 *Modern Healthcare* interview.[20]

Developing a Turnaround Plan

Creation of a plan took only four weeks, during which many options—some fairly dramatic ones—were considered and discussed. Alternatives included bankruptcy, resizing, contract management, mergers, divestiture, sale, conversion, closure, and turnaround. Turnaround was selected as the desired option because the organization had strong market share and good relationships with its physicians.[21]

The plan was constructed to help meet four performance goals:

- To have $10 million in cash on hand by August 31, 1990
- To achieve a net income of 1 or 2 percent of net revenues for the fiscal year (FY) ending August 31, 1990
- To achieve covenant compliance (debt service coverage of 1.1 to 1 or above) and make debt service payments on a current basis
- To make at least $5 million in cash available for capital expenditures for FY 1990[22]

Specific action steps were spelled out and presented by Arthur Andersen & Co. in a report dated April 17, 1989. The consultants recommended that these steps be implemented simultaneously.[23]

Governance Recommendations for the Board of Directors

Evaluation: The HealthEast Board of Directors consisted of 24 positions, filled by 6 candidates from each of the 4 HealthEast sponsor boards. This size board was too large for contemporary governance, and the complex board committee structure caused duplication of effort among the various committees.

Recommendations: Create a board committee of not more than five members to assist in and monitor the turnaround plan, reduce the size of the board, include at-large members from outside the metropolitan areas, restructure the committees of the board, and appoint the president and CEO of HealthEast and the president of the medical staff as ex officio members. The board should also clearly state its role and function, delineate management's responsibility and authority, and establish a self-assessment process and an orientation program.[24]

Management Recommendations

Evaluation: Management had made significant strides in building the system, but did not have sufficient credibility among operating unit managers and physicians. Corporate staff and functions had grown excessively, and information to adequately manage the organization was not easily obtained. In addition, the existing management structure did not focus on the key business units of HealthEast—the hospitals.

Recommendations: Create a turnaround management team with clearly defined roles and functions, retain additional manpower with experience in turnaround management, make the president responsible for the turnaround management team, and set specific goals and timetables for managers. Reevaluate current senior corporate management, reducing staff and focusing on resource allocation, strategy, and supporting operating units. Implement decentralized hospital management, and develop a comprehensive management evaluation strategy with specific criteria and objectives.[25]

Medical Staff Management Recommendations

Evaluation: HealthEast had expended insufficient effort to manage physician behavior or to recruit and develop medical staff. Paid medical staff leadership had not been emphasized, and the corporate staff included only a part-time medical director. Still, medical staff members seemed relatively satisfied.

Recommendations: Recruit a full-time, paid medical director to strengthen medical staff management and its involvement in managing the hospitals, and reorganize existing paid medical staff management. Investigate the expectations of group practices and heavy admitters, then design strategies to fulfill those expectations.[26]

Information Systems Recommendations

Evaluation: Information systems did not provide the timely information necessary to properly manage the organization. A systems implementation plan was developed but was not being implemented effectively. The kind of management information typically used to manage multihospital systems was not being regularly produced.

Recommendations: Immediately complete the installation of the MediPac patient accounting and medical records system. To focus on turnaround priorities and effectively utilize available funds, a short-term decision support system, including key executive information reporting, should be designed and implemented. Initiate steps to plan, design, and implement an integrated decision support system.[27]

Operations Recommendations

Evaluation: Corporate expenses approximated $11 million, and operating hospital expenses approximated $67 million. Because fully 72 percent of revenues were received through managed care, there were limited options for increasing fees and charges.

Recommendations: Corporate operations should reduce staff from 230 to 210 full-time equivalents (FTEs), establish goals and objectives for all personnel and monitor their performance, put detailed cash forecasting and management systems in place, and provide timely and accurate operating results and expenditures reporting. In the hospital salaries and benefits area, all administrative positions should be evaluated and realigned with an entity-specific focus; nursing management positions should be combined where possible; and ancillary, nursing, and nonclerical support departments should establish and follow hours-per-unit and financial goals. With supplies and other costs, the use of consultants should be evaluated and reduced, nonessential expenses (catering, cars, travel, entertainment, subscriptions, dues) reduced, contract services (housekeeping, maintenance, and so on) reevaluated, supply purchases standardized, parking and cafeteria prices increased, employee health insurance plans reviewed, and administrators held accountable for all expenditures and for detailed monthly variance reporting. In addition, various recommendations related to libraries, volunteer services, foundation support, and education could amount to $1.2 million in savings. For product line/hospital consolidations, no new major capital expenditures should be allowed, relocation of the transitional care unit from HealthEast Midway to HealthEast Bethesda should be considered, no additional programs should be immediately considered, and opportunities for HealthEast Divine Redeemer to become a joint venture with another organization or a specialized facility should be investigated.[28]

Care Management Recommendations

Evaluation: Commitment to utilization management has been varied, and neither physicians nor nursing personnel have been active participants. Information systems support for care management has been minimal. Nursing staff is not aware of terms of managed care contracts, resulting in potential overutilization of services.

Recommendations: Reduce resource consumption and educate patient care staff on utilization management, while ensuring maximum quality, and hire a full-time corporate vice president of medical affairs with a strong background in utilization management.[29]

Managed Care Contracts Recommendations

Evaluation: Seventy-two percent of hospital revenues were received under fixed-payment arrangements, information regarding the profitability of the various managed care contracts is minimal, and negotiations with providers appear to have been primarily focused on volume and market share, rather than profitability. Payments by managed care providers to HealthEast have been lower than those paid to the hospital community as a whole, and HealthEast has experienced very poor results on a number of these contracts.

Recommendations: Reopen managed care contract negotiations with each major payer within the next four months, and improve communication with physicians.[30]

Cash Management Recommendations

Evaluation: Operating losses, capital expenditures, and scheduled debt repayments had caused HealthEast's cash position to decline significantly since August 31, 1988. Cash flow was negative in FY 1989.

Recommendations: Make cash conservation top priority, develop a specific action plan, bring HealthEast Bethesda long-term care operations to a break-even cash flow position, set specific goals for accounts receivable and inventory, establish a crisis management plan in the event of a catastrophic event with a major cash impact, and investigate debt restructuring.[31]

Alliances and Collaborations Recommendations

Evaluation: Major health care organizations in the Twin Cities had discussed alliances or collaborative agreements with HealthEast.

Recommendations: Defer consideration of any alliances for at least six months, and remain open to collaboration opportunities that could bring mutual benefit.[32]

Marketing and Communications Recommendations

Evaluation: The marketing plan had been focused on establishing HealthEast as a major player in St. Paul.

Recommendations: Shift marketing activities from a HealthEast system identity focus to relationship management with physicians at each hospital and to the promotion of selected service lines and facilities.[33]

Nonobligated Group Recommendations

Evaluation: This group of diversified services (primarily nonhospital services such as long-term care, home-delivered products and services, and medical transportation) has experienced deteriorating financial results and has required substantial management attention. However, some of these entities have generated positive contributions or suffered only slight losses.

Recommendations: Classify nonobligated entities into three categories: (1) those that are a cash drain and provide no meaningful support; (2) those that are marginally profitable or experiencing small losses; and (3) those that consist primarily of real estate holdings.

Keeping Patients—and HealthEast—Healthy during the Turnaround

Aware that an attempt to create a turnaround through implementation of the consultants' recommendations would create stresses, fears, and reactions among its staff and constituencies, HealthEast set out to manage the expected response in several ways. Weekly senior management meetings were followed by middle management meetings, with common agendas to minimize miscommunication. A 24-hour rumor hotline was created, and rumors and answers were printed in employee newsletters. Recognizing that every constituent would be aware of HealthEast's situation, management supported open recognition of problems, solicited suggestions, and acted on them.[34] The board also appointed physician and hospital staff action committees that could communicate regularly with their constituencies.[35]

Additionally, the board, management, and medical staff wanted to avoid a decline in quality of care and service as a by-product of improved financial performance. Quantifiable quality objectives became an integral part of the turnaround plan. Managers at all levels were asked to identify at least two quality measures—such as medication errors, X-ray retakes, and patient waiting time—and to monitor and report on them routinely.[36]

Another step of the board was to appoint and empower the recommended turnaround action team. The action team functioned as the board's overseeing and reporting mechanism for implementation of the plan, and ensured that the management skill necessary to implement recommendations was in place.[37]

HealthEast also hired temporary management support services through the Hunter Group. Such services were deemed to be necessary because hospital management did not have experience working through a crisis situation.[38] Hunter provided an interim chief financial officer and representatives to manage selected projects, such as the sale of diversified services. The consultants also provided assistance with some of the tough decisions on layoffs, management shifts, and service reconfigurations. In addition, the interim support provided HealthEast with a much-needed "reality check," according to HealthEast Vice-President of Marketing Roger Green.[39] The permanent management team, including the CEO and hospital administrators, was set by April 1989.

The turnaround action team's recommendations were reviewed and weighed by the HealthEast board and then selected for implementation as the board so judged. Not every recommendation was implemented. The diversified companies, for instance, were not sold as the cash position improved because they were deemed integrally important to the organization's mission.

Enjoying the Results

For the fiscal year ending August 31, 1990, HealthEast showed a profit. *Modern Healthcare* reported that the system, though still burdened by high debt levels, was on the rebound.[40] Audited financial statements for that fiscal year reflected a modest operating surplus, cash reserves had grown to more than 30 days of operations ($30 million), and HealthEast was current with its vendors and its principal and interest payments.[41]

With the release of FY 1991 audited results, the debt service coverage ratio had increased to 1.61 and HealthEast was no longer in technical default. A payment default never occurred, and long-term debt had been reduced by $4 million down to $183 million. HealthEast was working to operate as a system, not just from crisis to crisis, and was improving its community image by meeting with business leaders, paying bills on time, and purchasing services and products locally.[42] (Figure 11-1 shows the progression of HealthEast's net income and invested cash scenarios between 1987 and 1991.)

Figure 11-1. HealthEast Net Income (top) and Invested Cash (bottom), 1987–1991

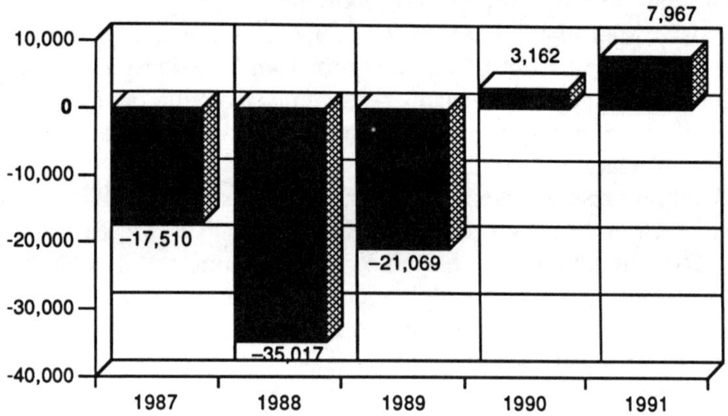

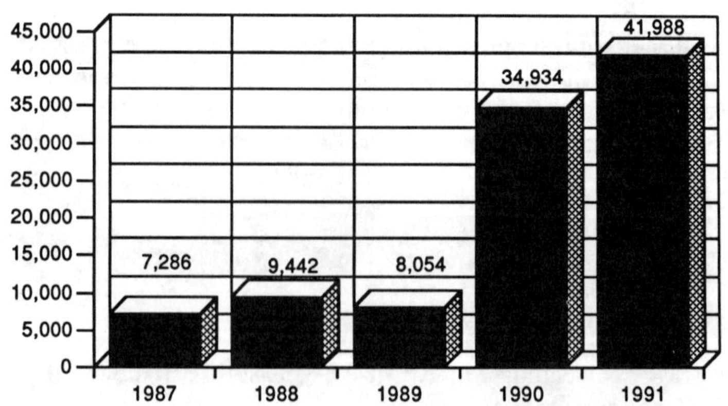

Following FY 1991, credibility in the credit markets began to return. This was HealthEast's second consecutive year with no event of technical default. By becoming partners with its community, managing considerable internal change with forethought, and implementing the carefully considered recommendations of its consultants, HealthEast had completed a successful turnaround.

By early 1992, HealthEast had obtained a credit upgrade by Standard & Poor's and a letter of credit from an international bank in support of certain bond financing. Normalcy was returning.

Conclusion

Following the policies that helped it through the turnaround years, HealthEast has set specific financial performance goals for itself into 1996. The system's future vision includes refinancing bonds in 1993, reaching and maintaining a debt service coverage ratio of 2.0, and creating a true, ongoing partnership of care givers dedicated to financial survival that will enable HealthEast to care for its community well into the future.

HealthEast commemorated its internal changes and growth by creating a succinct mission statement that more accurately reflects its future vision: "Rooted in Judeo-Christian values, our mission is to provide high-quality, cost-effective, compassionate health care to Twin Cities East Metro residents."

References

1. Foussard, R., and Perry, B. M. Board directs system turnaround. *Trustee* 43(11):20–21, Nov. 1990.
2. HealthEast Mission Statement, 1986.
3. Management interviews, 1992.
4. Management interviews, 1992.
5. Foussard, p. 20.
6. Southwick, K. *Healthweek,* Feb. 11, 1991, p. 15.
7. Greene, J. Three hospital systems on the rebound from financial and organizational woes. *Modern Healthcare* 20(50):31–32, Dec. 17, 1990.
8. Greene, pp. 31–32.
9. Foussard, p. 20.
10. Foussard, p. 20.
11. Greene, J. Management, policy decisions trouble HealthEast. *Modern Healthcare* 19(42):28–31, Oct. 20, 1989.

12. Arthur Andersen & Co. Final recommendations resulting from a comprehensive review of HealthEast, Apr. 17, 1989, p. 1.
13. Arthur Andersen & Co., p. 1.
14. Arthur Andersen & Co., p. 1.
15. Arthur Andersen & Co., p. 1.
16. Arthur Andersen & Co., p. 1.
17. Arthur Andersen & Co., p. 2.
18. Foussard, p. 30.
19. Foussard, p. 30.
20. Greene, Three hospital systems on the rebound from financial and organizational woes, p. 31.
21. Foussard, p. 30.
22. Arthur Andersen & Co., p. 23.
23. Arthur Andersen & Co., p. 4.
24. Arthur Andersen & Co., pp. 5–6.
25. Arthur Andersen & Co., pp. 6–8.
26. Arthur Andersen & Co., pp. 8–9.
27. Arthur Andersen & Co., pp. 9–10.
28. Arthur Andersen & Co., pp. 10–16.
29. Arthur Andersen & Co., p. 17.
30. Arthur Andersen & Co., p. 18.
31. Arthur Andersen & Co., pp. 18–20.
32. Arthur Andersen & Co., pp. 20–21.
33. Arthur Andersen & Co., pp. 21–22.
34. Foussard, p. 30.
35. Foussard, p. 30.
36. Foussard, p. 30.
37. Greene, Three hospital systems on the rebound from financial and organizational woes, p. 31.
38. Foussard, p. 20.
39. Foussard, p. 20.
40. Southwick, p. 15.
41. Greene, Three hospital systems on the rebound from financial and organizational woes, pp. 31–32.
42. Foussard, p. 20.

Chapter 12

Case Study: Turning Around an Independent Community Hospital

Patricia C. Breault

Dickson Hospital (a fictional name) is a hospital in serious distress, worse than many hospitals attempting turnarounds. If its turnaround, which is currently in progress, proves successful, Dickson's story will be an example of how to turn around a hospital with numerous internal and external problems. In particular, it will demonstrate that, even in the midst of immediate and severe crisis, it makes sense to focus first on the nuts and bolts of management and control.

Market and Environmental Factors

In order to begin to formulate an appropriate turnaround strategy for Dickson, the various external factors affecting the hospital's performance had to be examined so that the problem areas could be identified. Those external factors included the hospital's market position, its reimbursement environment and payer mix, its pricing strategy, the regulatory environment, the demographics and economics of its service area, and its size and utilization rate.

Market Position

Dickson has long been one of several providers sharing the same market area, in which it is the largest hospital and historically the market leader. The market includes two principal providers and has significant overcapacity; none of the hospitals has an occupancy rate over 50 percent. As the oldest hospital in the area, Dickson has considerable support in the community. This loyalty, which the hospital has worked to strengthen, will be particularly valuable throughout the turnaround period.

Historically, Dickson dominated the market for obstetrics, which accounted for 15 to 20 percent of its admissions. The hospital was perceived by the community as the leader in this area, and its most committed medical staff members were concentrated in this specialty. In 1989, another provider in Dickson's market area announced that it would begin offering obstetric services the following year. Though Dickson had time to plan its response, it did not take steps to protect its market share with either the physicians or the patients. By the middle of 1991, Dickson's obstetrics admissions had fallen by 30 percent and its pediatrics admissions by 10 percent.

Reimbursement Environment and Payer Mix

Reimbursement factors have been a significant element in Dickson's growing financial distress. Overall, 75 percent of gross revenues are derived from fixed-rate payers. However, this mix is representative of the market and is slightly better than that of the other area providers.

The state's Medicaid program, like many others, has been implementing strict cost-containment measures. Sharp reductions in the covered length of stay for several conditions commonly treated at the hospital will continue to adversely affect hospital performance until case management is improved and length of stay can be reduced to that covered by the state.

Managed care penetration is still comparatively low in the market, but forms a greater share of Dickson's mix than that of the other area providers. As occupancy dropped in response to the competition in obstetrics, the hospital sought out high-volume managed care contracts in order to rebuild census. The contracts often had both low per-diem payments and tight restrictions on covered days, so that even a hospital with effective utilization management would have had difficulty working within them. Dickson's aggressiveness in this area led the hospital to contract with some carriers with scant track records, uncertain financial conditions, and business systems that did not generate prompt payment. It was probably also the case that as Dickson's troubles deepened, insurers knew that the hospital was not dealing from a position of strength and structured their offers accordingly.

Pricing

With such a high percentage of fixed-rate payers, not only at Dickson but in the overall market, gross charges are largely irrelevant. To the extent that they matter, though, Dickson's gross revenue per discharge is within 5 percent of that of the other principal providers. For Dickson, the critical pricing issue is managed care contract rates.

Regulatory Environment

The hospital's JCAHO accreditation is threatened due to a multitude of noncompliance issues and facility problems. In addition, Medicare reimbursement is frequently delayed or denied due to lack of appropriate admission criteria.

Service Area Demographics and Economics

Demographics are not much of a factor, except for an unemployment rate slightly higher than the national average. Population growth is slow but stable, and per capita income is above the national average. One warning sign for the future is that area utilization rates are high compared to national norms and will likely be dropping in response to pressure from insurers.

Size and Utilization

In recent years, smaller hospitals have been more vulnerable to distress. Dickson is licensed for 300 beds and is larger than the typical hospital at risk of default. It is currently operating with 200 staffed beds, but its plant and other expenditures reflect some of the costs of maintaining a larger facility. However, because other area hospitals are no larger, size is not a relative disadvantage.

Dickson's occupancy rate declined from 50 to 42 percent over a period of two years. During this time, market area days fell by only 6 percent, although the average daily census of one of the other area providers increased by 10 percent. To avoid losses, the hospital would have to control expenses tightly, but historically it has had difficulty doing so.

Internal and Operational Factors

In addition to the factors in Dickson's outside environment that could be having an effect on the hospital's decline, an overall assessment also had to include examination of possible internal factors. These internal factors primarily involved Dickson's clinical and operational efficiency and the capability of its management staff.

Clinical Efficiency

Perhaps the most serious of the many problems facing Dickson is the efficiency of its clinical practice. The hospital's patients have long stays, high intensity of services, and a high percentage of special-care days, despite a fairly low case-mix index. Because of inadequate review and control procedures, management information in this area was essentially nonexistent. However, one clear indication of the problem was that overutilization had come to the attention of the local peer review organization (PRO), which reviewed a high percentage of the hospital's cases.

Overutilization had been recognized as a problem at Dickson for several years. The hospital had implemented various programs in utilization review and case management, but the resources committed were never adequate to the task, and physicians were not sufficiently involved in the effort. The need for improvement became more critical as reimbursement mechanisms evolved toward encouraging efficiency and as Dickson emphasized managed care contracting.

Dealing with medical staffs on utilization issues is always a delicate and difficult task. Dickson, never strong in this regard, was faced with the need to be strict in this area at the same time that strengthening physician commitment was necessary to shore up admissions.

Productivity and Operational Efficiency

Operational efficiency had also been a long-standing problem at Dickson. It became even more serious as reimbursement declined, the census fell rapidly, and expenses were not reduced accordingly.

Dickson's staffing in patient care areas is significantly higher than that of other area providers, without a higher case mix. In 1990, the hospital had 3 patient care full-time equivalents (FTEs) per adjusted occupied bed (AOB), whereas the other providers had between 2.1 and 2.5. Total FTEs per AOB were 5.4 by mid-1991. Overstaffing related to overutilization had also been a problem for some years.

The hospital has made heavy use of agency personnel. Agency staff were reduced as census declined, but the hospital FTE level remained essentially the same. Patient care staffing is not the only problem area; general and administrative FTEs are high as well, particularly in relation to the for-profit area provider.

Labor costs typically represent 60 percent of a hospital's total expense budget. Dickson's labor costs, including agency fees, were 48 percent of total expenses in 1991, suggesting that its other expenses are high as well. For example, use of consultants and outside services grew in recent years, as management correctly recognized the need to address many problems. However, the hospital usually failed to implement recommendations or otherwise realize the benefits of these services. The management information system (MIS) area was also the site of expensive and demoralizing failures. The hospital purchased a good system, but did not implement it fully or properly.

Hospital Management

For several years, Dickson had been experiencing high turnover in upper and middle management positions, including five chief financial officers (CFOs) in two years. In an understandable response to this, the hospital developed a pattern of promotion from within, on the assumption that this would provide much-needed continuity and cut down the time needed for new personnel to get up to speed. Unfortunately, the individuals promoted often lacked sufficient experience for the demands of their new positions. The negative consequences of this practice became more pronounced as the hospital's financial situation worsened to a point that would tax even the most seasoned professionals.

The particularly rapid turnover in the finance and accounting areas led to deficiencies in the most fundamental procedures and controls. Accounts were not reconciled for months. Basic financial and operating data were unreliable or nonexistent. With the focus on the immediate crises, there was little or no long-term strategic and financial planning. Even if this planning had been present, the information on which it would have been based was problematic.

The selected financial ratios in figure 12-1 show that, by almost every measure, Dickson has been in trouble for some time. Its one profitable year

Figure 12-1. Selected Financial Statement Indicators, Dickson Hospital

	1991	1990	1989	1988	1987
Profitability					
Operating Margin	−17.31%	−1.51%	1.83%	−1.07%	−4.31%
Total Margin	−15.96%	−1.41%	5.13%	−11.04%	−3.91%
Return on Equity	N/A	−0.15	0.49	−1.86	−0.22
Liquidity					
Current Ratio	0.89	1.13	1.25	1.19	1.05
Acid Test Ratio	−0.03	0.04	0.05	−0.02	0.04
Days Cash on Hand	−4.34	4.65	6.28	−2.57	5.02
Days in Accounts Receivable	118	116	129	129	106
Days in Accounts Payable	179	154	115	112	93
Capital Structure					
Long-Term Debt/Total Assets	0.72	0.66	0.67	0.71	0.72
Long-Term Debt/Net Fixed Assets	1.56	1.50	1.59	1.65	1.81
Long-Term Debt/Equity	−17.05	10.70	9.47	19.14	7.61
Long-Term Debt/Capitalization	1.06	0.91	0.90	0.95	0.88
Creditworthiness and Solvency					
Debt Service Coverage	0.17	1.18	1.79	0.13	1.04
Debt Service/Net Revenue	−0.72	−5.39	1.81	−0.79	−2.17

in 1989 was an aberration, not the beginning of the turnaround the hospital was planning when it issued its Series 1988 bonds.

The Decline into Default

As this discussion has shown, Dickson had for years presented all the warning signs of distress. Two developments helped to put it over the edge into default: Medicaid cutbacks and the competitor's initiation of obstetric services. Census fell quickly and cash collections soon followed. The hospital had always run with very little cash and now had to make do with almost none. Management had become proficient at survival-mode cash management, but the situation grew more serious than it had ever been before. As payables grew to 180 days, numerous vendors put the hospital on credit hold or cash-on-delivery (COD) status. As the hospital put in place payment plans with its highest-priority creditors, it had less and less flexibility. Out of cash and getting by on the float on its bank account, Dickson went into technical default on the Series 1988 bonds when the hospital drew on its debt service reserve to make an interest payment.

As census fell, that is what management attempted to fix. Although the most immediate sources of trouble were indeed recent and external, the sources of the hospital's vulnerability were its long-standing internal problems. Management's response, however, was to "grow out" of the problem. Although the hospital did begin to reduce staff and cut other costs, the emphasis was given to increasing volume. The drawbacks of this approach were that it was too long-term, given the immediacy of the crisis, and that it did not address the underlying problems. In addition, volume was to be gained mainly by signing managed care contracts with rates set at unprofitably low levels. There was not time to see the results of the strategy, though, because the technical default led to the bondholders getting involved.

The Option of a Workout

Dickson's crisis was pretty severe for a workout strategy, but one was pursued for several reasons. The bondholders' first choice was to sell the hospital as a going concern, but no acceptable offers were received. Bankruptcy was deemed too risky given Dickson's share of the market and its already declining occupancy. The liquidation value was estimated to be very low. Last, and perhaps most important, the majority bondholders were sophisticated institutional investors with experience and a record of success in the workout process.

Also, there was confidence that the hospital could be made to work. For one thing, there certainly was room for improvement in a number of areas. Falling census notwithstanding, the hospital still had the loyalty of its community and a payer mix no worse than that of its neighboring institutions, one of which, a for-profit, was doing very well.

Addressing Hospital Leadership

The first step was to address the leadership of the hospital. The board and bondholders hired a major national turnaround management firm, which provides a CEO, CFO, and key middle management positions and brings in specialists in other areas on a part-time basis. In this matter and others, the relationship between the board and the bondholders was cooperative from the early stages. There was a recognition of common interests, each party seeing the need to keep the other happy. The decision to bring in new management was made together, and the turnaround managers have a relationship with both parties.

After an initial review that found problems in all the areas discussed, the new management team developed its plan. The foundation of the plan, in the near term, was a focus on implementing basic management and control practices along with immediate and deep cuts in staffing and other expenses. The five-year forecast assumed only modest increases in census, emphasizing, instead, that which could be internally controlled.

Restructuring Debt

Setting the terms of the restructuring was an iterative process between management and the bondholders. During the process, the bondholders came to grant more indebtedness for a longer period than they had at the outset, and management's plan was modified where necessary to keep the hospital's projected cash requirements within acceptable confines. Significantly, management did not alter its modest projections for growth in census; changes were made primarily to the expense side. The original plan assumed some improvement in payer mix, but this was not changed during the negotiations.

The turnaround managers' plan formed the basis of the restructuring. Sources of available cash were defined to include:

- Earnings before interest, depreciation, crisis management, and restructuring fees (these last were segregated in the analysis to isolate the "normal" requirements of hospital operations)
- The proceeds of a working capital loan to be made by the bondholders
- The debt service reserve, which the bondholders decided could be used to make the current year's interest payment

Terms regarding uses of cash included:

- *Accounts payable.* On past due payables, the bondholders required that management negotiate with vendors a 50 percent discount—not unreasonable considering that the vendors' alternative would probably be filing a claim with the bankruptcy court. Past due accounts would be paid off over a one-year period; new payables would be kept at 45 days.
- *Capital expenditures.* It was agreed that the hospital would make the full amount of routine capital expenditures and also invest in additional projects important to keeping the hospital modern and attractive to patients.
- *Crisis management and restructuring.* Payments were to be kept current from the beginning of the workout process.
- *Working capital interest.* This would be paid on a current basis, even while the working capital principal was still increasing.
- *Cash on hand.* The hospital was allowed to keep an amount sufficient to establish sound cash management policies and to make the prompt payments critical to vendor relations and acceptance of the discount on the old payables.
- *Working capital principal.* Payments would be made next, if cash were available after meeting the higher-priority requirements listed above.
- *Bond interest and principal.* Once the working capital loan was repaid, first the interest and then the principal payments would be brought up to date.
- *Debt service reserve restoration.* This would be the last step in the workout, after bond interest and principal had been brought current.

The hospital's total new indebtedness at any given point was defined to include not only the working capital loan, but also the deferred interest and principal payments, and the usage of the debt service reserve. Two years into the workout period, it was projected to reach $13 million. To put this number in context, the Series 1988 bond issue was for $46 million; the net book value of hospital property, plant, and equipment at the time of the default was $30 million. The workout plan ends in 1999, when the additional debt is paid off and bond payments resume as originally scheduled.

Management's Plan for a Turnaround

Once Dickson's problem areas had been identified and a workout process had been determined and agreed to, the hospital's new turnaround managers began to carry out their action plan. The plan included effecting change in the hospital's leadership and culture, improving revenue and cash flow, implementing programs to improve utilization management, and soliciting the cooperation of the medical staff.

Leadership and Culture Changes

Dickson's extended crisis period set the stage for a real change in the culture of the institution. Employee morale had been understandably low because of management turnover, attempts at improvement that did not succeed, and as the crisis became acute, an atmosphere of impending failure, including late paychecks.

Even during the worst part of the default phase, the staff in general were cooperative and helpful in working with the many "outsiders" who became involved with the hospital. For the most part, the distress seemed to lead to a strong desire to improve things. The sense of working together to save the hospital—and it is no exaggeration to say that this is what was at stake—was a powerful motivation. The challenge for management was to foster this spirit and at the same time to implement major layoffs. The turnaround managers had seen and dealt with this problem many times before, and thus had an advantage over executives going through this for the first or even the second time.

It was important to make clear from the beginning of the turnaround process, in symbolic and practical ways, that things were changing. The benefit of new management control systems was clear early on in that paychecks were accurate and on time. Although staff had been through many leadership changes, each of which promised improvement that did not materialize or proved insufficient, this was by far the most dramatic, providing hope that this time could be different.

Revenue and Cash Flow Enhancement

Improving the hospital's cash collections was an immediate priority. New management found that the net accounts receivable on the books was inaccurate. For years, there had been considerable turnover in the business office management. In the midst of this, a new computer system was installed, and many relevant features were not properly implemented. Contractual allowances were not posted correctly, and the accounts receivable (A/R) balance was not correct. Though days in A/R is usually the key indicator of collection performance, management was not able to get a good figure on this. The turnaround managers wrote off many aged accounts, bringing the official days figure to 70, and started implementing correct recording of contractuals so that this would become a meaningful indicator.

Problems in medical records had also affected the billing operation. Coding was consistently backlogged and coders insufficiently trained. A review of a sample of Medicare charts showed that 45 percent of them could have had their diagnosis-related groups (DRGs) changed. Extrapolating these results, management estimated that the hospital could increase Medicare reimbursement by nearly $500,000 per year through better coding.

The hospital did not produce any reports showing actual contractual allowances by payer, so there was no way to monitor the performance of insurance carriers. This was particularly problematic given the high proportion of managed care, which requires sophisticated and intensive follow-up. Improving the handling of managed care accounts was designated a top priority in this area.

Utilization Management

Many of Dickson's problems were rooted in poor utilization management. Overutilization led to regulatory problems, delayed reimbursement, excessive contractual write-offs, overstaffing, and high costs. The turnaround managers placed the highest priority on developing case management and quality assurance programs, after finding that the hospital's controls were either inadequate or altogether missing.

Medical Staff

Medical staff involvement and support is always critical, but Dickson's case was especially difficult because of its utilization problems. Its doctors, many of whom also admit to neighboring providers, needed to become accustomed to working with leaner nursing staffs, to change their practice patterns, and become more responsive regarding documentation. The turnaround managers attempted to meet individually with each physician to secure their support and hear their concerns. In working with management, the physicians could help save the hospital. Also, because case management and managed care are clearly the wave of the future, the doctors at Dickson have a chance to work with a management team that can help them learn to work within the new rules.

In these early stages of the turnaround, the hospital did not focus much on market strategy, in either the short or long term. Even short-term positioning takes time and management resources. Dickson's internal problems were so acute that they required management's full attention if there was to be a long term.

Conclusion

Dickson's experience illustrates several useful lessons regarding turnarounds:

- For a severely troubled hospital, outside help, including the use of a turnaround firm, is probably essential, both for its expertise and the "outsider" perspective needed to make the very hard decisions.

- The basics matter, and the infrastructure of good management must be in place.
- Turning around a hospital with serious problems takes a long time, a fact that all parties involved need to recognize.

If management's plan can be successfully implemented, Dickson will be modestly successful, though getting to that point from where the hospital is now will be very difficult. If Dickson stays open long enough and improves enough to bring a reasonable sale price, the restructuring can be said to be a success from at least the bondholders' perspective.

Although Dickson's future is not necessarily assured, the undertaking of a turnaround process has at least offered the institution and its internal and external stakeholders hope that it will continue to provide needed services. Like so many other financially distressed hospitals today, Dickson has at least taken the first necessary steps toward financial viability tomorrow.